Justinian's Empire

Also by Nick Holmes

Books

THE ROMAN REVOLUTION

THE FALL OF ROME

ROME AND ATTILA

THE BYZANTINE WORLD WAR

Podcasts

THE FALL OF THE ROMAN EMPIRE

BYZANTIUM AND THE CRUSADES

Justinian's Empire

Triumph and Tragedy

The Fall of the Roman Empire
Book Four

Nick Holmes

Puttenham
Press

Published by Puttenham Press Ltd

ISBN 978-1-7397865-6-4

British Library Cataloguing in Publication Data.
A catalogue record for this book is available from the British Library.

Typeset in the United Kingdom by Indie-Go
https://www.indie-go.co.uk

In memory of my father

Here is a Roman General (Belisarius) whose victories are not less Roman, nor his strategical principles less classical, than Julius Caesar's. Yet the (Roman) army has by now changed almost beyond recognition...

– Robert Graves,
(Author of *I Claudius* and *Count Belisarius*)

The vain titles of the victories of Justinian are crumbled into dust

– Edward Gibbon,
(Author of *The History of the Decline
and Fall of the Roman Empire*)

Contents

Contents

Illustrations

Photographs are from the Author's Collection unless stated otherwise.

Maps

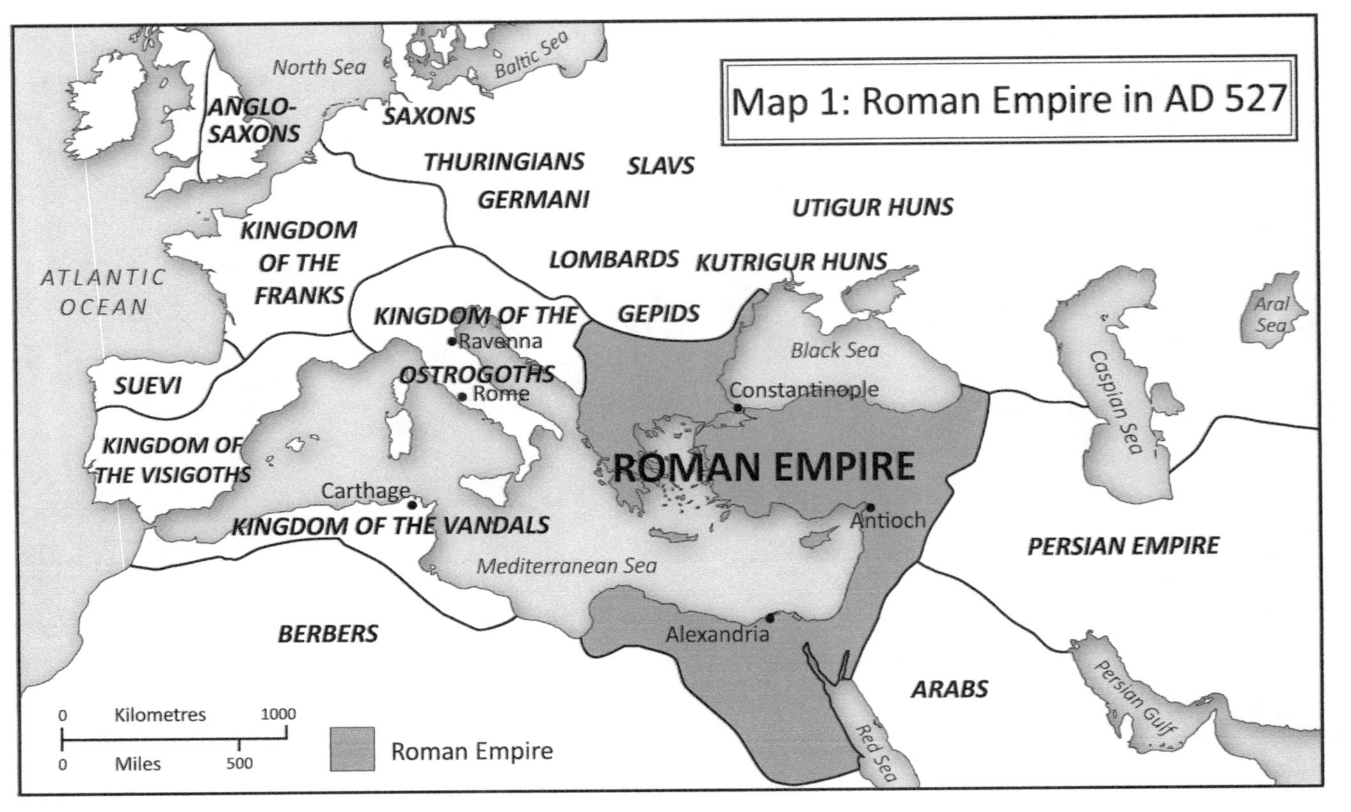

Map 1: Roman Empire in AD 527
North Sea
Baltic Sea
ANGLO-SAXONS
SAXONS
THURINGIANS
SLAVS
GERMANI
UTIGUR HUNS
KINGDOM OF THE FRANKS
ATLANTIC OCEAN
LOMBARDS
KUTRIGUR HUNS
KINGDOM OF THE
GEPIDS
Ravenna
Black Sea
Caspian Sea
Aral Sea
OSTROGOTHS
Rome
Constantinople
SUEVI
ROMAN EMPIRE
KINGDOM OF THE VISIGOTHS
Carthage
Antioch
KINGDOM OF THE VANDALS
PERSIAN EMPIRE
Mediterranean Sea
BERBERS
Alexandria
ARABS
Red Sea
Persian Gulf
Kilometres
0
1000
Miles
0
500
Roman Empire

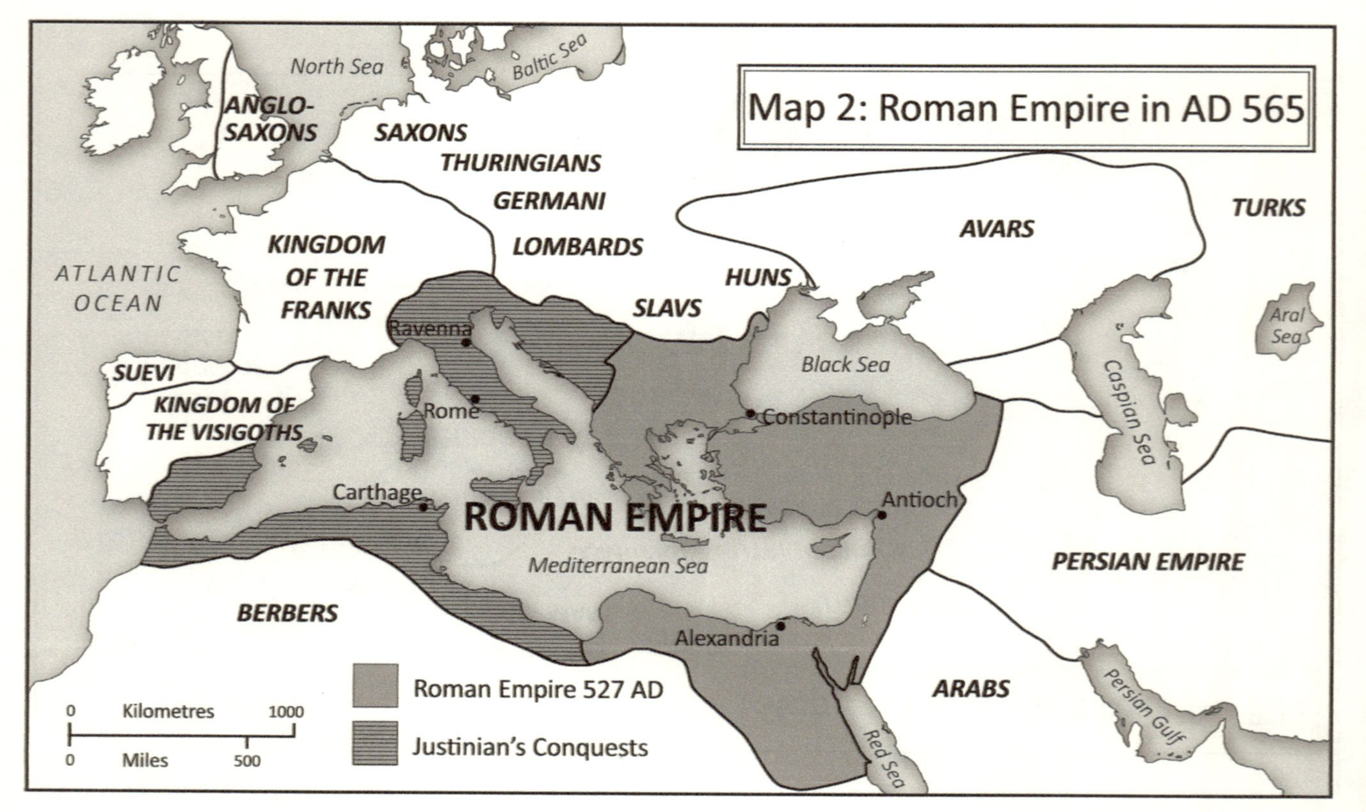

Map 2: Roman Empire in AD 565
North Sea
Baltic Sea
ANGLO-SAXONS
SAXONS
THURINGIANS
GERMANI
LOMBARDS
TURKS
AVARS
HUNS
SLAVS
KINGDOM OF THE FRANKS
ATLANTIC OCEAN
Aral Sea
Ravenna
Black Sea
Caspian Sea
SUEVI
KINGDOM OF THE VISIGOTHS
Rome
Constantinople
Carthage
ROMAN EMPIRE
Antioch
PERSIAN EMPIRE
Mediterranean Sea
BERBERS
Alexandria
Roman Empire 527 AD
Justinian's Conquests
ARABS
Persian Gulf
Red Sea
Kilometres
0
1000
Miles
0
500

Map 3: Central Constantinople

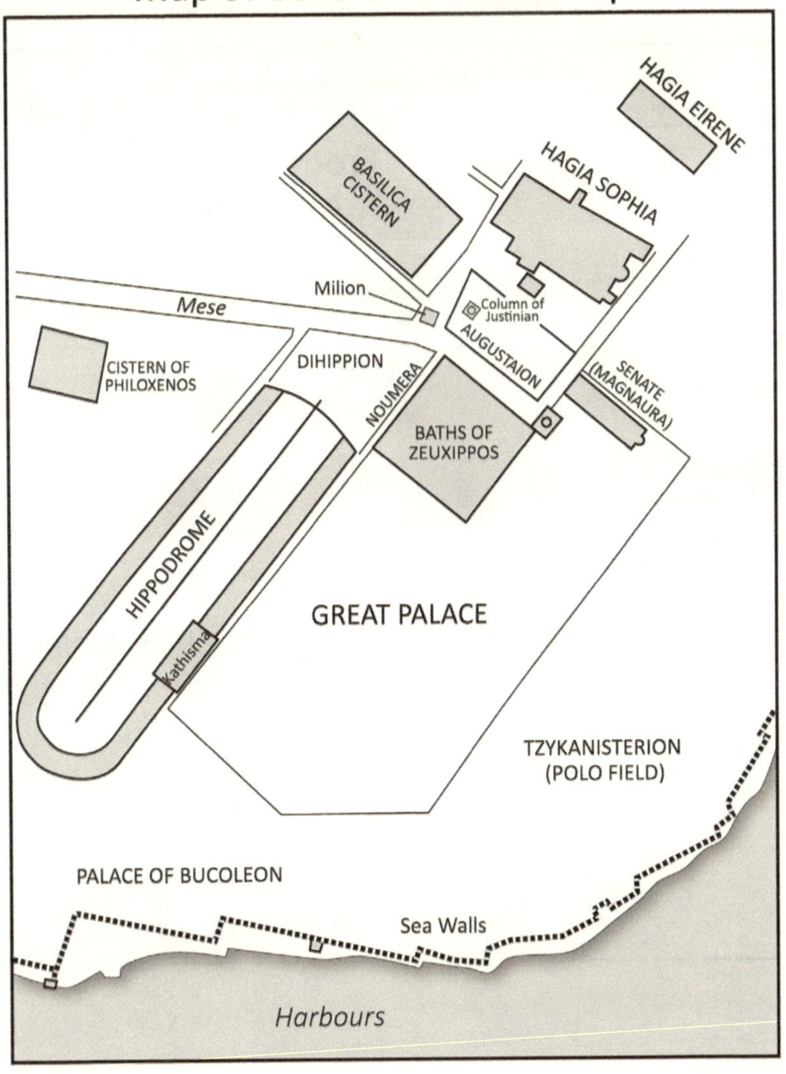

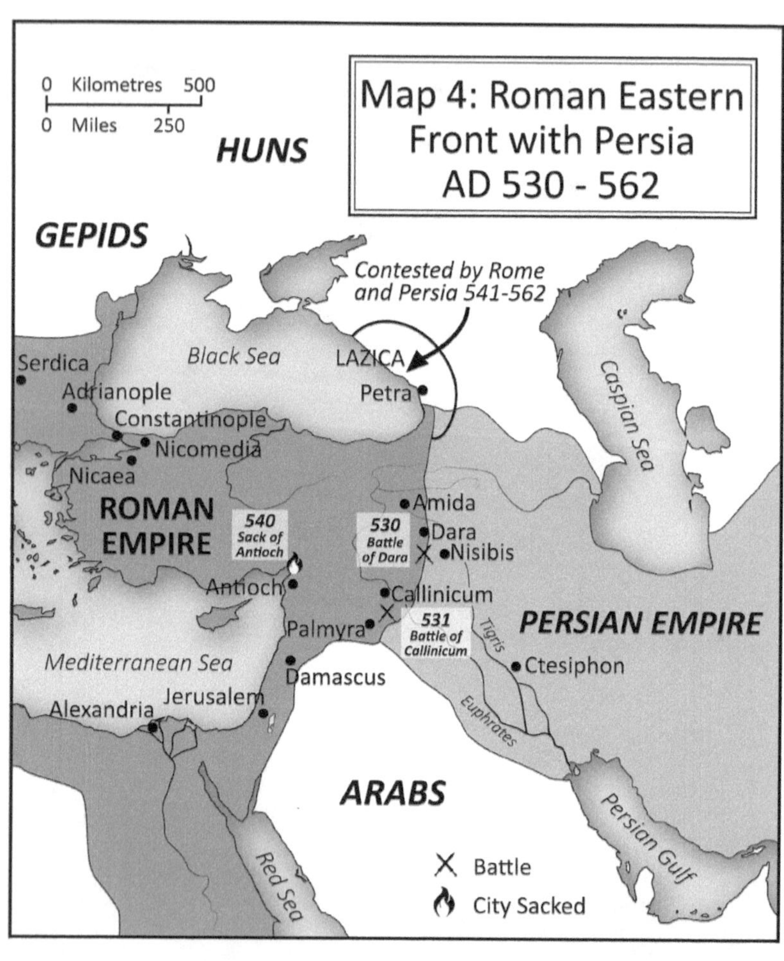

HUNS
GEPIDS
Map 4: Roman Eastern Front with Persia AD 530 - 562
0 Kilometres 500
0 Miles 250
Contested by Rome and Persia 541-562
Black Sea
LAZICA
Petra
Serdica
Adrianople
Constantinople
Nicomedia
Nicaea
Caspian Sea
ROMAN EMPIRE
540 Sack of Antioch
530 Battle of Dara
Amida
Dara
Nisibis
Antioch
Callinicum
531 Battle of Callinicum
PERSIAN EMPIRE
Palmyra
Tigris
Mediterranean Sea
Damascus
Ctesiphon
Alexandria
Jerusalem
Euphrates
ARABS
Red Sea
Persian Gulf
X Battle
City Sacked

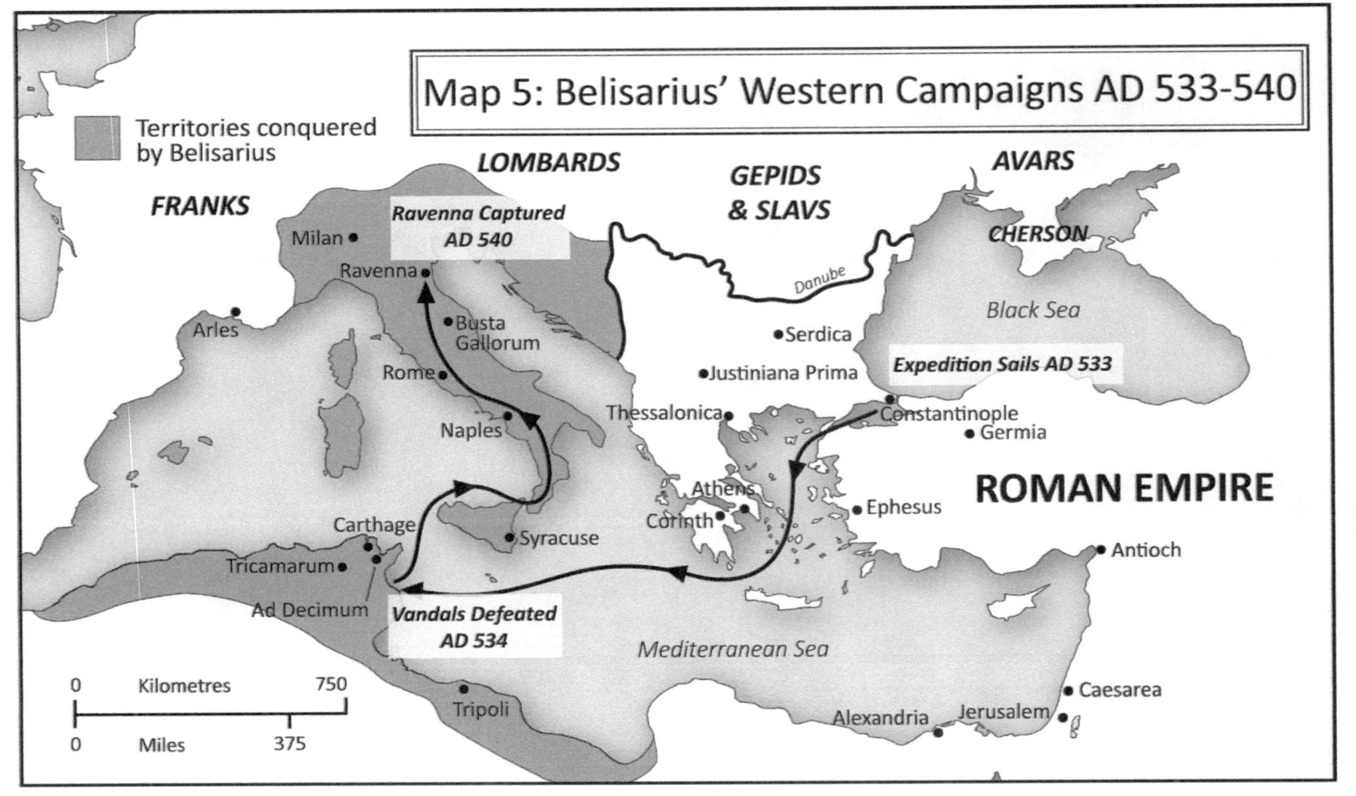

Map 5: Belisarius' Western Campaigns AD 533-540
Territories conquered by Belisarius
FRANKS
LOMBARDS
GEPIDS & SLAVS
AVARS
CHERSON
Ravenna Captured AD 540
Expedition Sails AD 533
Vandals Defeated AD 534
ROMAN EMPIRE
Milan
Ravenna
Arles
Busta Gallorum
Rome
Naples
Carthage
Tricamarum
Ad Decimum
Syracuse
Thessalonica
Athens
Corinth
Serdica
Justiniana Prima
Constantinople
Germia
Ephesus
Antioch
Danube
Black Sea
Mediterranean Sea
Tripoli
Alexandria
Jerusalem
Caesarea
Kilometres
0
750
Miles
0
375

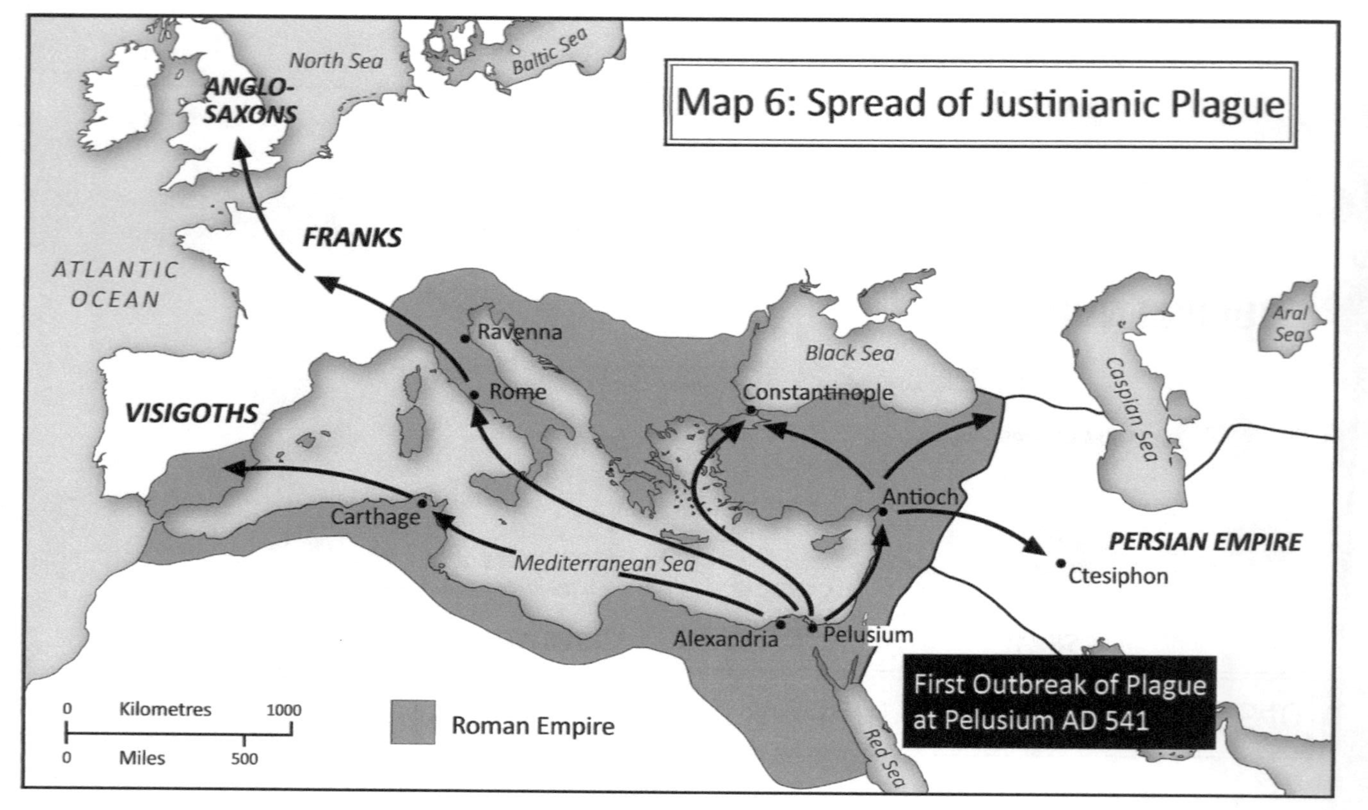

Map 6: Spread of Justinianic Plague
North Sea
Baltic Sea
ANGLO-SAXONS
FRANKS
ATLANTIC OCEAN
Black Sea
Aral Sea
Caspian Sea
Ravenna
VISIGOTHS
Rome
Constantinople
Antioch
PERSIAN EMPIRE
Carthage
Mediterranean Sea
Ctesiphon
Alexandria
Pelusium
Red Sea
First Outbreak of Plague at Pelusium AD 541
Kilometres
0   1000
Roman Empire
Miles
0   500

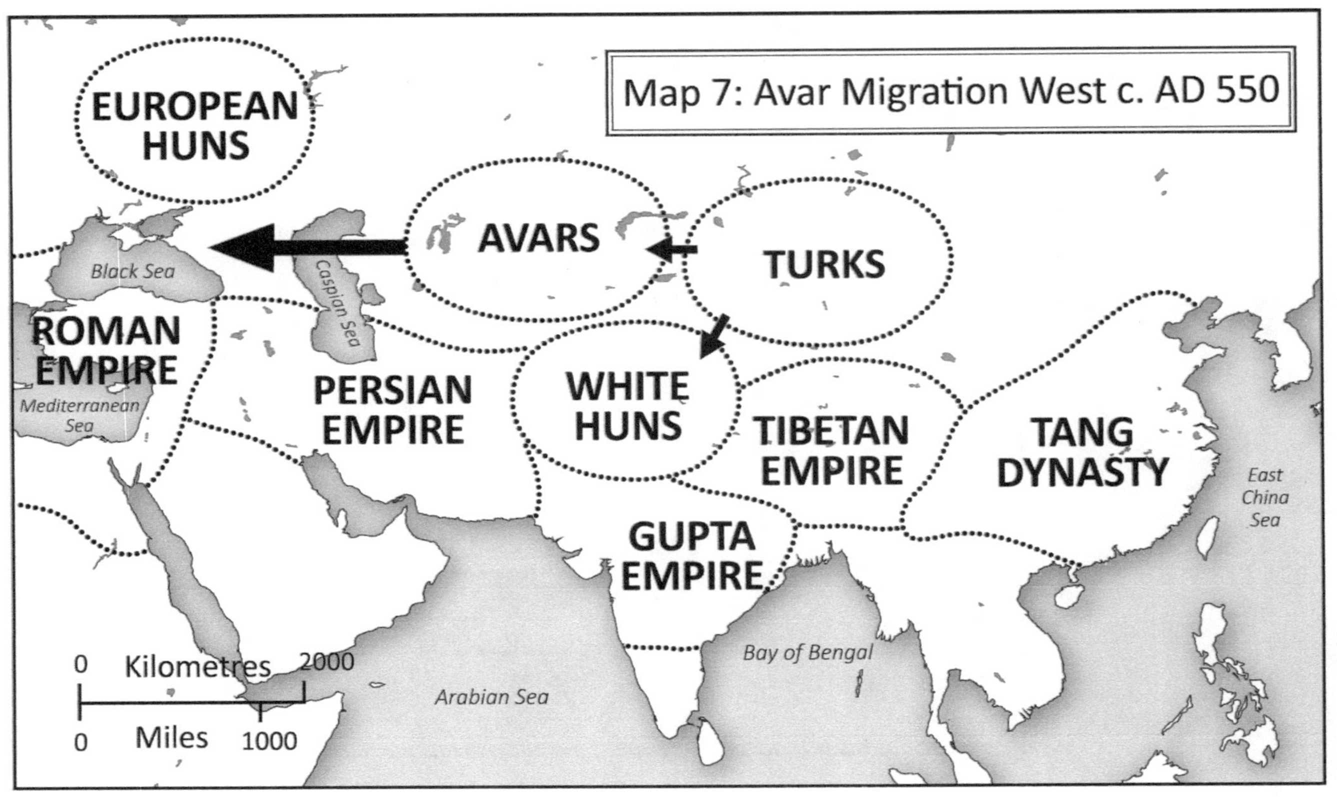

Map 7: Avar Migration West c. AD 550
EUROPEAN HUNS
AVARS
TURKS
ROMAN EMPIRE
PERSIAN EMPIRE
WHITE HUNS
TIBETAN EMPIRE
TANG DYNASTY
GUPTA EMPIRE
Black Sea
Caspian Sea
Mediterranean Sea
Arabian Sea
Bay of Bengal
East China Sea
0   Kilometres   2000
0   Miles   1000

Map 8: Ancient Rome

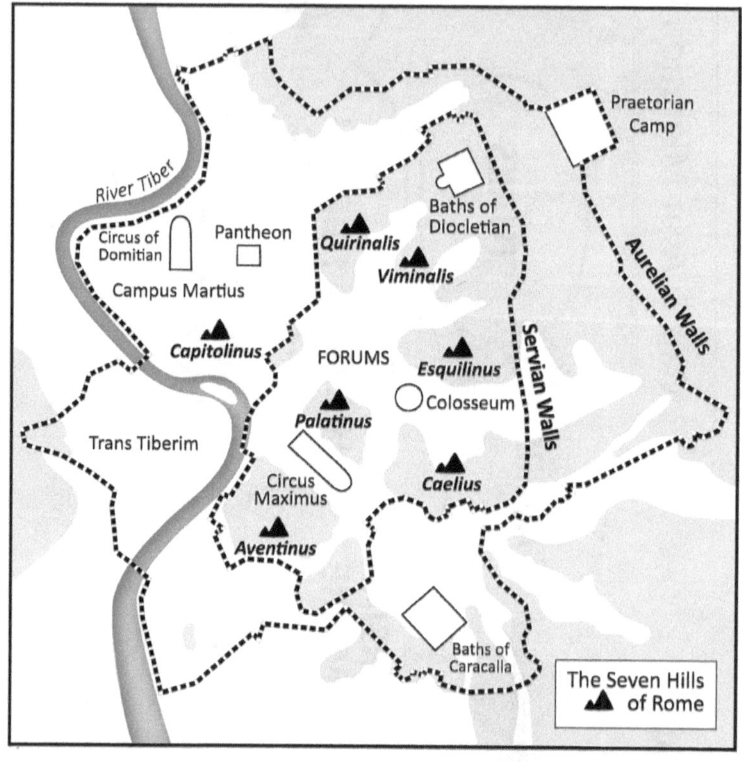

Map 9: Constantinople

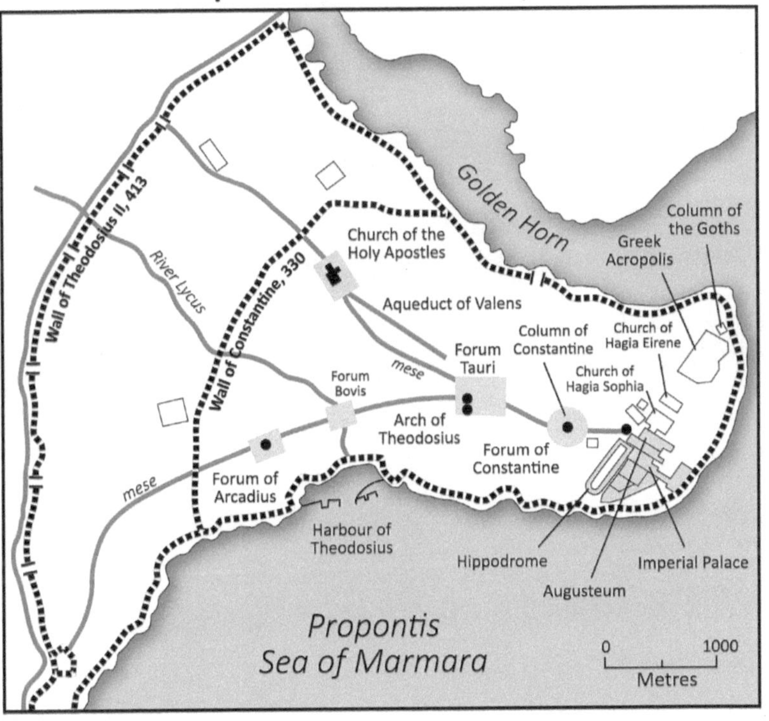

Introduction

A cold winter's day. Armoured horsemen ride along the Appian way. The 800-year-old road still looks modern. Its close-fitting stones pave its surface so neatly they could be a tessellated snakeskin. The horses' hooves clatter on it. Ahead of them lies a city.

Rome.

The day is 10 December AD 536, 60 years after the fall of the western Roman Empire.

So, who are these horsemen? Roman soldiers? Yet they look nothing like the soldiers we know so well, represented with rectangular shields and *lorica segmentata* – metal strips of armour – on Trajan's Column. Instead, they wear chain mail and ride horses with armoured plates covering their heads, necks and shoulders. On their left side hangs a sword. On the right, a quiver of arrows. One plucks an arrow and draws it back to his right ear. He releases it. The missile kills a spectating rabbit. The man laughs with his companions. What accuracy! What skill! These men are the new Roman army.

They ride to meet the barbarians. For Rome's great walls, built by the emperor Aurelian 260 years before to keep the barbarians out, are now keeping them in. The Goths hold the eternal city. But not for much longer. Belisarius, the most brilliant Roman general since Julius Caesar, is here.

Inside the city there is panic. The Gothic commander, Leuderis, looks out from the battlements of the Porta Asinaria. In the distance, he sees the Romans. He has 4,000 men. Belisarius 6,000. But Rome is difficult to defend. Its 12 miles of walls are too long. It cannot be provisioned from the sea. Leuderis turns to his second in command. 'We withdraw,' he says firmly.

Yet Leuderis has a trick up his sleeve. As the Goths march out of Rome's northern gate, the Porta Flaminia, and the Romans march unopposed into the southern one, Porta Asinaria, he remains behind. He removes his gilded chain-mail coat and discards his sword. At the Porta Asinaria, he meets Belisarius.

He kneels and looks up at the Roman general. The Goths admire him more than their own leaders. He proffers him the keys to the city. Belisarius dismounts from his horse. He is everything Leuderis expected. A soldier's soldier. His armour is battered. But his eyes are noble. Leuderis feels no fear. Belisarius tells him to stand. Then he shakes his hand. In Latin, which Leuderis understands, he tells him: 'In life, we have a choice. You made the right one. Henceforth, I appoint you a Patrician.'

Our foremost chronicler of the sixth century, and perhaps the greatest Roman historian of them all, Procopius, witnessed Leuderis' surrender. He wrote:

> *'So, after a space of sixty years, Rome again became subject to the Romans.'*[1]

Rome was back on the attack. The barbarians were retreating. We are in a new age – that of the emperor Justinian.

Justinian's reign (527–565) sits uncomfortably in the annals of history. It contradicts Edward Gibbon's celebrated *The History of the Decline and Fall of the Roman Empire*.[2] For we have a Roman Empire that is not declining or falling. The 530s were an age of spectacular reconquest. Belisarius seized North Africa and Italy. In a blitzkrieg-like campaign, he annihilated the Vandal kingdom of Carthage. Although it would take another 15 years for the Ostrogoths to be eliminated, they too would go the same way. The camera of history was in rewind, unravelling the fall of the western empire.

But stop the camera there. What really happened in these astonishing years? In this book, we'll try to understand the genuine sources of Justinian's success. Was it the military genius of Belisarius? Or the decay of the barbarian kingdoms? Or the remilitarisation of the Roman army, forged not in Justinian's day but in the ferocity of war with Attila the Hun?[3]

And there's an even more pressing question that demands to be answered. Fast forward the camera and we'll see Rome's fortunes change rapidly. In less than a century after Justinian's death, the Roman Empire died, replaced by a successor state we call Byzantium. But not just Rome died. So too did the entire ancient world. Sasanian Persia perished. Across the old territories of Rome, there was economic poverty. Falling populations. The disappearance of trade. The return of illiteracy except for a tiny minority. The magnificent cities of late antiquity vanished. Unforgiving religions fought for the hearts and minds of those who survived.

We have a name for it.

The Dark Ages.

So, what went wrong? Were the seeds of Rome's downfall planted in Justinian's reign? He said he wanted to restore the Roman Empire. But in reality, did he destroy it? In this book we will search for the answers. We will examine all the aspects of his reign. From Belisarius' campaigns to Justinian's reform of Roman law. From his monumental building programme, spearheaded by the mighty Hagia Sophia, which still stands in Istanbul, to the first bubonic plague in history. From the most cataclysmic climate event since the last Ice Age – the so-called 'dust veil event' of 536, when volcanic eruptions caused global temperatures to fall by three degrees centigrade – to the Roman obsession with chariot racing which so dominated the lives of every family, that Procopius wrote: 'I do not know what to call this if not a mental disorder.'[4]

It was an age of striking personalities, impossible to forget once met. Justinian was a peasant turned emperor. His wife Theodora, a prostitute turned empress. He was devoted to her and she to him. They were the ultimate power couple. They were joined by Belisarius and his wife, Antonina. According to Procopius, she was scheming and unfaithful, but the great general forgave her everything. These two couples were the fab four in this new age of the Roman Empire.

Supporting them came a captivating cast of characters from crooks to heroes. From the corrupt but gifted head of the Treasury, John the Cappadocian, the so-called 'Foul Cappadocian', to the erudite but greedy lawyer Tribonian. Procopius has left us with vivid portraits of the barbarians the Romans faced, from the terrifying Persian king Chosroes, who would slaughter thousands but yield to the words of a pretty girl or a brave man to Gelimer, the last Vandal king and a gifted musician who asked for a lyre with which to lament the fall of his kingdom, and to Totila, the macho Gothic king who, in his last battle, rode up to the Roman lines and performed a war dance, repeatedly throwing his javelin high in the air and catching it perfectly in his hand.

It was a magical age. Robert Graves, author of *I, Claudius*, said it stood at the cross-roads of history, between the twilight of antiquity and the dawn of the Middle Ages.[5] It captivated Dante, and in the *Divine Comedy*, he honoured Justinian with a place in the second sphere of heaven – the place for truly great rulers who were only limited by their lust for glory.

Let's begin our journey. We start with the age before Justinian. And no event dominated it more than the one we are about to discover now – one of the worst defeats in Rome's entire history. We begin in North Africa in the year 468.

PART I

New Rome, New Romans

1

Disaster at Cape Bon

It is a warm African night. A breeze blows inland from the sea across the sandy beach to a derelict, ancient temple that overlooks the wide expanse of the bay. The temple is long forgotten and has no roof, but its rows of columns once housed the god Hermes or, as the Romans called him, Mercury. Hence the name of this coastal town, Mercurium. Today, it's called Cape Bon.

Out in the bay, over a thousand Roman ships roll gently in the sea's swell. Smaller boats are bringing thousands of men and horses ashore. Horses, frustrated by their long time at sea, neigh and stamp their hooves before jumping into the sea spray when they land.

Further up the coast, in Carthage, Geiseric, king of the Vandals consults with African sailors. They tell him something. He nods and listens. An idea comes to him. It is his only hope against this vast Roman armada.

In 468, the eastern Roman emperor Leo mustered one of the largest invasion forces in Roman history. His mission was to destroy the Vandal kingdom in North Africa. We have various sources for this and they all agree on one point: the huge scale of the expedition. The sixth-century chronicler, Procopius, has left us with an account taken from the lost writings of Priscus. He says 100,000 soldiers were mustered for it. Another chronicler, Cedrenus, describes a huge armada of 1,113 ships. The number of ships is plausible given that many would have been quite small. The number of soldiers is more likely to have been around 50,000 at most. Not surprisingly, the cost to the eastern Roman treasury was said to be gigantic at 130,000 pounds of gold, according to Procopius, equivalent, for example, to nearly 62 years of annual tribute paid to Attila the Hun.[6]

The success of this expedition was crucially important to the eastern emperor Leo. He worked tirelessly on the plan of campaign. The main fleet would sail to Sicily and thence to Carthage. Roman troops from Dalmatia were to secure the island from the Vandals prior to the fleet's arrival, as well as ridding Sardinia of the Vandals. A third force, recruited from the army in Egypt, led by the general Heraclius, was to be transported to Tripolis in modern-day Libya, and would march along the Mediterranean coastline towards Carthage, taking the towns belonging to the Vandals along the way.

Despite Leo's wish to make the expedition a success, Procopius emphasised a fatal flaw on the Roman side. There was a bitter feud within their ranks. Leo gave overall command of the entire operation to his brother-in-law, the general Basiliscus. Although Basiliscus had proved himself a reasonably competent general in the Hunnic wars along the Danube, Procopius claims he had designs on the throne himself and wanted to discredit Leo. He also says he was in league with the prominent Gothic general, Aspar, who had fallen out with Leo. Indeed, he says Aspar wanted the expedition to fail.

Whatever the truth about the back-stabbing politics, the expedition started well. Marcellinus seized Sicily and Sardinia from the Vandals. Heraclius' Egyptian army landed in Tripolis and began its march towards Carthage largely unopposed. Meanwhile, the main fleet set sail for Sicily. One minor chronicler, Theophanes, quoting Priscus, suggests there was a naval battle off Sicily in which the Roman fleet triumphed over the Vandals: 'he [Basiliscus] engaged in naval battles with Gaiseric's force and sank many of his ships'.[7]

So far so good for the Romans. In June 468, Basiliscus crossed with the fleet from Sicily to North Africa. With a favourable wind, it might have taken only a day for it to reach the African coast. The armada anchored in the shelter of the bay of Cape Bon, about 40 miles from Carthage, between modern Ras el-Mar and Ras Addar in Tunisia. It was chosen because the winds in summer were normally easterly and would help a quick descent on Carthage. Historians think Basiliscus was probably aiming to land his army at the bay of Utica, a quick march from Carthage, since the harbour of Carthage was protected against enemy shipping by a chain.

Gaiseric must have been desperate by now. The Roman armada was far more powerful than his own forces. Procopius said that if Basiliscus '...had undertaken to go straight for Carthage, he would have taken it at the first onset, and ... reduced the Vandals to servitude without their even thinking of resistance...'.[8]

But it was not to be. Gaiseric was a cunning old fox. He wanted Basiliscus to believe that he had given up hope and was about to surrender. So, he sent a deputation asking for a five-day truce while in reality he prepared for war. Why did Basiliscus fall for this? Contemporaries and historians have universally labelled him either an imbecile or a traitor. Procopius' anger with Basiliscus leaps out from the pages of his history. He even suspected Basiliscus had accepted a bribe from the Vandal king: 'They say that he [Gaiseric] also, without the knowledge of Basiliscus's army, sent quite a sum of gold and in fact purchased this truce.'[9] In exasperation, he says Basiliscus fell into Gaiseric's trap for any of three reasons: one, he simply wanted Gaiseric's money; two, as previously mentioned, he was in league with Aspar against the emperor Leo and wanted the expedition to fail; or three, he was just plain stupid.

Perhaps the real answer was that, with an overwhelmingly large Roman fleet and army at his disposal, Basiliscus was simply too complacent. But if there was one lesson to be learned from fifth-century Roman history, it was never to underestimate Gaiseric. By offering the truce, Gaiseric was waiting literally for the wind of fortune to change. Advised by expert African sailors, for it is doubtful the Vandals ever truly mastered seamanship, he was told that victory or defeat depended on using the sea winds to your advantage.

The wind in question was an easterly one that was blowing when the Romans arrived and would have propelled them rapidly to Carthage. As Procopius said, if Basiliscus had attacked immediately, victory would almost certainly have been his. But he delayed. Gaiseric was hoping the wind would change to a north-westerly one that would pin the Romans to the coastline and allow him to launch his attack.

And again, no doubt advised by his African sailors, he had a trick up his sleeve. He was going to use fire ships. Procopius wrote: 'Arming his subjects in the best way he could, he filled his ships, but not all, for some he kept in readiness empty, and they were the ships which sailed most swiftly.'[10]

Fortune is fickle. Rome had had its fair share of luck during the centuries of its rise to greatness. But in the years of its decline, its luck ran out. And there is no better example of this than what followed next, as Procopius described:

> *But the Vandals, as soon as the wind had arisen for them which they had been expecting during the time they lay at rest, raised their sails and taking in tow the boats which, as stated above, had been made ready with no men in them, they sailed against the enemy. And when they came near, they set fire to the boats which they were towing, when their sails were bellied by the wind, and let them go against the Roman fleet. And since there was a great number of ships there, these boats easily spread fire wherever they struck, and were themselves readily destroyed together with those with which they came into contact.*[11]

Fire ships could be deadly in ancient warfare. Fire was one of the gravest threats to ancient wooden ships, whose sun-dried decks and sails burned quickly. Ironically, it was the Carthaginians, Rome's greatest enemy in its early days, and the predecessors to the Vandal kingdom of Carthage, who had used fire ships to devastating effect against a Roman fleet 600 years before in 149 BC. Centuries later, the Byzantines would learn how to use 'Greek Fire' to destroy several enemy fleets. And a more modern example was the English defeat of the Spanish Armada in 1588. Very similar to the Roman fleet in 468, the vast Spanish fleet outnumbered the small English navy. The situation looked hopeless for the English just as it did for the Vandals. Yet, only eight English fire ships caused enough damage to disperse and defeat the Spanish navy.

The same happened to the Romans at the Battle of Cape Bon in 468. We don't know how many Vandal fire ships were released into the midst of the Roman fleet. We don't know how many Roman ships were burned and sank. All we know is that Procopius says the Vandals destroyed the Roman fleet in a fiery haze. He praised the bravery of many of the Roman soldiers and sailors who fought to the death to prevent the fires from spreading while they also resisted the Vandal ships, in particular, a Roman general, named John, who went down with his ship rather than surrender:

> *He [John] stood on the deck and, turning from side to side, kept killing very great numbers of the enemy, and when he realized there was no hope left, he jumped wearing his heavy armour, from the deck into the sea … uttering that he would never surrender to the barbarian dogs.*[12]

The Romans fought bravely but in a few hours the wily Gaiseric had won by far his greatest victory.

Basiliscus, the architect of the disaster, survived the battle and sheepishly returned to Constantinople. Fearing for his life, he took sanctuary in the church of St Sophia. There, the formidable Verina, his sister and Leo's wife, intervened to save him. He had much to thank his sister for. Although he had been responsible for one of the Roman Empire's worst defeats in its entire history, he survived and we will soon hear more about him.

But the western Roman Empire was not so lucky. Its last hope was dashed. Within just eight years it had ceased to exist. As for the eastern empire, it took decades to recover from the catastrophe at Cape Bon. But recover it did, and the first part of this book will tell how that happened, so that by AD 533, Constantinople could send another expedition to Carthage. That time it was led by a brilliant young general, Belisarius, who would achieve a very different outcome. But before we get to that story, we must ask a question that historians still struggle to agree on. Who were the eastern Romans?

2

The New Romans

In modern Istanbul, a stone's throw away from Justinian's great cathedral of Hagia Sophia, lies another cathedral. But this one is underground. Referred to as the Basilica Cistern, or in Turkish *Yerebatan Sarayi*, meaning the underground palace, it is one of the most breathtaking places in the entire world.

Down a flight of steps, you enter a vast underground chamber, with a vaulted ceiling supported by 336 ancient columns, each 30 feet high (see Figure 6). Capable of containing nearly 3 million cubic feet of water, it is one of over a hundred underground cisterns built by the Romans to supply Constantinople. But this one is special. Commissioned by Justinian, it is not only the largest cistern in the city, but its mesmerising array of ancient columns provides us with one of our best insights into the late Roman mind.

For almost all the columns were plundered from classical buildings, not just temples but also from the forums, administrative buildings and palaces of the ancient world. Most striking are two Medusa heads, one placed upside down as a column base, and the other with its face sideways planted into the ground (see Figure 7). No one knows how or why they came to be there. They were clearly taken from some ancient building. But why go to the effort of transporting such colossal pieces of stone? The most likely answer is that these new Romans were as superstitious about their pagan past as they were about their newfound Christianity.

So, how should we imagine these new Romans? I suggest the key is to understand how the idea of 'Romanness' evolved during the long history of the Roman Empire. If we start with Julius Caesar, for him, being Roman meant belonging to an exclusive club of about 4 million Roman citizens who lived in an empire inhabited by perhaps 40 million people. In his time, the city of Rome was the undisputed centre of the Roman world, and overwhelmingly more important than any other city in the empire.

Fast forward 500 years and the eastern Roman Empire didn't even contain Italy or the city of Rome itself, both now subject to the Ostrogothic kingdom of Theodoric the Great. But the eastern Romans still thought of themselves as Romans. So, how are we to explain this?

Readers of the earlier volumes in this series will be familiar with how the concept of Romanness developed over the centuries. It was Augustus, the so-called 'grandfather' of Europe, who began the process of 'Romanising' the empire. For he saw that to govern an empire as large as Rome's, the diverse populations of the empire had to want to be Roman. He cleverly presented the alluring idea that the Romans were not oppressors but liberators. They offered not tyranny but the rule of a benign state, regulated by Roman law and protected by the Roman army. This was instantly attractive to the inhabitants of a world where tyranny and corruption were normal. Roman citizenship became the ultimate prize for the upwardly mobile people of the empire.

Unlike the Greek city states, who were fiercely protective of their citizenship, Roman citizenship was available to those willing to earn it. For example, 25 years' service in the army automatically bought you citizenship. Grants of citizenship were willingly made to foreign cities, allies and anyone contributing to the empire's well-being. Even Paul the Apostle was a Roman citizen.

In AD 212, the emperor Caracalla granted universal Roman citizenship to all free men in the empire (and free women were given the same rights as Roman women). Being Roman was no longer exclusive, it was inclusive. Let's not misread any benign intentions into this. Caracalla's motive was in fact a short-term policy to increase tax revenues by making more people liable for the inheritance tax that was levied on Roman citizens. On top of that, most wealthy and important people in the empire were already Roman citizens. But that should not detract from the significance of Caracalla's action which was to demonstrate that throughout the length and breadth of the empire *people wanted to be Roman.*

The trade-off was a dilution in the importance of Italy and the city of Rome. This accelerated in the 'crisis of the third century' when the Roman army was defeated on a scale never seen before. From the Rhine to Syria, Roman armies were destroyed. Emperors were captured or killed. The soldier-emperors, like Claudius Gothicus, Aurelian and Diocletian, saved the empire. But they did so by dispensing with the supine senatorial class, and relegating the city of Rome itself to a political backwater.

Henceforth, emperors hardly visited Rome let alone lived there. Diocletian lived in Nicomedia in western Anatolia, keeping a close eye on the Danube and Persian frontiers while his trusted deputy, Maximian, ruled the west and lived in Milan not Rome. As one Roman chronicler noted 'Rome was wherever the emperor was.'[13] And it wasn't just Rome that lost its status. Italy did as well when Diocletian withdrew the tax advantages that had distinguished it as the mother country and made it into just another province of the empire.

By this time, Julius Caesar would have been turning in his grave as all his 'Roman' biases and preconceptions were being challenged. And the next development would have sent him into a veritable spin. For there was a profound spiritual change in the concept of Romanness. The military invincibility associated with the Roman gods was shattered in the third century. The emperor Constantine took advantage of this by associating himself with a new religion that was growing strongly – Christianity. The soldier-emperors failed to find a new faith the Romans could embrace. Constantine made up for this by turning first to Sol Invictus, and then to Christianity, as his divine support. Constantine's message was simple: he was all-powerful and his rule was sanctioned by a Christian God. He founded a new city, Constantinople, to separate himself from the moribund image of the city of Rome.

New Rome was born.

3

The New Roman Army

By far the most important reason for the survival of the eastern Roman Empire was the revival of its army.

The western empire fell because of military failure. In the east, it was a different story. As discussed in the last book in this series, the catalyst for eastern Roman military recovery was Attila. A major Roman remilitarisation in the 440s was necessary to stop Attila's hordes from crossing the Danube and capturing Constantinople itself. Historians now think[14] two new field armies were created in the 440s besides the three that already existed, almost doubling the number of elite professional soldiers.

On top of increasing the numbers came a profound change in tactics and equipment. Although we have frustratingly little information about fifth- and sixth-century Roman armies (for example there is nothing similar to Trajan's Column in Rome which by itself provides a vast reservoir of pictorial detail about the classical army), Procopius has provided us with a valuable insight. He describes a type of Roman soldier that Julius Caesar and Augustus would not have recognised: an armoured horseman with sword and spear but also with a Hunnic-type composite bow he could use with deadly accuracy. I will quote the entire passage, since it is so important.

> *…the bowmen of the present time go into battle wearing corselets and fitted out with greaves which extend up to the knee. From the right side hang their arrows, from the other the sword. And there are some who have a spear also attached to them and, at the shoulders, a sort of small shield without a grip, such as to cover the region of the face and neck. They are expert horsemen, and are able without difficulty to direct their bows to either side while riding at full speed, and to shoot an opponent whether in pursuit or in flight.*[15]

Writing later at the end of the sixth century, the emperor Maurice, or one of his subordinates, penned an extraordinary military manual called *The Strategicon*,[16] which provides more information on this radically different Roman army. The regular Roman soldiers comprised the mounted archer/lancer supported by the traditional Roman heavy infantry, similar to but probably not as well trained or equipped as the legionaries of old. As will become clear in our history of Justinian's wars, light cavalry was also important, and usually recruited from barbarian groups. Elaborate tactics are described in *The Strategicon*, each one tailored to meet and beat the military skills of the empire's opponents, from steppe nomads to Persians and German barbarians.

Some historians have suggested Belisarius, in Justinian's reign, helped to invent this new type of Roman horseman.

The theory is that it was his and other generals' household guards' regiments, called *bucellarii* (literally the biscuit-eaters referring to the rations they were given) that developed them. I disagree with this. While the *bucellarii* were an element within the Roman army (and Procopius says Belisarius even had 7,000 of them – an exaggeration I think) they were not large enough to form its professional core. Nor would emperors have wanted this since it would have meant passing power to their generals' private armies. Instead, the powerhouse of the Roman army was its field armies, and these contained large numbers of armoured horse archers who required years of training and represented a considerable financial investment which only the state could afford.

The evidence for the strengthened eastern Roman army is that in 450, Constantinople stopped paying tribute to the Huns. The new emperor Marcian was willing to risk war with Attila. And the show of strength worked. Attila would not risk war with the eastern army and turned west instead. In 451, on the Catalaunian Plains, a coalition of Germans and Romans defeated him. It was the Germans, and the Visigoths in particular, not the weak western Roman army, who did most of the fighting and won the battle. Thereafter, it was the Germans and not the Romans who took the political gains in the west.

Meanwhile, the story in the east was the exact opposite. With its revitalised army, the eastern empire was ready to go on the offensive to save the west. This led to Leo's disastrous defeat at Cape Bon in 468, which stalled the eastern empire for at least two decades. But the eastern Roman army did eventually recover, as Belisarius' victories were to show.

What about numbers? Most historians think the chronicler Agathias was correct when he said Justinian's army was about 150,000 strong. This would have comprised a mixed force of elite field army troops and the second-rate garrison soldiers called *limitanei*. Back in the crisis of the third century AD, the legion-structured Roman army had broken into these two distinctive types of soldier, as emperors collected mobile field armies (with a large cavalry element) to strike at invaders or to fight rivals and usurpers and left cheaper, less professional troops to guard the frontiers. As mentioned above, in order to respond to Attila, the eastern empire probably created two new field armies, termed praesental (meaning 'with the emperor') to supplement the existing three field armies in the eastern empire, one based on the eastern front (*Oriens*) and two in the Balkans (the *Thracias* and *Illyricum* field armies). Assuming each of the five field armies had around 15,000 men, this would mean there were 75,000 top-quality soldiers, and probably another 75,000 *limitanei*, totalling 150,000.

In short, the military revolution in the eastern empire of the fifth century enabled the Roman army to become the best fighting force in the world just as it had been in the days of Julius Caesar and Augustus.

4

Zeno the Barbarian

In January 474, the emperor Leo, instigator of the disastrous expedition to Carthage, died. He was succeeded by Zeno, a man considered by most to be a barbarian.

This was because he was Isaurian. The Isaurians were a hardy people living in the Taurus Mountains in south-west Anatolia, widely regarded as barbarian despite being Roman subjects for over five centuries. Ignored until the threat posed by Attila in the mid-fifth century required the eastern Romans to rebuild their army, they suddenly became a sought-after source of recruits. Illyria (approximately modern Croatia and Serbia) had been the traditional recruiting ground for the Roman army ever since the crisis of the third century AD, when most of the soldier-emperors came from that region. But by the fifth century, the endless warfare with Germanic invaders decimated its population, and the Romans turned reluctantly to Isauria as a fresh and untouched source of tough, young men.

A parallel might be found with the recruitment of Scottish Highlanders by the British army in the eighteenth century. Faced with growing challenges in its American colonies, and an increasingly militant France, Britain had to increase rapidly the size of its small army, and turned, rather reluctantly, to creating regiments of Highlanders, who were exceptionally warlike and eager to take the king's shilling.

In Rome's case, unfortunately we have almost no information whatsoever about the numbers of Isaurians and the regiments they joined but I suspect they formed most of the new praesental field armies, as mentioned in the previous chapter, and were important in the battles fought against Attila in the 440s, and probably contributed a large proportion of the troops sent to Carthage in 468.

This created a tension within the eastern Roman army since Gothic mercenaries still dominated it, especially among its senior commanders. The background to this[17] was that in the late fourth and fifth centuries Gothic and other Germanic mercenaries had become the main troops within the Roman army in both east and west, pushing out the conventional Roman soldiers. This 'outsourcing' of their army had disastrous consequences for the Romans and was the main reason for the fall of the western empire. For example, two rival barbarian commanders, Stilicho and Alaric, had fought a bizarre duel in the 400s, culminating in Alaric's sack of Rome.

In the east, Stilicho's equivalent was Aspar, a Goth who had been head of the eastern Roman army since the 430s. He was powerful enough to become a kingmaker and promoted his protégé, Leo, to be emperor in 457 when Marcian died. But Leo feared he would become Aspar's puppet, so he promoted a military rival to challenge him. This was Zeno. Zeno might have been a barbarian in the eyes of many eastern

Romans but at least he was not Germanic. This was a vitally important step towards reclaiming the eastern Roman army as an indigenous force.

His Isaurian name was *Tarasicodissa Rousoumbladotes*, but he adopted the Greek name Zeno to integrate himself more easily within the Roman elite. Zeno's background is obscure, but it is likely that his father was a senior commander in the war against Attila in the 440s, and he was himself head of the palace guard when he came to the notice of the emperor Leo.

In the 460s, Leo and Aspar openly fell out and Leo made a point of siding with Zeno against him by marrying his daughter, Ariadne, to Zeno. Their son Leo became the heir apparent to the throne, displacing Aspar's son, Ardaburius, who Aspar was backing for the throne. In 471, Leo had Aspar assassinated and the problem of Gothic domination of the army was finally over. In January 474, Leo died and was succeeded by his seven-year-old grandson, and Zeno's son, Leo II. Zeno proclaimed himself co-emperor with his son on account of his young age, until his son unexpectedly died in November 474, when he assumed the sole position of emperor.

Zeno was now emperor. But people still regarded him as an outsider. Not least his mother-in-law, the empress Verina, who despite her husband Leo's death, was still a powerful force in politics. When Zeno married her daughter, Ariadne, she'd been happy to go along with this. But once he was on the throne, Zeno proved deeply unpopular with everyone, and not just his mother-in-law. The consensus was that Leo had made a terrible mistake making him emperor. And it was relatively simple for Verina to convince him he was about to be assassinated in order to get him to flee the capital.

One day in November 475, as he was watching the chariot races in the hippodrome, he received an urgent message from her that there was a conspiracy to assassinate him that day. He got up from the imperial chair and hastily beat a retreat from the hippodrome and later the same day slipped out of Constantinople with his wife Ariadne, and a retinue of servants to seek safety in Isauria.

In fact, Verina had made the whole thing up because she wanted to put on the throne her lover, a senator named Patricius. The moment it became known that Zeno had fled the capital, the mob rampaged through the city killing whichever Isaurians they could lay their hands on. Meanwhile, Verina's treachery backfired on her when the senate chose not her lover, Patricius, as emperor but her brother, Basiliscus, the man who had led the great Roman armada to destruction in 468. And Basiliscus was not afraid to confront his fiery sister and put her in her place by having her lover, Patricius, executed. Verina, terrified for her own life, backed off, perhaps ruing that she had ever conspired against her son-in-law.

Basiliscus was a man who, over the last 1,500 years, has received not one kind word from any chronicler or historian. He was universally detested in the sixth century and he still is. Indeed, it was truly remarkable that he attained the position of emperor at all, and once he did, he did everything possible to lose it. His first foolish action was to promote the lover of his beautiful wife Zenonis. Unknown to him, but known to everyone else, she was having a passionate affair with a senator called Armatus. A chronicler recorded:

> *Their relationship became intimate, and as they were both persons of no ordinary beauty they became extravagantly enamoured of each other. They used to exchange glances and smile at each other in public, scarcely concealing their passion.*

To make himself even more of a laughing stock, Basiliscus agreed to his wife's demand to make her lover the senior *magister militum* (head of the army), replacing the Thracian Goth, Strabo. Armatus then caused popular outrage with his vain antics:

> *When he was promoted by his mistress's husband, Armatus imagined that he was a man of valour, and dressed himself as Achilles, in which guise he used to ride about to the amusement of the people in the hippodrome. The mob named him Pyrrhus, on account of his pink cheeks, but he took this as a compliment to his valour, and became still more inflated with pride.*[18]

Basiliscus' unpopularity grew when it became known he was a Monophysite, a Christian sect we will discuss much more in later chapters, popular in some parts of the empire but deeply unpopular in Constantinople. The final straw was a great fire in the city which caused extensive destruction and burned to the ground an enormous library called the Basilica, founded by the emperor Julian the Apostate, and containing over 120,000 books. One victim of the fire was a famous copy of Homer's *Iliad and Odyssey*, written in golden characters on the intestine of a great serpent, 120 feet long.

This fire clearly had nothing to do with Basiliscus but the inhabitants of the city attributed it to divine vengeance for his idiotic rule.

Messages were sent to Zeno in Isauria, begging him to return and depose Basiliscus. Zeno gathered Isaurian troops and was joined by his fellow Isaurian, Illus, who had previously supported Basiliscus but who now switched sides and backed Zeno. Zeno marched on Constantinople.

Basiliscus responded by ordering Armatus, his wife's lover, to muster the troops in the city and march to meet Zeno in battle. But Armatus would not risk his life to save his mistress' husband. He sent messengers to Zeno, telling him he too would swap sides. He pretended to lose his way and led his soldiers in the wrong direction. Zeno entered the capital in August 476 with no resistance. Basiliscus fled with his family to the church of Hagia Sophia, not the one we can see today but the one that burned down before Justinian rebuilt it, just as he had done when he returned from his disastrous expedition to Carthage. Zeno persuaded the Patriarch Acacius to hand them all over by promising he would not shed their blood. Zeno was as good as his word. Instead of beheading them, Zeno sent Basiliscus, his unfaithful wife and their children to the bottom of a huge, dry cistern in Cappadocia where he left them, unable to escape or to eat, to die of starvation. At long last, the man who had led the great armada of 468 to destruction met his just deserts. Zeno had promised Armatus he would spare his life. He honoured this for a few months before assassinating him. He was fast learning that one of the main qualifications for a Roman emperor was not to have a conscience.

Against all expectations, the unpopular Zeno had triumphed and perhaps earned some respect. He had certainly learned some survival skills. He would need every one of those over the next 15 years.

5

Goodbye Goths

With Basiliscus out of the way, Zeno had no major contenders for the throne left. But he still faced three key challenges: first, the growing power of the Goths in the Balkans; second, an Isaurian rebellion against his rule since he was seen as a traitor to the Isaurian cause, and third, the continuing religious division within the empire over Monophysitism.

By far the most significant problem was the Gothic presence in the Balkans, and it was in this area Zeno achieved his greatest triumph. Let's begin by looking at the background to this.

After the collapse of Attila's empire in the 550s, two sets of Goths had migrated south across the Danube and occupied Roman territory in the Balkans. To the west were the Pannonian Goths led by Theodoric the Amal (the Amali being a leading dynasty), and to the east, the Thracian Goths led by another Theodoric, this time with the epithet Strabo, meaning 'the squinter' (we will refer to him as Strabo henceforth). During the 470s, Zeno kept negotiations going with both Theodorics, cunningly playing them off against each other. In 478, his plan was to persuade them to fight each other for Roman patronage, a bit like having two gladiators fight it out. He made overtures to both of them, promising huge rewards if they would defeat the other. For example, he told Theodoric (the Amal) a large Roman army would join him to attack Strabo. This was a complete lie, and the two sets of Goths met in the central Balkans in the Haemus Mountains. They realised Zeno had set them up and agreed to a truce. But this didn't last and Zeno sided with Strabo against Theodoric.

Facing both Strabo's Goths and the Roman army, Theodoric retreated west into Epirus and based himself at the Roman port of Dyracchium on the Adriatic which he had taken a few years previously. He thought of crossing to Italy. But he decided not to because Zeno and Strabo fell out when Strabo supported a Roman usurper, Marcian. Strabo advanced towards Constantinople but its walls deterred him from attacking the city. The Roman navy defeated his attempt to cross the sea of Marmara and Strabo resolved to take his people to Greece instead. But he never made it. One morning in 481, he mounted his horse which reared unexpectedly and threw him to the ground. He might have survived, but he fell straight onto a spear planted in the ground point up. Our sources don't suggest there was a conspiracy to kill him but it can't be ruled out. Strabo's son, Recitach, succeeded him, until he was killed in late 483 or early 484, on his way from having a bath to a feast. This time it was an assassination instigated by Theodoric, probably encouraged by Zeno.

Our sources describe this as a pivotal moment in Gothic history, for it enabled Theodoric to unite both the Pannonian and Thracian Goths into a Gothic supergroup.

Most historians[19] think this is a simplified view and the union of the two sets of Goths had been going on for some time. Whatever the truth, Theodoric emerged as the winner. What would he and his Ostrogoths do now?

Theodoric seemed unsure. He vacillated between alliance with the Roman emperor and defiance. At one point, in 484, he sought an alliance with Zeno and sent him troops to join the Roman armies fighting the Isaurians but in 486, he marched on Constantinople, where he cut the water supply and laid siege to the city. This was probably only a show of force since its formidable walls would have been far too difficult to storm.

As mentioned, he had looked at the possibility of taking his people to Italy before, and in the autumn of 488, Zeno and Theodoric agreed the Goths would leave the Balkans for Italy. Zeno permitted him to rule Italy as agent for the eastern empire, betraying Odoacer, his appointed patrician in Italy, who was doing the same job. In the autumn of 488, over 100,000 Goths, including women and children, left Moesia and took the road past Viminacium towards Italy.

This was a genuine turning point for both Goths and Romans. How did Zeno achieve it? It was obviously in his interests but why Theodoric's? I suggest the answer lies mostly with the recovery of the Roman military by the 480s. The defeat outside Carthage in 468 had left a military vacuum in the Balkans which the Goths filled. But by 488, 20 years after the Cape Bon catastrophe, the Roman army was stronger. Finally, it could challenge the Goths in the Balkans. Theodoric realised this and, like Alaric and his Goths nearly a century before, departed for Italy while the going was good. There he met with brilliant success. He defeated Odoacer, conquered Italy and created a powerful Gothic-Roman kingdom that we will revisit again in Chapter 31.

But if you think Zeno was now in for an easy life, you would be very wrong. His reign must count as one of the most fraught in Rome's entire history. Much of this was due to infighting within his own family. In particular, both his mother-in-law and wife opposed his Isaurian supporters, and in particular, his main Isaurian general, Illus. Verina hated Illus since she believed he had caused her brother's death. She planned his assassination. One day, an imperial slave was discovered lying in wait for him, sword drawn. Then another would-be assassin, an Alan, was caught who confessed under torture that the empress Verina had paid him to assassinate Illus.

Illus was understandably furious and forced Zeno to banish her to the castle of Dalisandus in Tarsus. But that was not the end of Zeno's turbulent domestic problems since his wife, Ariadne, protested that her mother, Verina, should be released. When Zeno refused, she plotted to kill Illus just as her mother had done.

One day, as Illus was walking to his seat in the hippodrome, an assassin jumped up and tried to kill him by bringing his sword down on his head. He only succeeded in cutting off his right ear. Under torture, the man revealed the empress had paid him. Illus protested to Zeno that he must have known what his wife was up to. Zeno protected his wife and denied all knowledge. To smooth things over, he ordered Illus to leave Constantinople to take up the position of *magister militum per Oriens*, the general in command of troops on the Persian front, hoping to get him out of harm's way.

I should mention at this point an added twist to the relationship between Zeno and Illus. Our sources are not completely reliable, but one of them says Illus was holding Zeno's brother, Longinus, prisoner. We'll hear more about Longinus in the next chapter. This might explain Zeno's reluctance to offend Illus. But when Illus refused to hand him over, there was a complete breakdown in relations between the two of them. Zeno relieved Illus of his command and appointed John the Scythian in his stead. Illus responded by gathering his Isaurian troops to oust Zeno from the throne. In 484, in a battle near to Seleucia, John the Scythian, leading regular Roman troops, defeated Illus and his Isaurian soldiers. Illus fled to the fortress of Papurius in the Isaurian mountains where the exiled Verina was living. In what has to be one of the most unexpected reconciliations in history, Illus and Verina became firm friends, united in their hatred of Zeno. The fortress held out for four years, Verina dying during this time, and in 488, it was finally taken by treachery and Illus was beheaded. His head was sent to Zeno in Constantinople, where it was no doubt prominently displayed.

It's hard to know what moral to draw from this tale, indeed if any exists. But it serves to illustrate just how uncomfortably Zeno's Isaurian identity sat, not just with the people of Constantinople but even with his own wife and mother-in-law.

Before we conclude with Zeno's reign, there is one last point to cover. This concerns religion, always a subject close to the hearts of the eastern Romans, and in particular the religious division over Monophysitism within the empire. We'll go into more detail on this in Chapter 10, but in 481, Zeno tried to heal the rift with a compromise called the *Henotikon*, or 'formula of union'. This worked to some extent in reconciling the Monophysites in Egypt and Syria with anti-Monophysite Constantinople, but it also caused a rift with the staunchly Catholic Church in Rome.

Against the odds, Zeno survived into old age, where he fell into despair, probably because his son, also called Zeno, born to his first wife Arcadia, died young after leading a dissolute life. With no obvious successor and fearing plots to assassinate him, he fell ill and died on April 9 491, at around the age of 70.

The question now was who would succeed him? And this time it was the people who would decide.

6

Give Us A Roman Emperor!

A cold, bright morning in Constantinople. Thousands of people pack the hippodrome. Wearing brightly coloured cloaks – blues and greens mainly, the colours of the Circus Factions – they chant the name of their favourite charioteers. Chariot racing is the lifeblood of the city. Almost everyone belongs to one of the so-called Circus Factions – Blue, Green, Red and White, although by this time it is the Blues and Greens who dominate. These factions run the chariot-racing teams but are also responsible for public festivals, law and order, and are highly political. Although sometimes compared with modern sports like American football and soccer, chariot racing in the sixth century was much more than that. It was like a cross between a political rally and a sporting event.

Today, the mob is intimidating. It wants to make its point. The people are fed up with the Isaurians. Barbarians in Roman clothes. They want a true Roman emperor. They chant: 'Give the world a Roman emperor!'

Suddenly, figures are visible in the imperial box, on the eastern side of the hippodrome, closest to the imperial palace. They see Zeno's widow, the empress Ariadne, surrounded by ministers. They chant: 'Long live the Augusta!' Then they repeat their demand for a Roman emperor. Ariadne's reply is given by the Master of Offices, whose voice was no doubt louder than hers:

> *In order that the choice may be pure and pleasing to God, we have commanded the ministers and the Senate, the vote of the army concurring, to make the election, in the presence of the Gospels, and in the presence of the Patriarch, so that no one may be influenced by friendship or enmity, or kinship, or any other private motive, but may vote with his conscience clear. Therefore, as the matter is weighty and concerns the welfare of the world, you must acquiesce in a short delay, till the funeral rites of Zeno, of pious memory, have been performed, so that the election may not be overly hasty.*[20]

These words and the description above are not fiction. They are taken from the unusually detailed record of this event, left to us thanks to the work of the tenth- century Byzantine emperor, Constantine Porphyrogenitus, who preserved a remarkable list of documents from antiquity, one of which is a detailed account of the proceedings that followed Zeno's death.

Let's return to our narrative. Ariadne and her ministers withdrew from the imperial box to discuss candidates. Eventually, a suitable candidate was chosen to meet everyone's requirements, except those of the Patriarch, as I will explain in a moment. This was Anastasius, a man who had held a long and distinguished career in the imperial treasury. He was well known in Constantinople as a capable administrator and incorruptible. In his sixties, which was old by the standards of the age, he'd been born around 430 in Dyracchium into a high-ranking Illyrian family. He was a man of tall stature and remarkable for his handsome eyes, one blue and one black, which caused him to be called *Dikoros*, meaning 'two-pupiled'. Our sources describe him as intelligent, well educated, courteous and energetic in pursuit of his administrative duties. Known to be a devout Christian, he had sympathies for the Monophysites, which caused the Patriarch Euphemius to oppose his selection and later demand he sign a declaration of orthodoxy.

For once, the empire had chosen an emperor for his merits, not because of his dynastic lineage, or because he was a stooge of the most powerful military faction. Anastasius was the first emperor to be genuinely popular since Marcus Aurelius. And he would prove to be an excellent choice.

His first challenge was one he was well prepared for. He had been selected because he was Roman rather than Isaurian. Therefore, a showdown with the Isaurians was inevitable. The Isaurians were still a powerful faction in Constantinople, and some of them had been hoping Zeno would make his brother, Longinus (as mentioned in the last chapter), his successor. But Longinus did not help matters by leading a life of debauchery that ruled him out as an imperial candidate. When Anastasius became emperor, tensions were running high. A riot in the hippodrome gave him the pretext to drive them out of the city. The riot was directed against the Prefect of the City, Julian, for reasons that have never become apparent. It may or may not have been incited by the

Isaurians. When Anastasius himself was present, the rioters set fire to the hippodrome and pulled down some bronze statues of the emperors. Anastasius called in the palace guards to restore order. But instead of punishing the rioters, he appealed to their sympathies by blaming the Isaurians. He passed a decree expelling them from the city. Longinus was forced to take holy orders and banished to far-away Thebes in Egypt. Anastasius confiscated Zeno's property, even selling his imperial robes, and withdrew the large allowances Zeno had been paying his fellow countrymen, amounting to 1,400 pounds of gold.

The result was a rebellion in Isauria. Anastasius had expected this. He sent the praesental armies led by John the Scythian and John the Hunchback against them. The Isaurians were said to have put together an army 100,000-strong, clearly a huge exaggeration but still a formidable force. At the battle of Cotyaeum in Phrygia in 492, the regular army proved its worth. It routed the Isaurians who never recovered as an independent force. Although the survivors fled into the Taurus mountains, and the last of them did not surrender until 498, the Isaurian problem was now well and truly over. Anastasius settled many of them in Thrace, still depopulated after the Gothic occupation.

Anastasius' next challenge was much more serious. This was the return of an old enemy. The Sasanian Persians.

7

The Old Enemy

The image of disciplined Roman soldiers fighting wild, long-haired barbarians dominates almost every Hollywood film about ancient Rome. But do you see this portrayed in the beautiful frescoes and mosaics that once decorated the houses of the rich inhabitants of Pompeii and other Roman cities? The short answer is no. Instead, there is another enemy depicted. An enemy regarded as far more frightening than the disorganised barbarians to the north of the civilised Mediterranean world.

These were the Persians.

Ever since the Parthian Persians crushed Crassus' six legions at the Battle of Carrhae in 53 BC, Persia had been Rome's only serious rival. And Rome's legionaries were afraid of Persian horsemen – the so-called 'boiler boys', or *clibanarii* – because of their heavy armour.

While Parthian Persia was no match for the might of classical Rome in the first and second centuries AD, in the third century the new Sasanian dynasty proved far more of a challenge. In AD 260, the first Sasanian shah, Ardashir, destroyed a huge Roman army at Edessa and captured the emperor Valerian. It was the ultimate insult to Roman authority and a clear sign the world order was changing.

Fighting was fierce in the fourth century. The emperor Julian the Apostate launched an invasion of Persia in AD 363, emulating Alexander the Great. But this ended in personal tragedy when a Persian spear killed him, and his great army was dispersed. Then something unexpected happened. For most of the fifth century, there was peace between Rome and Persia. This was because of the emergence of an even bigger threat to the Persians than the Romans – the Huns. In the early fifth century, more and more steppe nomads appeared on Persia's eastern borders. To begin with, it was fairly chaotic with various tribes fighting the Sasanians and each other until one group, referred to by contemporaries as the White Huns (also called the Hepthalites who were their ruling dynasty), rose to dominate the region.

In 484, matters came to a head when the Persian shah, Peroz, was killed and most of the Persian armoured horsemen slaughtered in a battle somewhere between Herat and Balk in modern Afghanistan. The Roman historian, Procopius, says the White Huns laid a trap for the Persians by tricking them into charging towards a concealed trench they had dug. Inside the trench were thousands of sharp wooden spikes. The Persian cavalry tumbled headfirst into the trench, impaling themselves and their horses on the wooden spikes. The slaughter was so large that in the following decades the Persians became the vassals of the White Huns and paid them tribute.

In this way, the White Huns succeeded where Attila failed. They subjugated Persia while he failed to subjugate

Rome. And the benefits to Constantinople were enormous. Almost a century of peace allowed the eastern Roman Empire to thrive in stark contrast to the almost complete economic collapse of the west.

But as the sixth century dawned, the eastern Romans were in for a shock. After a century of almost perpetual peace, Rome's old foe was back on the war path.

The reason for this lies with a remarkable young shah called Kavad, and we need to spend some time looking at his rise to power to understand why he, and Persia, suddenly presented Rome with the first serious threat on its eastern frontier for over a hundred years.

Kavad was only 15 in 488 when he became shah but he quickly displayed an astonishing political acumen way beyond his years. Born into an almost hopeless position in which the Persian monarch was not only the puppet of the White Huns but also of the Persian nobility who treated him merely as a figurehead and instrument for their own political ambitions, he displayed a Machiavellian ability to further his own cause by exploiting the political differences between his opponents. His first task was to remove the nobleman who was the real power behind the throne: Sukhra. To do this, he cleverly sowed discord among the nobility, causing a civil war that led to Sukhra's downfall and execution.

His next target was the powerful Magian priesthood, followers of Zoroaster and curators of Persia's official religion, who supported the nobility and opposed Kavad's growing power. To counter them, Kavad resorted to a remarkable strategy of supporting a fast-growing new cult among the lower classes, led by a controversial Zoroastrian priest called

Mazdak. Mazdak was a religious and social revolutionary who preached that all men were equal and called for far-reaching political and social reforms. These included a communist-style sharing of property and even, according to some sources, their wives. But even Kavad made mistakes. By supporting a sort of fifth-century hippy commune, he went too far and the nobility arrested and imprisoned him in the so-called castle of oblivion in Khuzestan.

According to Procopius, Kavad's wife helped him escape by sleeping with the castle commander and suggesting Kavad then dress in her clothing and escape disguised as her. Rather surprisingly, this ruse proved successful, and he escaped. He was welcomed by thousands of his peasant supporters and ran away to the court of the Persians' great enemy – the White Huns.

In 499, he returned with a Hunnic army, having married the Hunnic leader Akhshunwar's daughter. There's no mention of what happened to Kavad's other wife who had bravely helped him escape from the castle of oblivion. Faced by the Huns, the Persian nobility capitulated and agreed to reinstate him and removed his brother, Jamasp, from the throne on the promise that neither Jamasp nor the Persian nobles responsible for Kavad's imprisonment would be punished. Our sources are vague but we know Kavad didn't keep his promises. He blinded his brother, although he didn't actually kill him, and executed many of the nobility who were hostile to him.

But at this stage, Kavad was still merely a puppet of the Huns. Yet duplicity was his major strength. While pretending to be the Huns' friend he was plotting against them. He would do the same in later years with the followers of Mazdak, and murder the chief priests by burying them alive. With the Huns, his aim was to rebuild the Persian army, overtly with the purpose of using it to secure tribute from the Romans to give to the Huns, and then at some future point, to rebel against his overlords.

Meanwhile, Kavad worked to reduce the power of the Persian nobility and restore the authority of the Persian monarchy. He embarked on a number of initiatives to achieve this. He centralised government and taxation by dividing the empire into four regions with a military commander in charge of each region reporting to him. He undermined the power of the nobility by sponsoring the *dehqan*, a new class of small land-owning magnates, who provided a professional cavalry force managed and paid for by him. This reduced his dependence on the heavy cavalry provided by the nobles, a feudal force called the *wuzurgan*, which had formed the backbone of the Sasanian army for centuries. He also reduced the power of the Magi by establishing a new priestly office to help the poor – this ensured he remained popular among the peasantry, something he had originally achieved by supporting Mazdak and his followers.

But for the time being, Kavad still depended on the White Huns for their military muscle to maintain his authority. And to keep their support he needed gold. A lot of gold. This led him into conflict with the Romans, since he regarded war against the eastern empire as a way of meeting all his main aims – first, raising tribute to appease the Huns, second, testing out his new army, and third, building his own reputation as a national champion against the hated Romans.

So, in 502, Kavad cast aside a century of peace between Rome and Persia and led a combined force of Persians and White Huns into Armenia, breaking the 100-year peace that had been signed 80 years previously in 422.

It was the end of an era.

8

The First Persian War

Kavad's invasion took Anastasius by surprise. The fortress city of Theodosiopolis fell into Persian hands in the first attack, either through treachery or because the garrison was under-manned. He marched south to Martyropolis, where its governor surrendered and gave the Persians two years' worth of taxes provided they did not sack the city. Kavad kept his word and advanced to the important Roman city of Amida, located today in modern south-eastern Turkey. There, he met stiff resistance and powerful walls built over 150 years before by the emperor Constantius II. Battering rams couldn't dent them and when the Persians built an artificial hill beside the walls, the inhabitants tunnelled underneath it causing it to collapse.

The city held out in this way for four months from October 502 until January 503, when Procopius[21] says the Persians were ready to abandon the siege, but just as they were leaving, the city's inhabitants lined the walls to jeer at them, with prostitutes rather prominently lifting their skirts and waggling their bottoms at them. This was a bad mistake. For it outraged Kavad, and the Persians stayed to finish the job. Their opportunity arose when some monks entrusted with the defence of a tower, drank so much wine one night celebrating a religious festival they didn't notice the Persians scaling the walls.[22] The monks were butchered, and the city subjected to a hideous massacre although a brave priest allegedly saved some by confronting Kavad and telling him such slaughter was beneath the dignity of so brave and great a king. Kavad's pride was flattered, and he called a stop to the killing. The survivors were led away into captivity in Persia or allowed to stay and tend to the Persian garrison.

Anastasius may have been taken by surprise, but his response was quick and determined. According to the Roman sources, 52,000 soldiers were mobilised against the Persians and began a major offensive in May 503, led by three generals—Areobindus, Hypatius and Patricius. Unfortunately, none of them got on and since Anastasius didn't appoint a commander-in-chief, the result of this great offensive was disappointing. An advance on the Persian fortress of Nisibis by Areobindus, with 12,000 men, was beaten off, and an attempt to retake Amida with a much larger army of 40,000 led by Hypatius and Patricius was also pushed back by the Persians.

Anastasius quickly sorted out the disagreements at the top of the army. He sacked Hypatius, and appointed Celer, an experienced Illyrian soldier who was head of the imperial guard, as supreme commander. The Roman army was probably larger than the Persian since it's likely Anastasius sent most of the two praesental armies[23] that were still stationed around Constantinople to support the field army of the *Oriens*, meaning that the Romans had three of their five field armies facing the Persians. This would fit well with the number of 52,000 Roman soldiers, since a field army had 15,000–20,000 men. And the Romans would have had even more troops if we include those on garrison duty – the *limitanei* – meaning the Romans may have had up to 100,000 troops in total on the eastern front.

Meanwhile, Kavad focused his attention on taking the fortified city of Edessa. This was significant because of a legend dating back to the days of Jesus Christ, who had reputedly promised the citizens their city would never be taken by an enemy. This legend began when Abgar, the then prince of Edessa and a close friend of the emperor Augustus, had invited Jesus to leave Palestine, where he said the Jews would never accept him, and live in Edessa. Because of this legend, and afraid the local Jews would try to prove it wrong and betray the city to the Persians, the Christian population began by rounding up and massacring all the local Jews.

Rather more helpfully, Areobindus headed there with his troops and garrisoned the city strongly. Kavad's attacks on its walls were easily repulsed. When the Persians had been beaten back, Areobindus delivered a message to Kavad saying: 'Now thou seest that the city is not thine, nor of Anastasius, but it is the city of Christ who blessed it, and it has withstood your hosts.'[24]

Another less prominent source says Areobindus paid Kavad 2,000 pounds of gold to retreat. Whatever the truth, the Persians were now clearly losing the war in the face of superior Roman forces. This continued when Celer and Areobindus invaded Persian Armenia and devastated many Persian-held towns. Patricius advanced to besiege Amida.

The siege became protracted and lasted through the winter of 504–505. Both the garrison and what remained of the Roman population began to starve to death. One source tells a grizzly story that people: 'Used to go forth by stealth into the streets of the city in the evening or in the morning, and whomsoever they met, woman or child or man, for whom they were a match, they used to carry them by force into a house and kill them whereupon they were either boiled or roasted.'[25]

The Persians discovered this cannibalism when they smelled cooking. They instituted a death penalty but allowed the corpses to be eaten. Finally, the Persian garrison surrendered, although its commander struck an agreement with Patricius to let them go unharmed and with 1,000 pounds of gold in their pockets.

Anastasius had won. He had broken Kavad's offensive. Amida had been recovered. Persian Armenia was mostly in Roman hands. Meanwhile, Kavad was in trouble. He was not only losing the war, but he had to deal with the breakdown of his peace with the White Huns. He offered Celer an armistice. A truce was agreed in 507 to last for seven years. In fact, peace lasted for longer than that. Anastasius strengthened Roman defences along the eastern frontier. In particular, he built a large, fortified town at Dara close to the Persian fortress of Nisibis. He named it Anastasiopolis but in later years it reverted to its original name of Dara. Replete with a gigantic citadel, storehouses, cisterns and even public baths, it became the headquarters for the Roman army in the east. It would also become the site of one of Belisarius' most famous battles.

Anastasius had won the first round in this new conflict with Persia. But we need to take a wider perspective and lament the tragic new era that had begun. For Rome and Persia had returned to their perennial and pointless struggle. The previous century of peace had profited them both. From now on, the resumption of hostilities would bring nothing but death and destruction.

9

Money, Money, Money

The eastern Roman Empire was full of surprises. One of these was an economic boom in the late fifth century. The limited archaeological evidence we have in the eastern Mediterranean supports this view. A striking example is floor mosaics. Elaborate and extensive Roman floor mosaics from the fifth and sixth centuries have been unearthed in recent years in Greece, Turkey and Crete, suggesting a prosperous society.

So, where did this prosperity come from? We know that in the west, the opposite was true, and Roman civilisation had all but collapsed, with the end of the plentiful supply of ceramics, roof tiles, building materials and other industrialised products that had defined Roman civilisation for centuries.[26] The definitive study of this subject is still waiting to be written. Given the paucity of information, it will probably remain that way. But one fairly obvious reason for increased prosperity was that the eastern provinces, from Anatolia through the Levant to Egypt, enjoyed an almost unparalleled century of peace in the fifth century. In contrast, the west was being torn apart by barbarian invasions. As discussed earlier, peace was mainly caused by an unprecedented *entente cordiale* with Persia throughout the fifth century, which was fully occupied dealing with its own barbarian problems in the form of the White Huns.

Another ingredient was a fairly benign environmental record. Increasing focus on climatic and disease history has led historians[27] to point to an absence of droughts, earthquakes, famine and pestilence in the fifth century. This stands in marked contrast to the middle of the sixth century, as we will discuss in later chapters, which was shaken by significant natural disasters, such as earthquakes and the extraordinary 'dust veil event', followed by the first bubonic plague to hit humanity.

I suggest another factor has been overlooked by most historians. Economic growth was also favoured by Anastasius' good leadership. Having spent a lifetime working in the Roman treasury, he was uniquely well qualified to know what was wrong with the Roman economy and how to repair it. Indeed, perhaps his most important achievement in his entire reign was his economic reform, in particular his overhaul of the Roman monetary system and changes to the tax system.

Most historians believe the success of the Roman economy depended on one thing more than any other: a monetary system. Without coins to pay for goods, trade was severely limited, and long-distance trade almost prohibited. Of course, coinage was not a Roman invention or unique to Rome. Far from it, coins, or at least a form of recording monetary values, even on clay tablets, went back thousands of years in Mesopotamia, Egypt and China. But the existence of a huge supply of many different types and values of coins was a striking feature of Roman civilisation. Indeed, so many coins were minted during the millennium and more of Rome's existence that they are relatively cheap and easy to buy today for personal collectors.

A monetary system was challenging to operate. This was shown in the third century AD, when the empire faced rampant inflation as the currency was debased because of a shortage of gold. This is discussed in some detail in the first book in this series when the Romans tried and mainly failed to control monetary policy, even inventing the first fiat currency which is used today in almost all countries – i.e. currency printed with the government's guarantee of value. Roman innovation didn't stop. Diocletian tried and failed to control inflation with price controls.

The economic chaos of the third century ultimately caused a return to a gold standard. It wasn't until Constantine introduced a pure gold *solidus* in 312 that monetary stability was restored. Made of pure 24 carat gold, the coin was struck at a rate of 72 coins to a Roman pound (which weighed 11.6 ounces). It was not devalued for centuries (except briefly in Justinian's reign as we will cover in Chapter 45), and became the dollar of the ancient world, ensuring monetary stability even during the turbulent fifth century.

Although Anastasius didn't have to face high inflation, he was the most sophisticated of all the late Roman emperors in understanding the details of the empire's economy. And he knew the Roman monetary system needed a radical overhaul in two respects: first, taxation was more efficient when it was paid in coins rather than 'payments in kind'; second, there was a desperate need for copper coins to enable the majority of the population to use coins for transactions every day.

With the first point, in the fifth century, taxation had become complex and irregular, with the breakdown of the western empire in the fifth century. Many taxes had started to be collected in kind – such as grain and other agricultural products – since monetary payment was difficult with devalued and increasingly scarce coins. For example, 'in kind' arrangements – wheat, wine and other foodstuffs – had been arranged in particular to feed troops stationed on the frontiers. But as the frontiers changed and the troops moved elsewhere, payment with provisions no longer made sense, and large amounts of agricultural produce was left to rot because it was too expensive to transport. Anastasius changed this by abolishing payments in kind wherever possible. Instead, taxes were paid in coins. Although we don't know the numbers involved, at his death, Procopius says he left an extraordinarily large treasury surplus of 320,000 pounds of gold which stands as evidence for a far more efficient tax system.

With the second point, Anastasius was determined to resolve the lack of small-value copper coinage in circulation. This was preventing people paying for small transactions in coins and stifling small businesses. It seems surprising but copper coins in circulation in the early fifth century had no marks of value at all, making it difficult to pay for small transactions in coins and to pay labourers' wages in coins.

Anastasius solved this by introducing a new set of copper coins, starting with a large copper *follis*, equivalent to 40 sesterces, and smaller coins to the value of 20, 10 and 5 sesterces. The effect was transformational. It was easier to pay labourers, and for those labourers to stimulate the economy by buying goods and services with coins.

It's hard to explain why such an obvious improvement was not made before. One answer is that the turbulence of the mid-fifth century distracted attention from this issue. Another is that it took an emperor like Anastasius with sufficient economic know-how to push through such a large-scale monetary reform.

Anastasius also reformed the tax system itself. As discussed in the first book in this series, the last major reform of the Roman tax system occurred back in the late third century, when the emperor Diocletian implemented the most thorough overhaul of Roman tax in its entire history. This proved to be a turning point, allowing the Romans to fund an enlarged army that successfully defended the empire for a century.

In comparison with Diocletian's reforms, those of Anastasius were not motivated by a need to raise money for an emergency, or a political tactic designed to reward supporters, but by a genuine wish to improve the efficiency and fairness of the entire fiscal system coming from his long years working in the treasury and his intimate knowledge of the deficiencies of the tax system.

He started by abolishing a tax which he thought wasn't worth collecting called the *Chrysargyron* which was levied on fees paid to merchants, artisans, money lenders, and famously, prostitutes. The Church was pleased with the abolition for the latter since it had long argued it conferred legitimacy on a sinful activity. Our sources describe almost hysterical joy at its abolition. In the city of Edessa: 'The entire city rejoiced, and they all put on white garments, both small and great, and carried lighted tapers and censers full of burning incense.'[28]

The festivities lasted an entire week and the happy citizens resolved to make the celebrations an annual event. Why was Anastasius happy to cancel this tax and lose revenue? The answer was its collection was scarcely worthwhile since it was only collected once every four years and the amounts weren't large.

But this was small fry. Anastasius had much bigger ambitions in mind. His primary target was the *annona*, the central plank of Roman taxation introduced by Diocletian. This had two elements: a wealth tax and a poll tax, which he left unchanged. His innovation lay with the method of collection. Diocletian had originally used government agents to collect it, thereby creating a large administrative bureaucracy. Julian the Apostate had changed the system, giving town councils responsibility for tax collection, which had been the classical Roman system of devolved administration. The problem Anastasius found was that this encouraged corruption and, in particular, large-scale tax evasion by the wealthy landowners who often dominated the town councils.

His solution was to revert to Diocletian's centralised tax system by restoring tax collection into the hands of government-appointed officials called *vindices*. Our sources are divided on whether this cured corruption since some say the *vindices* were open to bribery, but the consensus seems to be that the power of the big landowners was reduced and they paid more tax. There was also less exploitation of the poorer farmers who had in the past been victimised by the landed aristocracy. Accompanying this change was an increase in government bureaucracy although it remains unclear whether the actual tax collectors remained the same people with a different reporting line, i.e. to the central government rather than the local one. Whatever the case, the treasury department in Constantinople became hugely powerful, with its head, Marinus, who had been Anastasius' deputy when he used to head it, becoming Praetorian Prefect. He was also rumoured to be handsomely paid.

Another reform concerned the taxation of farms that fell out of cultivation because of the farmers' bankruptcy. This happened frequently, and the tax regulations required neighbouring farmers to make good the tax liability through an addition to their tax contributions called the *epibole*. Although our records are thin, it seems Anastasius eased the burden of this on poorer farmers by requiring the larger landowners to pay this tax. This was another example of his attempt to strengthen the authority of the state over the big landowners.

Finally, we know he confiscated property belonging to Zeno and all his Isaurian supporters, who were now hiding in the Taurus Mountains, and appropriated their wealth for the state. This was a useful boost to the imperial estates. To manage them more productively, Anastasius appointed a finance minister dedicated to maximising returns.

As mentioned, Procopius says Anastasius left a huge treasury surplus of 320,000 pounds of gold on his death worth, for example, two and a half times the cost of the entire North African expedition of 468 (130,000 pounds of gold). This was an extraordinary achievement. He describes him as 'the most stewardly and bursarial of all the emperors'.[29]

Anastasius has been largely forgotten in most histories of this period which concentrate instead on Justinian. This is a serious mistake since it was he, not Justinian, who reformed the tax and monetary systems in the most effective way for 200 years. This strengthened the eastern Roman economy which was essential to the Roman expansion in this period. In short, Anastasius funded Justinian.

10

The True Nature of God

Living in the twenty-first century, it can be difficult to understand the religious disputes that were so divisive in the Christian Roman Empire. One of these was over Monophysitism, and it was serious enough in Anastasius' reign to lead to rioting in Constantinople and to civil war, both of which threatened to topple him. But it was not the only dispute – another was Arianism. For example, the German barbarians who occupied the western empire in the fifth century were mostly Arian (not to be confused with the word Aryan denoting racial origins).

So, what were these disputes about?

The disputes boiled down to whether Jesus Christ was a man, God, both, or neither. The question was not unreasonable given Christ appeared on earth as the 'son of God' but not God himself. What was surprising was the ferocity with which the theologians argued. And the reason for this, I suggest, was that religion was 'weaponised' to further political ends.

A brief history of these disputes begins in the second century AD, when the early Christian writer Tertullian first articulated the concept of a trinity comprising God the Father, who lays out the divine plan, God the Son who carries out the Father's will, and God the Spirit who motivates the Father's will in believers. All were, so he contended, equal and part of the same divine authority.

But there the problems began. A division within the empire arose when the bishop of Alexandria, Arius, declared that Christ was the son of God and therefore couldn't be co-existent with him. Instead, he was subordinate. This view became popular and was referred to as Arianism. At Constantine's groundbreaking Council of Nicaea in 325, when a single doctrine was supposedly established for the Christian Church, Arianism was rejected, and the Holy Trinity was adopted as the official Nicene Creed which is today still the view of the Catholic Church.

But Arianism was slow to die out. Some Roman emperors, like Valens who was killed at the Battle of Adrianople in 378, were Arian. It wasn't until Theodosius I implemented an empire-wide anti-Arian policy that it was largely eradicated within the territories of the Roman Empire. For this the Catholic Church awarded him the title of 'the Great', which I suggest was otherwise inappropriate to describe his poor leadership of the Roman Empire.

That point aside, Arianism remained far from dead *outside* the empire. For early Christian missionaries, who had been Arian, had converted Germanic tribes like the Goths to Arianism. When they invaded and occupied the western empire in the fifth century they remained Arian. Therefore, the Ostrogoths, Visigoths and Vandals, who had occupied over half of the territories of the western empire were Christian but ideologically opposed both to the eastern empire, and also to the former Roman inhabitants of the conquered territories, who remained true to the Nicene Creed. This will be an important point when we consider Justinian's western conquests.

Enough of Arianism. The theological division that divided what remained of the Roman Empire, especially in the east, was Monophysitism. The point in dispute was about the true nature of Christ and, in particular, whether he was just divine or both human and divine. Monophysite means in Greek *monos*, single, and *physis*, nature – so, a single nature. For Monophysites, Christ was divine with no human frailties. This went against the doctrine agreed at the Council of Nicaea in 325. There it was agreed Christ was both divine and human (a difficult concept) – which became known as the Nicene Creed and is still the position of the Catholic Church to this day. But in the fifth century, the powerful Egyptian church challenged this view, led by Cyril, the Patriarch of Alexandria, who believed Christ was only divine.

And to complicate matters, Cyril was also in conflict with the Patriarch Nestorius of Antioch, the third big city in the eastern empire, who held yet another view – that Christ was human before he was divine.

So, you may be wondering why people cared about this. In an age of poverty, war, foreign invasion and the ever-present threat of famine and starvation, didn't they have better things to worry about?

I suggest the answer was yes. It was only a tiny minority of theologians who even knew about these disputes, let alone cared. Although I cannot prove it, I strongly believe that to the man or woman in the street, these religious nuances would have been as incomprehensible as they are to us today. Liberal intellectuals were equally unimpressed. The superbly well-educated Procopius famously dismissed this ecclesiastical wrangling as nonsense: 'I consider it a sort of insane stupidity to investigate the nature of God, asking what sort it is. For man cannot, I think, accurately understand even human affairs, much less those pertaining to the nature of God.'[30]

So, why were these disputes important? I think the answer, as with so many religious disputes throughout history, was that they masked a political battle. This was a power struggle between Constantinople, Alexandria and Antioch, the three biggest cities in the eastern empire. The Patriarchs in each city were battling for supremacy. Doctrine was their weapon. Constantinople was aggressive because it was a relative newcomer to the establishment. Antioch and Alexandria were older and more prestigious, at least in the eyes of their clergy.

Constantinople wanted to assert its authority, and it did just that. At the Council of Ephesus in 431, during Theodosius II's reign, Nestorius was removed from his position and his views declared heretical. Indeed, his supporters fled to Persia, where they developed a separate Nestorian church that ultimately spread all over Asia and even to China. But that, as they say, is another story.

The Nestorians may have got the bullet, but it wasn't long before Alexandria, where the Monophysites reigned supreme, suffered the same fate. Their turn came at the Council of Chalcedon, convened by the emperor Marcian, in 451. There, he turned against the Monophysites. Since the

Patriarch Cyril was now dead, anger was directed against one of his most vehement supporters, the Monophysite priest, Eutyches, who was exiled.

Constantinople wanted to rule the roost but Alexandria and Antioch were still powerful. The Monophysites made a comeback under Basiliscus who, during his short usurpation in 475–476, championed the cause in Constantinople only to anger the capital's mob which led to his downfall and the return of Zeno. Zeno sought a compromise, and in 482 he issued the *Henotikon*, as I mentioned in Chapter 5, hoping to persuade the Chalcedonians (as I shall now call the anti-Monophysites) and Monophysites to agree by uniting in their condemnation of Nestorius and Eutyches. This fudge worked to some extent, but the underlying rift was still there.

And in Anastasius' reign it would explode again with spectacular fury.

11

The Gamble

In religious matters, a sixth-century Roman emperor could not win. The religious divisions within the empire were so deep he was damned no matter which side he supported. However, endorsing the Monophysites was particularly risky since it could incite the wrath of the Chalcedonian mob in Constantinople. And they lived just outside the palace gates.

This didn't stop Anastasius from harbouring Monophysite sympathies. He was keenly interested in theological matters and genuinely believed their view was right. He was also aware most Romans in the eastern empire were Monophysites, especially those in Syria and Egypt, and with a more militant Persia, the last thing he wanted to do was to alienate the clergy and the populations of those important provinces.

We also haven't mentioned what was happening in the city of Rome until now. You may be forgiven for thinking that no one cared about Rome, which was the former capital of a forgotten empire, now ruled by the Ostrogoths, and with a population a fraction of what it had been in its glory days.

Think again. Rome was still important. Not only did it have the legacy of the Saints Peter and Paul, and the huge basilicas built in their honour, but it also housed a formidably militant clergy, uncowed by the Ostrogoths, who left it a free hand to do as it wanted.

Rome's position was strengthened by calls from the Patriarch of Constantinople to stand united against the Monophysites. As I mentioned in Chapter 6, before Anastasius was made emperor, the Patriarch of Constantinople, Euphemius, objected to his nomination on account of his Monophysite leanings, and matters came to a head when he appealed to Felix, the bishop of Rome, for his help. Anastasius had little choice but to depose Euphemius in 496, and replaced him with Macedonius, who was a suitable compromise candidate since he was a Chalcedonian but a less virulent one than Euphemius, and did not mind signing the *Henotikon*.

But the people of Constantinople were not happy. Serious rioting broke out in 498. In the hippodrome, the Greens threw stones at Anastasius, some of them nearly hitting him. The imperial guard was called in to restore order, and the man who had been throwing stones at Anastasius was executed. This just caused further rioting, and the Greens set fire to the bronze gate of the hippodrome. But eventually they went home and order was restored.

Peace returned to Constantinople for most of the next 14 years. The only disturbances were over Anastasius' banning of some of the mob's favourite festivals, which ironically were mostly pagan in origin, including wild animal fights and a festival of the Brytae, involving lascivious dancing. This shows just how skin-deep religious devotion was in Roman society. Fast forward a decade and by 511, Anastasius was becoming more overtly Monophysite. This might simply have been because he was becoming old (he was about 80 in 511) and cranky. Whatever the reason, in 511 he made a Monophysite, Timothy, Patriarch of Constantinople. On top of that, a Monophysite monk, Severus of Sozopolis, arrived in Constantinople and was received with honour by Anastasius. He shocked the Chalcedonians by holding services in which the chant of the Trisagion – *Holy, holy, holy, Lord God of Hosts* – included the Monophysite addition of *Who was crucified for us* which had been introduced at Antioch 50 years before.

This was going too far. On Sunday 4 November 512, an orthodox multitude in Saint Sophia drowned the chanting of the heretical priests with their shouts. Fighting broke out between the imperial guard and the people. Two days later, an enormous collection of citizens formed a camp in the Forum of Constantine. The discontent was now breaking into a serious rebellion to overthrow Anastasius. His statues were pulled down, and the mob called for general Areobindus, the veteran of the Persian war, to be emperor. He was married to Juliana Anicia, the granddaughter of Valentinian III, and thus claimed some connection with the distant house of Theodosius. What Areobindus' reaction to this was has not been recorded, but another veteran of the Persian wars, Celer, now the head of the praesental armies, stayed loyal to Anastasius. He advanced with soldiers to enforce peace. But Anastasius didn't want bloodshed. When the soldiers were pelted with stones, Anastasius told Celer to retreat without fighting.

Then, he did something remarkable. He sent heralds to the mob, proclaiming that he was ready to abdicate if they wanted, but asked them to listen to what he had to say. It was a desperate gamble. The next day, a crowd of 100,000 gathered peacefully in the hippodrome, and Anastasius appeared in the imperial box without his crown, ready to abdicate if they wanted. It's unfortunate we have no record of what he said, but in some extraordinary way, he calmed the mob and won their confidence. When he finished speaking, they were cheering him and begging him to put on his crown and in return they promised him good behaviour. The gamble had worked.

What he said has never been discovered. But there's no record he bribed the rioters or made concessions to them. We can only assume that his skills as an orator must have been as spectacular as those of Cicero or Julius Caesar. He was also a man of humility and compassion, unwilling to risk bloodshed. I think this makes him one of the most remarkable of all Roman emperors – a point seldom made in the few histories of this neglected period.

12

The Last Days of Anastasius

If you thought Anastasius deserved a quiet end to his reign, think again.

In 513, a Roman general in Thrace called Vitalian raised a rebellion against him, ostensibly in indignation at the appointment of a Monophysite patriarch in Constantinople. He also claimed his soldiers – so-called federates – were being deprived of provisions by Hypatius, his boss and *magister militum* for the Thracian field army.

Vitalian is a puzzling character and historians have never been sure what his true agenda was. Our few sources on him are inconsistent, with some describing him as a Goth while others say his mother was the sister of Macedonius II, the patriarch of Constantinople from 496 to 511, putting him in the upper echelons of Roman society. Contemporaries described him as an unlikely military leader – short with a bad stammer – but he was apparently brave and well liked. He commanded the federate forces in Thrace which, by this time, Procopius points out, were not barbarian allies, such as Alaric's Goths had been, but high-quality Roman cavalry, initially recruited from barbarians under the command of

Roman officers, and by Vitalian's time, mainly recruited from the Roman populations in Thrace and Anatolia, making them indistinguishable from the regular Roman troops.

Vitalian marched on Constantinople, ostensibly to restore a Chalcedonian patriarch. Crowds of supporters, reportedly 50,000 strong, joined his troops and altogether they arrived before the gates of the city. Anastasius was caught by surprise. But he didn't panic. He instructed the *magister militum*, Hypatius, not to offer resistance but to withdraw his troops inside the city walls, and set up bronze crosses in front of the city's various gates, with inscriptions appealing for order and setting out his view of what the cause of the rebellion was. We don't know what that was, but perhaps the message contained the offer of a peaceful solution. And that was Anastasius' aim. Above all, he wanted to avoid bloodshed.

To maintain peace, Anastasius sent Patricius, a highly regarded general and veteran of the Persian Wars, to negotiate with Vitalian in his camp. Patricius was actually a friend of Vitalian's and persuaded him to send his officers to discuss the cause of their resentment with the emperor personally. Vitalian himself refused to go, suspecting a trap, but his officers met Anastasius who, displaying the same personal charisma that had won the city mob over to his side, reassured them about his Monophysite views.

Appeased, the officers returned to Vitalian, who had no choice but to return with his soldiers to barracks. For a while it looked as if Anastasius had won the day. But no. Vitalian assassinated a general called Cyril sent to negotiate with him. This was an outrage not to be tolerated. The senate declared

Vitalian an enemy of the Republic. An army was sent from Constantinople under the command of Hypatius.

His army was said to be 80,000 strong, a ridiculously large number. Our sources are vague but Hypatius is credited with a victory over Vitalian in the autumn of 513 followed by a disaster in which the Roman army was said to have been driven over a cliff by trickery in the dark, assisted reputedly by black magic, leading to the loss of 60,000 men, again a massively exaggerated number. Hypatius escaped the slaughter by jumping into the sea but was rescued and taken to Vitalian as a hostage.

Even if Hypatius' force was in fact only a couple of thousand men, as I suspect, this was still an unmitigated disaster for Anastasius. It allowed Vitalian to march on Constantinople a second time with his federates, aided now by a fleet of 200 ships which had sided with him. This time, Anastasius caved in. He promoted him to *magister militum* for Thrace and promised to convene a general council at Heraclea the following year in July 515, to discuss Monophysitism at which he agreed the Pope's representative should be represented. He also promised to restore all the Chalcedonian bishops who had been replaced by Monophysite ones.

It was a humiliation for Anastasius but it quickly became clear his promises were hollow and he had no intention of giving in to Vitalian. The council never took place. No Monophysite bishops were replaced. In fact, nothing changed. Furious he'd been tricked, Vitalian marched for a third time on Constantinople and occupied the northern shore of the Golden Horn, known as Sycae (now known as Galata). This time Anastasius was ready for him. He'd gathered troops and ships and appointed his trusted finance minister, Marinus, as commander-in-chief. There was a naval battle at the mouth of the Golden Horn, in which Vitalian's ships were burned, apparently with a chemical compound that was the forerunner to the famous Greek Fire that would save Constantinople in centuries to come. Marinus landed at Sycae, and defeated Vitalian's land forces, capturing his chief lieutenant, Tarrach, who was burned to death. Vitalian fled to Thrace, where he went into hiding and disappeared for the next three years. He would make a reappearance after Anastasius' death, which we will hear about in the next chapter, but Vitalian's revolt was no more and Anastasius had triumphed.

The way Anastasius dealt with Vitalian was impressively non-confrontational. A different emperor might have used more force. Anastasius was more subtle. Instead, he used minimum force and maximum diplomacy.

Not long afterwards, he died on the night of 9 July 518. He was 87 years old, the oldest Roman emperor in history. His reign is both fascinating and frustrating. Fascinating because he achieved so much. Frustrating because we know so little about it. His achievements merit a short summary, especially because they stand as an invaluable yardstick against which to measure the successes, or otherwise, of his much better-known successor, Justinian.

First, his economic success was unparalleled as mentioned in Chapter 9, when he left the treasury 'overflowing with gold' as Procopius said,[31] with an astonishing surplus of 320,000 pounds of gold. Second, his military legacy was strong. The Roman army had mustered to fight Persia, with reasonable success in the war from 502 to 506. Third, he'd avoided any serious religious conflict, and although his Monophysite sympathies alienated people in Constantinople, they earned him support in the eastern provinces. Overall, when he died, the empire was probably more religiously united than it ever was under Justinian.

Zeno, and most of all Anastasius, restored the eastern empire's strength and prestige after Leo's disastrous defeat in 468. They remind me of the Illyrian soldier-emperors who rebuilt Rome in the third century like Claudius Gothicus, Aurelian and Diocletian. These fifth-century emperors have been largely forgotten, and most history books only spare them a few paragraphs in contrast to the copious pages written about Justinian. But it was these men, and especially Anastasius, who made the age of Justinian possible.

PART II

The Peasant and the Prostitute

13

A Long Walk to Constantinople

Three young men walking in the sun. Tall and strong, they laugh as they stride along the Via Egnatia, the main road from Dyracchium on the Adriatic coast to Constantinople. On their backs they carry heavy sacks, full of dried biscuit. In their pockets are a few copper coins. In their hands stout sticks, ready to ward off any unwanted attention, and in their belts sharp hunting knives in case anyone wants to have more of a go at them.

Their names are Zimarchus, Dityvistus and Justin. They come from Vederiana, a village in Illyria. Their aim is to escape a life of poverty. To find something more than pigs and horses to tend. They know the army is short of men and that it can pay well. But they don't want to join any old regiment. Not the frontier soldiers whose pay is forgotten more than it's remembered. They want to join the imperial guard. So, they're heading 300 miles along the paved road to the mother of all cities. Constantinople.

Their hopes will be rewarded far beyond their expectations. For one of them will become emperor.

And so, they march on.

Procopius has left us with a vivid description of Justin and his friends leaving their life of 'grinding poverty'[32] to find fame and fortune in Constantinople. When they got there, they easily found employment as soldiers for, as Procopius described, they were tall and strong, young men, just the type the Roman army wanted. Indeed, they joined the best of the best, the palace guard, known as the *Scholae Palatinae*, where they suddenly found themselves at the centre of the eastern Roman court.

We don't know what happened to his two peasant friends but Justin embarked on a long and highly successful career in the imperial guard. He would probably have spent his time not just on ceremonial duties around the palace but also on campaign, especially during Anastasius' reign when the Scholae fought with the regular army, first against the Isaurian rebellion that lasted from 492 to 497, then in the Persian War of 502 to 506, and also against Vitalian after his revolt in 515. Before Vitalian's revolt, Justin's military career continued its ascent when he transferred from the Scholae to the Excubitores, a 300-strong elite guard regiment. By 515, he was commander of the Excubitores, putting him in an influential position, given his proximity to the imperial family.

Justin's personal life is every bit as surprising as his meteoric rise to power. For instead of searching out a well-connected woman to be his wife who could help him cultivate useful contacts, such as, for example, Stilicho had done when he married the emperor's niece, Serena, 100 years before, he married a woman of very low social standing with whom he had forged a strong relationship early in his life. She was a former slave girl of barbarian origins called Lupicina, best translated as 'Foxy'. Instead of casting her off as he rose to power, he married her and changed her name to Euphemia, meaning 'Of Good Repute', thereby distancing her from her lowly origins. Procopius said she became a pious woman, although, like Justin, she was nothing more than an illiterate peasant.

Cue the event that would now turn the world upside down for Justin. On the night of 9 July 518, Anastasius died. He was 87 years old. He had no obvious heir apparent. Of his three nephews, Probus, Pompeius and Hypatius, none of them it seems was particularly ambitious or keen to become emperor. Hypatius and Pompeius were both generals and were stationed some distance from the capital, Hypatius in Antioch and Pompeius in Marcianople. The civil servants – called *silentarii* – who discovered Anastasius' dead body sent news of his death to the two heads of the imperial guard, Justin and Celer. They told their troops to wait until a successor was chosen. In these circumstances, the senate was expected to make the choice, and the next day it duly met to vote on candidates. Meanwhile, news of Anastasius' death spread like wildfire and when the senate was meeting, not far away in the hippodrome, the mob started chanting: 'A God-given emperor for the army! A God-given emperor for the world!'[33]

But the problem was the senate couldn't agree on a candidate. As the day wore on, the mob in the hippodrome lost its patience. In response, the palace guard started calling the shots. The situation became farcical when Justin's excubitores declared a tribune and friend of Justin's, John, emperor, only to be shouted down by the Blues. The *scholarii* (headed by Celer) were not to be outdone and proclaimed their own emperor – a friend of their boss Celer, a general named Patricius. We have an account of this from a leading diplomat of the time – Peter the Patrician[34] – whose record of the antics in the palace is almost beyond belief. He tells us the *excubitores* didn't approve of the *scholarii's* nomination, and for the first time in our history, we encounter Justinian – Justin's nephew and the future emperor – in his capacity as a senior member of the guards. It was only his intervention which stopped a fight between the two sets of guards. Remarkably, the *excubitores* then asked Justinian himself to be emperor, but he refused, presumably because he felt he was too junior and it would only lead to trouble.

Back to the senate, where reports were coming in of the scandalous attempts by the *excubitores* and *scholarii* to nominate their own candidates. The senators finally decided they needed to nominate someone. And fast. So, almost at random it seems, they turned to Justin as a well-liked soldier and asked him to be emperor. Justin accepted, although not without some protests made by Celer's *scholarii*, one of whom apparently even punched him. Justin was about 68 years old and known to be a brave soldier, loyal and sensible, as well as an anti-Monophysite so, although he had no imperial pedigree he ticked a lot of boxes, similar, for example, to the emperor Marcian when he was raised to the purple back in 450 to succeed the incompetent Theodosius II.

When Justin went to the hippodrome, both the Blues and Greens cheered him. This sealed his selection. The patriarch of Constantinople and Anastasius' ministers gave him the imperial diadem, spear and shield. He received an ovation from the crowd who chanted: 'Justin Augustus, may you be victorious.'[35] He immediately bought the support of the army by announcing that every soldier would receive a donative of five gold coins and a pound of silver to mark his accession.

Had Justin planned this all along? I think the answer has to be no. Most historians accept his later statement to Pope Hormisdas in Rome that becoming emperor was a total surprise, and he was at first unwilling to accept the nomination. I'm a bit more sceptical and I think Justin grasped the opportunity with both hands when it arose. This view is echoed by one chronicler[36] who says he purloined money given him by the court chamberlain Amantius to buy support for himself from the imperial guard when it was intended for a senator named Theocritus. Later on, Justin had both of them murdered. Make no mistake, Justin was no innocent when he seized the throne. He knew exactly what he was doing.

Procopius is scathing about his lack of education, claiming he couldn't read or write, and when he became emperor, he could only sign documents with the help of a stencil in which he traced the words saying, 'I have read it.' Most historians regard this as an exaggeration and think Justin probably learned to read and write as a soldier, although, as Procopius noted, it was truly remarkable that an emperor should come from such a lowly background.

Reflecting this, and the fact he was 68 years old when he ascended the throne, he didn't bring the energy to his new role that a younger man might have done, and his reasonably short reign was largely uneventful, if not in fact deeply forgettable, except in one respect. For he spent most of it nurturing a successor, and that man would be everything Justin was not – highly educated, immensely ambitious and with a gimlet-eyed intelligence. His name was Petrus Sabbatius. We know him better as Justinian.

14

Petrus Sabbatius

It is now time to meet Justinian properly. And the real reason for the origins of his elevation to power lay not so much with his own abilities but a cruel twist of fate for his uncle Justin and his wife, Euphemia, the barbarian girl to whom he was so devoted. For despite their apparent love match, they could not have children. But Justin was family minded, and he contacted his sister, whose name has not been recorded, who was married to a poor peasant, Sabbatius, just as Justin had been, and asked them to send their son, named Petrus Sabbatius, to join him where he would use his good fortune to provide the boy with an excellent education and career prospects he could never have dreamed of at home.

Petrus was born about 482, and Justin summoned him to Constantinople in around 490, when he was only eight years old. Justin looked after him as if he were his own son, and paid for an education so he could read and write both Greek and his own native Latin. He added the adoptive name of Justinianus, or Justinian to use the anglicised form, which was more Roman-sounding, and thereafter he was always referred to by this name.

When he was a teenager, Justin secured him a position in the imperial guard, in the *candidati* who served as the emperor's personal bodyguard, an exclusive unit which gave the young Justinian an ideal opportunity to see the workings of court life at first hand. Although he almost certainly never saw active service on the front line, as Justin did, he became an experienced and senior member of the imperial guard.

Although Justin's nine-year reign was relatively uneventful in terms of foreign policy, he made some important decisions. The most significant of these was his attack on Monophysitism. He persuaded the patriarch of the city, John, who had been appointed by Anastasius as a pro-Monophysite, to re-affirm his allegiance to the Chalcedonian definition of the faith. He also got him to condemn Severus, the outspoken Monophysite patriarch of Antioch, who fled to Egypt. Next was the recall of Vitalian, who as we discussed in Chapter 8, was passionately hostile to Monophysitism and had rebelled against Anastasius and was now in hiding in Thrace.

Vitalian was welcomed back like the prodigal son and given the office of *magister militum* of the praesental armies, although this title was largely honorary since the praesental armies were now stationed along the Persian frontier since the war of 502–506. Justin also made him consul for the year 520, an even higher honour.

At the same time, he sought to repair the rift with Rome by sending a letter to Pope Hormisdas asking him to pray for his success. This was code for saying that the Chalcedonian faith – i.e. the opposite of Monophysitism – would now be promoted throughout the eastern empire. In March 519, a papal delegation was received in Constantinople led by Vitalian, Anastasius' nephew, Pompey, and Justinian. It's interesting to note at this point Justinian was much the junior partner, with Vitalian the most powerful man in the empire after Justin. But once the people were happy with Vitalian's recall and the new alliance with Rome, Justinian quickly asserted his authority. In the summer of 520, Justin made him *co-magister militum* of the praesental armies with Vitalian. Justin was manoeuvring Justinian into prime position. And what followed next was shocking.

Only a few months after being made consul, in July 520, Vitalian was suddenly and unexpectedly murdered in a parade ground near the imperial palace in Constantinople. Also murdered were the court chamberlain, Amantius and his protégé, Theocritus. As mentioned earlier, Amantius had given Justin money to promote Theocritus when the senate was debating imperial candidates, which Justin used to buy support for himself.

Much scholarly ink has been spilled over whether it was Justin or Justinian who was behind this. In my view, it was almost certainly a concerted effort. Justin had long regarded Justinian as his own adopted son and inheritor of his life's work and was eagerly planning for him to take power after he died, especially since he was approaching 70 years old. The purge shows just how brutal Justin and Justinian could be when they wanted.

In 521, Justinian was proclaimed consul, taking Vitalian's position, and embarked on a charm offensive to secure his succession to the throne. It was traditional for the consul to court popularity with the people of Constantinople by staging lavish entertainments in the hippodrome. This harked back to the classical empire when the orgies of bloodshed in the Colosseum became a ritual for emperors to display both their power and their gratitude to the people of the capital. For example, when the Colosseum, or Flavian Amphitheatre as it was known to the Romans, was completed in AD 80, the emperor Titus held 100 days of games and gladiatorial combats.

Over 400 years later, and despite the adoption of Christianity, the format in the hippodrome in Constantinople kept much of its original pagan character. Although gladiatorial combat was banned, many other spectacles were the same as those in the past. For example, there were wild animal hunts. One source records Justinian exhibited 20 lions and 30 panthers, besides other wild beasts. Lions and panthers were among the most exotic and expensive of wild beasts and the crowd loved it. There was also prize fighting and wrestling. One of the mob's favourites was the so-called parade of the whores, which proceeded through the streets to a theatre close to the hippodrome. Actors, actresses and prostitutes would even dress up as monks and nuns, to the wild amusement of their audience. Of course, the church strongly disapproved, and later in the century, when plague and famine brought an end to this age of prosperity, the event was abolished.

The cost of this entertainment was prohibitive. According to Procopius, a consul would normally be expected to spend 2,000 pounds of gold a year – a huge amount of money. Traditionally, this was paid out of the consul's own pocket, and in return, they could attract massive popular support, an ideal platform for an aspiring politician. But by Justinian's day, consuls were reclaiming this expenditure from the state, and we can be fairly certain that Justinian was doing just that.

By 521, Justin's health was failing. He was over 70 years old, troubled by an old war wound and, according to Procopius suffering from what we would call today dementia: 'Justin was in his dotage and quite senile, so that he became the laughing stock of his subjects.'[37] Justinian took over government in all but name. He wanted to eliminate any opposition. His lavish entertainments had won over the mob, in particular the Blues, who shared his pro-Chalcedonian stance in contrast to the Greens who were more aligned with the Monophysites. Most of the senate also backed him and his supporters called for him to be given the honorary rank of *nobilissimus* (most noble). In 525, Justin formally made him his deputy or *Caesar*. Everything looked set for a smooth succession.

But there was still some opposition. In 523, major riots occurred in Constantinople and other cities in the empire orchestrated by the Blues. The urban prefect of Constantinople, Theodotus, nicknamed 'the Pumpkin', was rumoured to be on the verge of arresting Justinian for inciting these given his support for the Blues. This was probably a pretext to oust him from power. If so, it failed, but it was still a threat to Justinian. Justin had to intervene to get Theodotus dismissed. Justinian tried to get his own back by inventing charges of murder and sorcery against Theodotus, who employed the most brilliant lawyer of his age, a barrister by the name of Proculus, to defend him and got off scot-free. But, fearing for his life, he still had to flee the capital and found refuge in a monastery in Jerusalem. The lesson was obvious. Justinian was not to be trifled with.

Nevertheless, opposition to him was still building. In the senate, Anastasius' nephew, Hypatius, was regarded as a serious alternative to Justinian. The aristocratic families in the capital still resented Justin and Justinian as peasants. Justin was now senile and incapable of ruling, and Justinian had to act fast to stop Hypatius being put forward as an imperial candidate. In 527, the succession was rushed through. Justinian told his supporters in the senate to call for him to be made *Augustus* on account of Justin's ill-health. On 1 April 527, the doddering Justin appointed him *Augustus* and co-emperor in the palace. Three days later, the imperial guard proclaimed him emperor. Shortly after that, Epiphanius, the patriarch of Constantinople and an ally of Justinian's, formally crowned him. Justinian's opponents in the senate had no choice but to accept this as a fait accompli. Justin was probably bed-ridden by this time. He died on 1 August 527.

Justinian was 45 years old when he became emperor, and the chronicler, John Malalas, has left us with this description:

'He was short with a good chest, a good nose, fair-skinned, curly-haired, round-faced, handsome, with receding hair, a florid complexion, with his hair and beard greying.'[38]

We can see this image in the beautifully preserved mosaic of him in San Vitale, Ravenna (see image 1), pictures of which adorn so many books. He looks formidable, intelligent and energetic. Justinian can be seen through many different lenses. First and foremost is through that of his main chronicler, Procopius. He provides us with by far our best insight into the peasant who became emperor. Many historians also regard Procopius as the last great Roman writer, and perhaps the greatest of them all.

It is to him we now turn.

15

Procopius

Procopius was of Palestinian origin, coming from Caesarea Maritima, now located in Israel (not the Caesarea in Anatolia), and a thriving port in the sixth century. Extensive Roman remains are still visible there including an aqueduct and a well-preserved theatre. We know little about his early life but he clearly had a first-class education and became a lawyer. His historical significance began when he became Belisarius' legal adviser and accompanied him on his campaigns on the Persian front, North Africa and Italy. He recorded his experiences in three works which have survived intact and make him by far the most important Roman historian since Ammianus Marcellinus who wrote about the fourth century and has featured so much in the earlier books in this series.

The first and most well-known of his three works is called the *History of the Wars*. Seven books describe events to 551, including primarily Belisarius' campaigns against the Persians, Vandals and Goths. An eighth book covers the events of 552 and was probably written in 553. By far the longest of all his works, it was a success both in his own lifetime and afterwards, with many copies preserved in the libraries of Constantinople and elsewhere.

Written in an accessible and objective style, similar to the prose of classical writers like Thucydides, Tacitus and Suetonius, it contains no overt religious message as many late Roman sources do. Indeed, although Procopius was nominally a Christian, his style was influenced more by the classical tradition of antiquity than the fiery Christian texts that were common in his day. In the *Wars*, his hero is undoubtedly Belisarius, the general on whose staff he worked and who he knew well. He presents Belisarius as an almost ideal soldier; tough, unflappable, rigorously professional and endlessly resourceful. He is unsurpassed in his ability to manage and inspire his troops, command them in action, spot the weaknesses in his enemies' armies and use the strengths of his own soldiers to exploit tactical opportunities. Belisarius is, in short, a military genius. However, he presented an altogether different view of him in *The Secret History*, which we will consider in Chapter 47.

In the *Wars*, his portrayal of Justinian is factual rather than flattering and one senses reserve in praising the emperor. Indeed, his admiration for Belisarius is such that it could be seen as critical of the great emperor. Was Belisarius really more important than Justinian? That is the lingering suspicion.

Clearly, Justinian thought this as well. Procopius' second major work called *The Buildings*, probably written in the mid-550s, presents Justinian as the ideal Roman emperor: '…in our own age has been born the emperor Justinian, who, taking over the state when it was harassed by disorder, has not only made it greater in extent, but also much more illustrious'.[39]

The contrast with the *Wars* is striking. Although the book is a description of the many buildings begun in Justinian's reign, such as Hagia Sophia, there's no doubt Justinian commissioned it as a eulogy to himself. Procopius probably had little choice but to comply. However, reading between the lines of his descriptions, there's plenty of evidence that his praise is ironic, his flattery a deceit.

If Procopius had stopped there, he might have gone down in history as one of Justinian's admirers. But that's not what happened. He wrote a third work probably completed around 551, and therefore contemporary with the publication of the *Wars*, which was only discovered in the seventeenth century in a corner of the Vatican Library in Rome, still today one of the oldest and most important libraries in the world. And what it says has left people dumbfounded ever since.

Called the *Anecdota*, and commonly referred to as *The Secret History*, although the literal translation is *Unpublished Writings*, it is a fantastical depiction of Justinian, Theodora and Belisarius, portraying them respectively as a demon, a harlot and a cuckolded husband. He writes in a style unrecognisable in his other works. Instead of the measured and urbane prose in the *Wars* and *The Buildings*, *The Secret History* is a deeply insulting and often lewd account of the people he praised in his other works. For example, he claimed Justinian was a demon in human form:

> *And some of those who were present with the emperor late at night, conversing with him in the palace – men of the highest possible character – thought they saw a strange demonic form in his place. One of them declared that he*

more than once rose suddenly from the imperial throne and walked round and round the room, for he was not in the habit of remaining seated for long. And Justinian's head would momentarily disappear while the rest of his body seemed to continue making these long circuits. The witness himself, thinking that something had gone seriously wrong with his eyesight, stood for a long time distressed and quite at a loss. But later the head returned to the body, and he thought that what a moment before had been lacking was, contrary to expectation, filling out again.[40]

Many commentators have dismissed it as a joke. I suggest it is a work of genius; witty, insightful and passionate about a man and a regime that he detested. So, why did Procopius write *The Secret History* and what is its genuine message? The fundamental challenge to answering that is our almost complete lack of knowledge about his life other than his appointment to Belisarius' staff in around 527. He seems to have left that position by 544, and thereafter we know nothing about his life, not even when he died. There was an urban prefect of Constantinople called Procopius in 562 but historians don't think this was the same man. How long Procopius lived is anyone's guess, but his writings don't include any historical events after 554.

Many answers have been suggested to explain *The Secret History* ranging from, for example, putting distance between himself and Justinian in case there was a regime change, to following the literary traditions of antiquity which included writing invective-filled lampoons of rulers, a bit like those written today in publications like Britain's *Private Eye*.

My sense is that the truth behind *The Secret History* is much more straightforward. It represents Procopius' true feelings. He was intensely critical of the people in his time. He disliked religion, especially Christianity. The fanaticism of the Circus factions seemed to him a 'form of mental disorder'. He wrote in the style of the classical authors like Tacitus. He was an enlightened, liberal thinker, in tune with the philosophy and culture of the rapidly fading classical world. He was in many ways the last great Roman writer.

Some historians dismiss *The Secret History* as a personal vendetta. Yet I suggest it offers much more than personal invective. It provides an insightful analysis of Justinian's regime. This is especially true of the third section of the book called *Anatomy of a Regime* which makes serious and considered allegations against Justinian: first, he bankrupted the state; second, he undermined the quality of the army; and third, his wars in the west devastated the conquered lands in Italy and North Africa, rendering them largely valueless acquisitions.

These sections are often ignored in favour of the more scandalous personal invective, but they are essential to any analysis of Justinian's reign, and we will return to them many times in this book. Procopius is our eyes and ears for the age of Justinian. He was a writer of prodigious talent, and his bravery in confronting the tyranny of Justinian's rule was second to none. We need no better recommendation than that of Edward Gibbon who said of him:

> *I neither have nor desire another guide than Procopius, whose eye contemplated the image, and whose ear collected the reports, of the memorable events of his own time.*[41]

16

Theodora

Procopius has left us an account of Justinian's wife, Theodora, which has become famous for being scurrilous. He describes her as an actress, which at that time meant a prostitute, with a voracious sexual appetite. Written in an almost tabloid style, there's a comic inversion of the classical literary model in which the ideal Roman woman was typically presented as chaste in youth, faithful in marriage and a devoted mother. In contrast, Theodora is presented as a prostitute who delights in her trade and had frequent abortions rather than raising children.

There's certainly more than a grain of truth in what Procopius wrote but what I find most surprising is that, without meaning to, he elicits our sympathy for a woman abused in her youth. As mentioned, Justinian was the son of illiterate peasants, and Theodora was almost certainly a prostitute in her early life. However, what actually emerges from Procopius' account is that she had suffered appalling abuse as a child. Her father was the bear-keeper for the Green faction in Constantinople, where the bears would have been made to fight and trained to dance. But he died early, putting his wife and family of three little daughters on the street. Although Theodora's mother hastily remarried to save the family from destitution, and tried to secure the same bear-keeping job for her new husband, the Greens refused to co-operate. Eventually, her husband found work with the Blues. But this wasn't sufficient to stop the daughters becoming actresses or, in other words, prostitutes.

The truth was that Theodora probably endured a life of back-street abortions and abuse as she entertained rich men connected with the Blue faction. She hated the Green faction since they had abandoned her mother when her father died. We know that she eventually became the mistress of an imperial official called Hecebolus who she accompanied to Egypt. But the relationship broke up when she became pregnant and gave birth to a daughter.

She returned to Constantinople, via Alexandria and Antioch, plying her trade as a prostitute according to Procopius, until she met Justinian probably around 518, when Justin became emperor and Justinian's own star began to rise. Although we have no records of exactly how they met it was probably at a function organised by the Blues, who Justinian backed to increase his popularity. She was presumably a dancer when he first saw her. To quote Procopius, who disliked her intensely, but had to admit, 'She (Theodora) had an attractive face and a good figure.'[42] When Justinian saw her, he was immediately captivated by this attractive and fiery, young woman. Procopius says:

When she arrived back in Constantinople, Justinian developed an overwhelming passion for her. At first he consorted with her only as his mistress, though he did promote her to a patrician rank. This at once enabled Theodora to obtain vast influence and very considerable wealth. For, as so often happens to men consumed with passion, it seemed to Justinian's eyes the most delightful thing in the world to lavish all his favours and all his wealth upon the object of his passion.[43]

Like his uncle Justin, Justinian was a romantic. You recall Justin had fallen in love with a barbarian slave girl and defied all social conventions to marry her and make her empress. There's no doubt Justinian had the same strong and genuine feelings for Theodora. His scandalous relationship encountered serious obstacles to begin with. First, it was actually illegal for a senator, like Justinian, to marry an ex-actress which as I mentioned was considered a disreputable profession. Second, Justin's wife, Euphemia, the former slave girl, rather ironically given her own past, couldn't stand Theodora. Perhaps the two shared too many similarities. But these problems were resolved when Euphemia died sometime between 521 and 522, and Justin, who seems to have fully supported Justinian's passion for Theodora, enacted a law allowing ex-actresses to marry men of high status provided they repented of their past sins. This fitted well with Christian thinking on redemption. Theodora and Justinian were married and made a devoted couple.

Theirs was a marriage of equals, to Procopius' dismay, and Justinian consulted her on all important matters of state. She became a powerful political figure in her own right. She had a sharp intelligence and a capacity for loyalty to people she liked, as well as a strongly vindictive streak against those she disliked. While devoted to her husband, she was also an independent thinker who was not afraid to disagree with him and objected to some of his political appointments. They had no children which may be because of the abortions she had had in her youth although she had a daughter from her liaisons before meeting Justinian. Procopius lamented Justinian's love for Theodora saying:

> *So it came about that Theodora – born, brought up and educated as described (i.e. disreputably) – despite all these obstacles attained imperial rank. For it never even occurred to her husband (i.e. Justinian) that his conduct was shocking, though he was in a position to take his pick of women in the Roman Empire and select one of the most nobly born women in the world who had enjoyed the most exclusive upbringing, and was thoroughly acquainted with the claims of modesty, and lived in an atmosphere of chastity, and in addition was superbly beautiful and still a virgin.*[44]

Theodora had certainly lived a scandalous life before she met Justinian but there was a transformation in her behaviour after she married him. For example, she spent many years championing women's rights, and especially helping young women who had been forced into a life of prostitution against their will, just as she had been. This shows a sympathetic side to her character, and it is perhaps surprising Procopius was so hostile to her. But her vindictive streak was frightening. She was a street fighter, happy to demolish her opponents.

An example was her treatment of John the Cappadocian, Justinian's capable but corrupt finance minister, who refused to pay her the respect she thought she deserved. So, in 541 she engineered his downfall with the help of Belisarius' wife, Antonina, who tricked the Cappadocian by telling his daughter Euphemia that Belisarius was disenchanted with the emperor and ready to rebel. When Euphemia conveyed this to her father, he expressed similar feelings and agreed to meet Antonina to discuss a plot against the emperor. Antonina had troops in hiding who jumped out and arrested him. When led before Justinian, the emperor dismissed him, confiscated his property and exiled him to Egypt but he didn't execute him, a sign of his lingering fondness for the old rogue. This was Theodora's high-water mark when she, Justinian, Antonina and Belisarius were regarded as the fab four of their time.

Her power and vindictive temperament terrified Procopius and many like him. In *The Secret History*, he writes of her 'swarms of spies' and his fear he would be put to death if she discovered what he was writing. It was her intolerance that he resented most. Theodora will remain a critical part of our story until her premature death in 448, probably because of cancer.

But for now, we need to return to the narrative of Justinian's early reign and consider his first major challenge. War with Persia. Enter a new character in our story, and one who will prove just as important as Justinian himself. This is Belisarius, the young general who would become perhaps the greatest soldier in Rome's entire history.

17

Belisarius

In the early morning sunlight, the horsemen ride through the Golden Gate, the grand gateway into Constantinople. About 50 of them canter along the road leading into the heart of the city, their horses' iron shoes clattering on the stone paving. Finally, they reach the imperial palace. Leading them is a youth, no more than 18 years old. He wears the plumed helmet of a senior officer in the imperial guard. Once inside the walls of the palace, where few of the city's inhabitants have ever been, he's met by the emperor's nephew, the future emperor Justinian.

He dismounts and bows before him. Half a foot taller than Justinian, broad-shouldered and with long, flowing locks of brown hair, he looks like a reincarnation of Achilles. Justinian smiles at him and asks him about the expedition. The young man is vocal. Enthusiastically he tells him his horsemen have crossed the Danube and raided the lands of the Huns. He wanted to see if they could out-shoot the famous nomadic warriors, out-ride them and, in short, prove they are the better warriors. 'Everyone is afraid of the Huns,' he tells Justinian, 'but once we're better than them, we'll rule the world.'

Justinian clearly likes this young officer. You might think he was his father, for Justinian is 20 years older, in his late thirties and laughs and talks with him completely at ease. The youth asks for more recruits to his regiment. He wants to expand his small unit into a full cavalry regiment of expert horse archers, even better than those who exist in the praesental armies. They walk into the interior of the palace together, engrossed in conversation.

This young man talking so earnestly to the future emperor is called Belisarius. And he, more perhaps than Justinian himself, will transform his reign into one of the most memorable eras in the entire history of the Roman Empire.

Belisarius' early life is obscure. He was probably born around 505 based on Procopius' observation that in 526, when he engaged in his first recorded military action, he was 'a young man wearing his first beard'.[45] Procopius says he was born in a small town called Germania, right in the centre of the Balkans, between Thrace and Illyria, but we know nothing about his family and his upbringing. Given Procopius' criticism of Justinian and Theodora in *The Secret History* for being low born, we can assume his silence about Belisarius' family suggests they were respectable but perhaps not wealthy or illustrious. Just like Justinian, and before him his uncle Justin, Belisarius enlisted in the imperial guard in Constantinople. It was there he formed a personal connection with Justinian which was to change both of their lives. We don't know the details but Justinian was clearly impressed with this resourceful young officer and promoted him rapidly through the ranks. Given that we know Belisarius was allowed, early in his career, to have his own regiment of elite horsemen, it is quite possible Justinian allowed him to develop this corps while he was still a teenager, as imagined in the description above.

By 526, Procopius tells us he was a senior officer in the guards and, along with another senior officer, Sittas, he led a raid into Persian Armenia. This was a success and the Romans returned with plunder and captives, although Procopius also mentions a second raid later in 526 which was a failure.

What these raids tell us is that both Belisarius and Sittas were among Justinian's favourites. His aim was to build a network of loyal supporters through whom he could rule. And he still had enemies. Once Vitalian had been assassinated, the next threat was Hypatius, Anastasius' nephew and a potential imperial rival. Justin could not eliminate or sideline Hypatius, and thought it best to make him *magister militum* for the east, the position Justinian himself had had before he was promoted to *co-Augustus*. Thus, Hypatius was Justinian's only potential rival to the throne. And his principal aim was to oust him.

The problem was Hypatius was doing rather well in negotiating a peace with Persia. Although the Persian shah, Kavad, had started a war with the eastern Romans in 502, discussed in Chapter 7, 20 years later he preferred peace. He even wanted an alliance with Rome to counter threats to his position from the Persian nobility and offered his son, Chosroes, for adoption by the emperor Justin.

Although this sounds extraordinary, it wasn't without precedent. Something similar had happened a century before when the pro-Roman Persian Shah Yazdegerd had adopted the emperor Arcadius' son, the future Theodosius II. Kavad opened negotiations with Hypatius, who was only too eager to take the credit for himself, making Justin and Justinian determined to derail the peace plan. When a Persian embassy arrived in Constantinople in 525, Justin and Justinian rejected it outright, claiming it was a Persian trick to set Chosroes up to inherit the Roman Empire. They used this idea to discredit Hypatius. Then they offended Kavad by offering to make Chosroes effectively the vassal of Rome rather than the adopted heir of the emperor. When this was presented to a Persian delegation led by Chosroes himself he was deeply offended, as Procopius describes: 'Chosroes left and went off to his father with nothing accomplished, deeply injured at what had taken place and praying that he might exact vengeance for their insult against him.'[46]

The price was war. Keen to bolster his authority by taking the initiative, Justinian gathered a field army in Armenia and, in 527, the year when he became sole emperor, he unleashed it against the Persians, led by Sittas. It achieved some success. Meanwhile, Justinian had plans for Belisarius. He promoted him to Dux of Mesopotamia and instructed him to advance towards the key Persian stronghold of Nisibis in central Mesopotamia (see Map 4) and build a new fortification at Mindouos, only four miles from Nisibis. This was a blatant provocation to the Persians who sent an army to destroy it in the summer of 528.

Justinian reinforced Belisarius' troops with detachments led by the generals Boutzes and Koutzes. These were routed and Boutzes captured. Both Procopius and our other main chronicler, Malalas, are vague about this battle and it might not have been that large. Belisarius was involved, but he wasn't in overall command and escaped punishment for the defeat. Indeed, he benefited since, with Boutzes captured and Koutzes in disgrace, he was promoted to the supreme command of the armies in the east, ousting Hypatius which had been Justinian's intention all along. In 529, Belisarius went to Constantinople where Justinian personally appointed him to this high rank.

Belisarius' rise to power had been nothing short of meteoric for a young man in his mid-twenties. A special relationship between the two had been well and truly established. But Belisarius now had to earn Justinian's trust. In 529, an outraged Persian embassy arrived in Constantinople, demanding tribute from the Romans. Kavad was now playing a dangerous card. The Persian nobility regarded tribute as a test of his strength. If tribute was paid, they would respect him. If not, they would overthrow him. On the Roman side, there was a history of making payments to the Persians to subsidise their defence of the Caucasus mountains against the Huns. Kavad now asked for this to be increased. Kavad was offering Justinian a face-saving device since the Caucasus payment was not technically regarded as tribute by the Romans. But Justinian wasn't interested. With Hypatius now out of the way, he wanted war and victory over the Persians.

In the spring of 530, he instructed Belisarius to muster the army of the east for battle. Troops began arriving at Dara, opposite the Persian stronghold of Nisibis (see Map 4). Simultaneously, the Persian army was mobilising. Justinian's schemes to oust Hypatius had led to a dangerous war with Persia. Everything now depended on Belisarius. Could this young man deliver?

18

The Battle of Dara

The Battle of Dara in 530 was Belisarius' first great test.

He had under his command around 25,000 troops, mostly regular units helped by some auxiliaries, principally 1,200 Huns and 300 Heruli cavalry. Against him, Kavad sent the main Persian army comprising probably around 40,000 men with most of its elite heavy cavalry, under the command of Perozes. This was to be a test of strength between the two superpowers of the ancient world. True to Persian etiquette, Perozes sent Belisarius a message instructing him to prepare a bath and a feast to celebrate the impending Persian victory.

Meanwhile Belisarius was at his most resourceful. The Persian heavy cavalry were famous for the ferocity of their charge and he was worried they might break through the Roman lines, so he tried to limit the impact of their charge with an ingenious series of trenches. He didn't dig these in a straight line but had the central section set back so that the trenches on either side of it were further forward. He positioned his most mobile and dangerous force – the Huns – in the centre to strike at attackers on either flank. He hoped this would surprise the Persians who had no idea the trenches were dug in this fashion. He also put a group of 300 Heruli horsemen – Germanic warriors like the Goths – concealed behind a hill on the Roman left flank.

Battle was slow to be joined. When the Persians arrived, regiments of cavalry and infantry massed in front of the Romans but Perozes was only reconnoitring his enemy and didn't order an attack. There was a small skirmish between some Roman and Persian horsemen on the Roman right wing leaving, according to Procopius, seven dead Persians without any Roman casualties. But nothing else happened until a young Persian nobleman rode right up to the Roman trenches and offered single combat to anyone brave enough to fight him.

Procopius says no one in the Roman army responded until the soldiers looked around in astonishment to see a young man walking through their ranks to challenge him. He was Andreas, a bath attendant who trained youths to wrestle in Constantinople. The Persian was equally surprised but, as he hesitated to run this non-combatant through with his sword, Andreas grabbed a spear from a soldier and hit the Persian so hard he fell from his horse whereupon he jumped on him and slit his throat. An enormous cheer went up from the Roman lines.

Not surprisingly, this infuriated the Persians who, according to Procopius, sent another warrior, a man of huge stature, who rode up and down the Roman lines, calling out for a challenger, and cracking his whip violently. No Roman soldier came forward but the bath attendant reappeared, disobeying orders not to repeat his unprofessional performance, and this time wearing armour and riding a horse. He charged at the Persian and they knocked each other off their horses but, using his wrestling skills, Andreas tripped up the bigger man as he rose from the ground, and slit his throat. Round two to the Romans.

Procopius' account of Andreas' exploits may be exaggerated but there's probably some truth to it since single combat was widely practised before pitched battles, although the outcome seldom had much influence on the course of the battle. So, it was that day. There was no battle. The Romans did a lot of cheering and the Persians regarded Andreas' antics as a bad omen and withdrew to their camp.

On the next day, 10,000 Persian reinforcements arrived. Further messages were exchanged. Perozes called on Belisarius to come to terms and pay tribute rather than face battle. When he refused, he reminded him to prepare his bath for him. In true Shakespearian fashion, Procopius has recorded the speeches delivered by both Perozes and Belisarius to their troops. Perozes called the Romans cowards for digging trenches to hide behind while Belisarius exhorted the Romans to scorn the Persian infantry: 'For their whole infantry is nothing more than a crowd of pitiable peasants'.

The next morning, Perozes was ready to attack. He led the Persian army up to the Roman lines. He held half of it in reserve, including the elite Immortals regiment, and put Pityaxes in charge of the right wing and Baresmanas, a very experienced Persian general, famously called the one-eyed since he had previously lost an eye in battle, in charge of the left. According to Procopius, the Persian cavalry cantered towards the Romans at noon to disrupt their midday meal. At first, there was an aerial battle as both sides showered each other with arrows. Procopius says the Persians shot more arrows in a 'vast cloud'[47] but the wind blew unfavourably against them, checking their force.

With most of the arrows used up, Perozes struck against the Roman left wing. A large group of armoured Persian horsemen followed behind an advance guard of White Huns, called Cadiseni by Procopius. The Roman heavy cavalry met them and were pushed back. But this was what Belisarius had expected. Giving orders from the central trench, he unleashed his own Huns, led by their fierce chieftains, Sunicas and Aigan, against the Persians as they pursued the retreating Romans. This surprised the Persians and caused their advance to falter. But his masterstroke was to unleash the 300 Germanic Heruli horsemen, concealed behind a hill, into the Persian rear.

Belisarius had discussed this with the Heruli, who liked the idea of plundering the corpses of the dead Persians, and agreed to strike when the Persians had advanced past them. Procopius says the Heruli were like a bolt of lightning, particularly savage and brave. The Persians didn't know what had hit them and panicked. They fled back to their own lines but left 3,000 dead on the battlefield. Wisely, the Romans didn't pursue them, and the Huns and Heruli stopped to strip the Persian bodies of their gold and silver. It was payment for a job well done.

Belisarius must have been delighted his tactics had worked so well. But this was just the start of the Persian attack. In fact, Perozes had used it as a diversion to distract Belisarius from his main attack which was now directed against the Roman right wing, commanded by the one-eyed

Baresmanas. An enormous group of Persian heavy cavalry, with the 10,000 Immortals leading them, advanced against the Roman trenches. The Romans were forced back behind their trenches. Again, this was what Belisarius expected. It meant his mobile force in the centre could attack the Persians in the flank.

When the Persians advanced too far in pursuit of the retreating Romans, Belisarius sprang his trap. Into the Persian flank, poured the Hunnic and Roman cavalry. As they had already done on the Persian right wing, according to Procopius, it was the Huns and their leader Sunicas, who did most of the damage. Procopius says Sunicas himself found the Persian standard bearer and hacked him down whereupon the Persian cavalry rallied around their leader, Baresmanas, before the illustrious Persian general was himself killed by Sunicas. This caused panic in the Persian ranks and many fled, leaving those who had advanced deep into the Roman lines, including the Immortals, surrounded. Procopius tells us: 'And the Romans, having made a circle as it were around them, killed about five thousand.'[48]

With so many of its best troops surrounded and slaughtered, the Persian army caved in and fled back towards Nisibis. As Belisarius had predicted, the massed ranks of Persian foot-soldiers threw away their shields and ran off. Procopius says thousands were killed as they fled although Belisarius called a halt, fearing the Persians might turn around and counterattack. Persian casualties must have been well over 10,000 including the slaughter of the infantry and the 8,000 Persian horsemen who Procopius says were killed. We have no record of Roman casualties but they were probably little more than a thousand or two at the most. It was a glorious victory, extraordinary for a young man only 25 years old. Alexander the Great had been 22 when he inflicted his first major defeat on the Persians at the Battle of the Granicus River. Had the Romans now discovered their own Alexander?

Procopius summed it up modestly: 'For on that day the Persians had been defeated in battle by the Romans, something which had not happened for a long time.'[49]

19

Taxes and Lawyers

The Battle of Dara was a military turning point for the eastern empire. It was the most important victory over the Persians since the emperor Carus sacked Ctesiphon, over 200 years before, in AD 283. For Justinian, it boosted his prestige immeasurably but that prestige was about to suffer a series of blows which would lead, in less than two years' time, to an attempt to overthrow him.

So, what went wrong?

Although we have very little detail about the political situation in the early 530s, there was a segment of aristocratic Roman society which viewed Justinian as an upstart, just like his uncle Justin had been, a peasant with pretensions way above his station. And Justinian's wife, Theodora, only added to this sense of outrage. In short, many people wanted a regime change and thought men like Anastasius' nephews, Hypatius and Pompeius, were more deserving of imperial office than Justinian.

And one area that excited the resentment of not only the senators but a broad cross-section of the population was taxation. We have almost no information about it but it seems resentment was growing against Justinian's increasingly aggressive tax regime and in particular, against his newly appointed finance minister, John the Cappadocian. Justinian made him chief finance minister in the role of praetorian prefect for the east in about 531, but he seems to have held this role unofficially for years before then. According to an account by a bureaucrat called John Lydus,[50] John the Cappadocian came from the city of Caesarea in Anatolia (not to be confused with the Palestinian city of the same name located in modern Israel), and served as a financial officer in the army based in Constantinople where he came to Justinian's notice when he was in the imperial guard, just as Belisarius and Sittas had done. Justinian observed in John two of the features he most highly valued – ruthless efficiency and complete loyalty. As Justinian's star rose, so he helped John rise to a senatorial rank and then to his position as chief finance minister. John Lydus nicknamed him 'the foul Cappadocian' and wrote: 'Cappadocians are always foul; fouler, however, when appointed to office, and at their foulest when in pursuit of profit.'[51]

Lydus says John was keeping money for himself, and his tax collectors became so severe that they would torture people to death who they suspected were hiding money. He claims that in Lydia in Asia Minor, John's agents overtaxed the inhabitants such that the province 'became bereft not only of money but also of human beings'.[52]

Procopius is also particularly critical of Justinian's budgeting. In *The Secret History*, he describes him sucking the sea dry as he overtaxed the empire and still failed to balance the budget or pay the army.

I shall now proceed to relate how he [Justinian] appropriated all the money he could lay his hands on, first mentioning a dream-vision which at the beginning of Justin's reign appeared to one of the senators. He reported how in his dream he seemed to be standing somewhere in Constantinople on the seashore exactly opposite Chalcedon, and that he saw Justinian standing in front of him right in the middle of the channel. First, Justinian drank up all the water of the sea, so that from then on he seemed to the dreamer to be standing on dry land, as the waves did not break on the shore at this point; then more water appeared there, choked with masses of filth and rubbish and pouring out of the sewers on both sides. This Justinian drank this up as well, laying bare once more the bed of the channel.[53]

Justinian's budget deficit would become a major feature of his later reign which we will examine in future chapters, but even in his early years there seems to have been a problem balancing the books which led to a rapacious tax system.

Another cause of resentment lay with a seemingly benign project – the codification of Roman law – for which Justinian has become especially famous. This began in his first year as emperor, on 13 February 528, when he announced it to the senate. Why did he want to do this? The answer was that it was one of the best ways of making your mark as an emperor. However, this was not easy. The last legal codification had been the Theodosian Code of 438 which had taken nine years to complete. But in almost exactly a year, in April 529, Justinian delivered his *Codex Justinianus*. It was hugely ambitious since it represented an updating of Roman law stretching back beyond the Theodosian Code to Hadrian's reign in the second century AD (117–138).

What exactly was in this new Code? To understand it, we need to take a step back and revisit the origins of Roman law in a text known as the Twelve Tables written in the early days of the Republic in around 450 BC. These legal principles formed the basis of Roman law which had been clarified and updated over the subsequent centuries with legal opinions given by authorities like judges called *praetors*, and since the days of Augustus, by individual emperors who became a favourite source of petitioning by plaintiffs and made an endless number of legal rulings. This led to an enormous amount of case law, or precedents, that lawyers struggled to interpret. Consequently, any codification of these precedents into a user-friendly document was welcomed and seen as a mark of authority by whichever emperor would take on the role of supreme lawmaker. The first to do this had been the superb administrator Diocletian who had issued two major compilations called the *Codex Gregorianus* and the *Codex Hermogianus*. The next one was the *Codex Thedosianus* produced in 438, but by the late 520s it was 90 years old and needed updating.

Justinian jumped at this opportunity, partly because he liked administration and preferred making laws and regulations than leading soldiers into battle. Known as the 'sleepless emperor', he also enjoyed hard work. For example, when he became co-emperor with his uncle Justin in April 527, he issued more laws in the five months of his joint rule than Justin had done in his entire eight-and-a-half-year reign.[54] Indeed, during his first nine years as emperor Justinian was especially prolific, issuing over 400 new laws compared with some 30 issued by Justin and a similar number issued by the emperor Anastasius who'd ruled for 27 years.

Justinian applied this same energy to his new codification. But there was a problem that became apparent in April 529 when the new Code was delivered. It had been done too quickly. It caused more problems than it solved. Justinian had to go back to the senate to tell them that the work would have to be re-done. He got it right second time around. One of his greatest gifts was to spot talent, and just as he had singled out Belisarius as an able general, so he appointed a capable barrister, Tribonian, as *quaestor*, or chief legal officer, to implement the second version of this new codification but this time with a detailed compilation of the ancient laws on which it was based called the *Digest*, a term close to the modern word 'encyclopaedia'.

Tribonian has become synonymous with Justinian's legal reforms in the same way Belisarius has with his wars of reconquest. In 530, he said he wanted at least three years to gather, analyse and reissue under the emperor's signature, case law which was said to take up 2,000 books or some 3 million lines of Latin text. Tribonian's revised version of Justinian's Code would become the definitive one, but it was only issued in 534. And the point that caused dissatisfaction was that up until this date, his attempts at legal reform had failed. This wouldn't have been apparent to the general public but it would have been visible to the senate, in which Justinian's most influential opponents resided, i.e. those who wanted Hypatius to replace him.

Of course, his legal reforms would eventually become one of the most enduring legacies of his entire reign. This was because of his perseverance and commitment. For example, he instructed Tribonian to produce a condensed and introductory textbook of the new reformed laws called the *Institutiones* (Institutes). These provided lawyers with a framework explaining how the new Code worked and how the different parts of it related to one another. It was published in 533 at the same time as the *Digest* and just prior to the reissue of the Codex in 534. Justinian's legislation didn't stop there. As I mentioned, he was a prolific maker of new laws, and during his reign, he also issued the *Novellae Constitutiones*, literally the 'New Constitutions', or, as they are almost always called today, the 'Novels'. These were various new laws issued during his reign, many of them in the later 530s, which Justinian himself never compiled into a single document but which were collected and recorded by others.

Taken all together, the Codex, the Digest, the Institutes, and the Novels are today referred to as the *Corpus Juris Civilis* or *Body of Civil Law*, or more simply as the Code of Justinian. This established the basic principles and practice of civil law (not common law which developed independently in medieval England) used in most of continental Europe for over a thousand years until they were updated by the legal code of another famous emperor, Napoleon, in the *Code Napoléon*. Justinian's Code stretched beyond Europe, since it was influential on Islamic law as well.

But let's get back to the year 530. Justinian's first attempt at codification had been a failure. Resentment against him, especially in the senate, was building. But of course, Justinian had a trump card – Belisarius. But even he could make a mistake.

20

Defeat at Callinicum

After the victory at Dara things continued to go well for the Romans. They won another battle against the Persians, this time in Armenia, where the generals Sittas and Dorotheus met a Persian army outside the town of Satala. Unlike at Dara, Procopius wasn't present at the battle so our information is limited, but he says the Romans had some 15,000 men, comprising the typical mix of armoured horse archers and heavy infantry. Sittas concealed his cavalry in some woods as the Persians advanced up to the town, which was defended by Dorotheus. As the Persians attacked, Sittas unleashed his cavalry into the Persian flank, who fled with heavy casualties. After that, the Romans captured two fortresses, Bolum and Pharangium.

Justinian was delighted with these two victories and keen to make peace with Kavad, so he even offered him a one-off cash payment, but Kavad's regime was now in crisis and he needed some sort of success to counter the growing criticism of him at home. So, in the spring of 531, another Persian army advanced into Syria. By this time, the Persians were short of manpower and they employed a large force of Arab allies, the Lakhmids, under the leadership of al-Mundhir. Led by a skilful Persian general, Azarethes, this force consisted entirely of cavalry, leaving behind the large numbers of inferior-quality infantry that boosted Persian numbers but seldom made a positive contribution in battle. As such, it was a highly mobile force capable of making a lightning raid into Roman territory, sacking a city or two, and withdrawing, claiming some sort of victory which would help bolster Kavad's standing. To achieve an element of surprise, they took an unusual route into Roman territory, going along the Euphrates, far to the south of the normal battleground of Dara and Nisibis (see Map 4).

The attack caught the Romans unawares since they thought the war was as good as won. Belisarius took charge of the Roman response but he wasn't sure whether Azarethes' attack was a diversion to cover for a larger Persian attack around Dara, so he garrisoned the fortresses around Dara, and marched to meet them with an army of some 20,000, including the Romans' Arab allies, the Ghassanids led by Harith. When Azarethes realised Belisarius was coming to meet him head-on, he retreated rather than give battle. What happened next is unclear since we have two differing accounts left to us by Procopius and Malalas.

Procopius provides the most detail and emphasises that Belisarius did not want to fight the Persians since they were retreating and it was Holy Week, with Easter Sunday fast approaching, which was a strict day of fasting for Christians. But his troops thought differently. They were keen to fight and, according to Procopius they 'mocked him, both officers and soldiers, although no one reproached him to his face'.[55]

Procopius says Belisarius addressed his men, telling them he thought it was the wrong time to fight, especially since Easter Sunday fell on the next day when they would be expected to fast, and emphasising they had nothing to gain since the Persians were already retreating. But the soldiers refused to accept this and when some officers accused him of cowardice, it was too much for him. Belisarius offered battle beside the town of Callinicum, positioning his army next to the Euphrates on his left, putting himself with the regular heavy cavalry in the centre, most of the Roman infantry on the left beside the Euphrates, and the right wing comprising a mixed force of Arabs, Huns and newly recruited regular infantry from Isauria and Lycaonia in Anatolia under the command of Longinus and Stephanacius, bolstered by some regular cavalry led by Ascan.

The Persians stopped and turned to face the Romans. There was a long archery battle, as happened at Dara, with both sides shooting enormous quantities of arrows. However, unlike at Dara, where a wind had favoured the Romans by denting the force of the Persian arrows, this time they rained down more heavily on the Romans although Procopius says the Roman archers had more powerful bows but they couldn't fire as quickly as the Persians.

When this archery contest ended in a stalemate, Azarethes launched a powerful attack against the Roman right wing where the Roman's Arab allies – the Ghassanids – fled. Procopius blames the Arabs for retreating although he says they often did this to feign a retreat. However, there was no feint this time, and they fled off the battlefield, leaving the Roman heavy cavalry and the Isaurian and Lycaonian infantry surrounded. They fought bravely and both the infantry generals Longinus and Stephanacius were killed, as was the Roman cavalry commander, Ascan, who Procopius says slew many Persians before he too was slain. Eight hundred of the 3,000 Roman heavy cavalry died before they fled leaving the 2,000 Isaurian and Lycaonian infantry to be slaughtered. Procopius grimly notes these new recruits had been the keenest to fight.

The collapse of the right wing was catastrophic for the Romans but instead of the entire Roman army being routed, Procopius tells us the regular heavy infantry on the left wing beside the Euphrates conducted a successful rearguard action, holding out until nightfall when the Persians withdrew. Here, Procopius and Malalas disagree about Belisarius' actions. Procopius says he left the cavalry to join the infantry and led the resistance. However, Malalas says he fled the field leaving the infantry to fight on by themselves under their commander, Peter. He claims the Hunnic leaders, Sunicas and Simmas, bravely joined the infantry.

One thing both chroniclers agree on is the infantry put up a heroic resistance, forming a dense shield wall or *fulcum* as the late Roman version of the classical *testudo* formation was called. From behind the shields Roman archers shot arrows at the attacking Persian cavalry, finding their mark, according to Procopius, rather more effectively than the Persians who charged again and again in vain against the Roman shields until 'their horses, annoyed by the clashing of the shields, reared up and made confusion for themselves and their riders'.[56]

Most historians believe Malalas' version that Belisarius fled the field with his cavalry. I disagree. Procopius' version sounds more true to his character. The infantry certainly saved the defeat from becoming a rout. Procopius was at pains to point out the Persians' victory was a pyrrhic one as, with casualties just as high as those of the Romans, and embellishing this with a story that the Persians counted their war dead by requiring soldiers to leave a weapon in a basket when they marched away. On their return, the army would file past the baskets and pick out their weapons. The number of unclaimed weapons therefore equalled the number of dead. Procopius tells us: 'Since there were many weapons left, Kavad rebuked Azarethes for the victory and thereafter ranked him among the most unworthy.'[57]

However, despite the rearguard's heroic defence and the Persians' heavy casualties, Justinian dismissed Belisarius from his position as *magister militum per oriens* and set up a commission of enquiry into the defeat. Belisarius was recalled to Constantinople to face the enquiry. However, this may have been done more for show than anything else since he was soon reprieved.

After Belisarius' recall for court martial, the war in the east continued to be an embarrassment for Justinian. Things had returned to a stalemate until the Roman general Bessas launched a raid into Persian territory from the frontier fortress city of Martyropolis to regain the initiative but this only provoked the Persian Shah Kavad to focus all the Persian forces on besieging the city. Three veteran Persian generals took command of the attack, Chanaranges, Aspebedes and Mermeroes. It looked as if the city would fall but Bessas maintained a brave defence and Sittas, Belisarius' erstwhile companion, who had replaced him as *magister militum per oriens*, took the main Roman army to Attachas, about a hundred miles from Martyropolis, to harass the besieging Persians.

Martyropolis was holding out but for how long? Procopius says Justinian was terrified its fall would damage his reputation further, so he resorted to an espionage trick to save the city. Spies were everywhere in the Roman and Persian armies, and they were often double agents working for the highest bidder. One such was spying in the Roman camp for the Persians when he changed sides and sought an interview with Justinian himself. He told him the Persians were actively looking to buy an alliance with the European Huns for a combined attack through the Caucasus on Roman Syria. Justinian was horrified but saw an opportunity to double-cross the Persians. He paid the spy an enormous sum of money to return to the Persian forces outside Martyropolis and tell them the Romans had bribed the Huns to join them instead. This alarmed the Persians who stopped their attack on the city and considered how best to respond to the possibility of a Hunnic onslaught. In addition, they were distracted by the Shah Kavad's death in September 531. The nobles gathered in Ctesiphon to choose his successor. The Persian army withdrew and Martyropolis was saved.

Justinian had managed to avert another defeat. But he'd achieved nothing he could boast about. Meanwhile, discontent with his rule was growing in a new quarter that had enormous political power: the Circus Factions of the hippodrome.

21

Blues and Greens

Chariot racing was the lifeblood of late antiquity. In Constantinople, the hippodrome occupied a pivotal position, not just for racing but for political and social life. Almost everyone belonged to one of the so-called Circus Factions – Blue, Green, Red and White – although by Justinian's day it was the Blues and Greens who dominated. Charioteers were sporting superstars. For example, one named Porphyrius was commemorated with statues and plinths all over the city, several of which have survived to this day.

Although sometimes compared with modern sports teams in American football and soccer, the Circus Factions were much more than that. They ran the chariot racing teams but were also responsible for public festivals, law and order and were highly political. People went to the hippodrome not just to see the races but also to see the emperor and to call out political messages. The hippodrome was the town hall of late antiquity. Emperors delivered key political speeches there. Indeed, emperors' careers were often made or broken in the hippodrome, as we shall shortly hear.

The Blues and Greens also had a large hooligan element

in them. In Justinian's time, this was growing. Procopius was unforgiving about this:

> *They fight against the rival faction without knowing why they are putting themselves at such risk…So there grows in them against their rivals a hatred that has no cause…all that matters is that it goes well with their 'faction', for so they name the bands of partisans. Even women join them in this unholy strife, and they not only follow the men but even fight them if that is how it turns out, even though they neither go to the spectacles at all nor are led by any other cause to get involved. So that I, for my part, do not know what to call this if not a mental disorder.*[58]

Chroniclers like John Lydus pointed to the hooligan element growing because of an influx of migrants from Anatolia into the city who, he claimed, had been bankrupted by John the Cappadocian's aggressive tax regime. He referred to a growing underclass in Constantinople of 'useless mobs'.[59]

But another reason for the influx of migrants might have been the strong economy with people flocking to Constantinople to seek jobs and better prospects. Certainly, the eastern empire's economy was booming in the first half of the sixth century, and by 532 Constantinople was an enormous city by late antique standards, perhaps the largest in the world, with probably over 600,000 inhabitants.

Justinian had a close relationship with the Blues because, before he was emperor, he'd publicly sought their support to gain popularity. As I mentioned in Chapter 14, he had spent a fortune when consul, paying for entertainment in the hippodrome, not just chariot racing but also animal fights and lewd pantomime shows. The Blues were associated with him and also Theodora, who had in effect been a prostitute working for them. Indeed, it's highly likely they first met at a function organised by the Blues where she was a dancing girl.

But when he became emperor, Justinian didn't see the need to pander to the Blues any more. The same was even more true of Theodora when she became empress. Indeed, one senses both of them wanted to reject their previous associations with these odious organisations. And this created a problem since, not surprisingly, the Blues were offended by this.

And this was increasingly voiced in the hippodrome in Constantinople where the mob gathered to chant their views. Normally, these were respectful towards the emperor, along the lines of 'Long may you live, Justinian'[60] but towards the end of 531 the chanting took a decidedly more threatening tone, and the Greens, in particular, taunted Justinian with chants of 'Would that Justinian had not been born'.[61] A few years before, the Blues would have silenced them with their own chanting but now they didn't bother. Anger was building. And it was about to boil over.

22

'You Are a Stuffed Ass'

The trouble began on 10 January 532, when seven Circus Faction members, a mix of Blues and Greens, were sentenced to death for murder. Transported by boat across the Golden Horn to the suburb of Sycae (modern Galata), they were hanged but the scaffold broke and two of them (one Green and one Blue) miraculously survived and fled to a nearby church for sanctuary where the urban prefect, Eudaemon, dared not send troops to arrest them on sacred ground.

Three days later, on 13 January, a new series of races began in the hippodrome presided over by Justinian. Both Greens and Blues chanted appeals to him for the two survivors to be allowed to live. Justinian chose to ignore them. By the end of the day, the mob was getting impatient. Using a new slogan, *Nika*, meaning 'Victory', the war-cry of the Roman army, they started to riot.

Their first destination was the headquarters of the urban prefect called the praetorium, a building which included the main city prison and administrative offices. They broke into it, released the prisoners and then burned it down.

Despite this outrageous behaviour, the next day (14

January), Justinian allowed the second day of races to continue. But the mob had scented blood and wouldn't be appeased. They started burning down the upper tiers of the hippodrome. The blaze got out of control and spread to the Baths of Zeuxippus which contained many famous statues from antiquity. These were destroyed.

Justinian and his ministers were shocked by how this disturbance was getting out of hand. But they didn't know how to respond since it wasn't clear what the rioters wanted. The two condemned murderers had been rescued by the mob. What more did they want? One source[62] says that Justinian was told, probably by Theodora, that he needed to listen to their demands. Three high-ranking officials, including the general Mundo, were sent from the palace to speak to them. The mob responded by demanding the resignation of Justinian's main ministers, starting with Eudaemon, the city prefect who had originally refused to release the two condemned men, and also John the Cappadocian.

More surprisingly, they also wanted to sack Tribonian, the barrister working on Justinian's legal reforms. This was surprising because he wasn't a well-known member of the administration. So, the call for his dismissal probably indicates senatorial involvement. Justinian's legal reform was in its early stages and would have been largely unknown to most ordinary citizens. But in the senate, it was a main talking point with many conservative senators suspicious of Justinian's true intentions and sensing a potential betrayal of traditional Roman values. For example, the bureaucrat, John Lydus even disliked the idea of issuing new laws in Greek instead of Latin (as Justinian proposed) since this would be a betrayal of Rome's traditional focus on using Latin for all legal and administrative business.

Justinian was alert to the danger of mob violence turning into a call for regime change. So, he gave way to the rioters and dismissed all three of his top ministers. But it seems what he feared most was a coup in the palace itself. This was a possibility since Procopius says the palace guard were staying neutral during the rioting, waiting to see if rivals made a bid for power. To prevent any sudden *coup d'état* in the palace itself, he sent Anastasius' nephews, Hypatius and Pompey, to their homes in Constantinople, thinking they posed less of a threat at this distance. This would prove to be a major mistake.

However, Justinian did have one supporter. Belisarius. He had returned from the eastern front to face the court of enquiry into his defeat at Callinicum, although the fact he had a group of his best troops with him suggests he either had already been pardoned or was going to be. It is at this point that our three main sources on the Nika riots diverge. Malalas describes Justinian ordering Belisarius to restore order with his troops. According to him, on Friday 15 January, Belisarius' soldiers killed some of the rioters protesting in front of the imperial palace which he said only made matters worse and encouraged the mob to call for a new emperor.

Although Belisarius might have tried to stop the mob from attacking the palace, there was no large-scale fighting since two days later, on Sunday 17 January, another chronicle, the anonymous *Paschal* or *Easter Chronicle*, says Justinian made a last appeal to the mob by going to the hippodrome, standing in the imperial box, or *kathisma*, and in front of a vast crowd who had gathered specifically to hear him, he offered to pardon all the rioters under oath:

> *'By this power (i.e. holding the bible), I forgive you this error, and I order that none of you be arrested but be peaceful; for there is nothing on your head but rather on mine. For my sins have made me deny to you what you asked of me in the hippodrome (i.e. the release of the convicted murderers).*[63]

This was an extraordinary capitulation by the proud Justinian. He was in effect telling the mob the problem is me, not you. Although not mentioned by Procopius, I suspect he was hoping to emulate the emperor Anastasius' successful appeal to the mob in the hippodrome, described in Chapter 7. If he was, he was to be sadly disappointed. Justinian no doubt hoped to defuse the insurrection with a few choice words. Unfortunately, the mob had a few choice words for him. Although some Blue supporters shouted out their support, a chant quickly took hold in the hippodrome calling out: 'You are a stuffed ass.' Before long, the entire hippodrome was shouting out this humiliating put-down. Justinian nervously exited the *kathisma*, probably hoping not to trip up as he walked back down the steps that led into the palace (the hippodrome was directly linked to the Great Palace).

Back inside the palace, he had one thought – to run for it.

23

Murder in the Hippodrome

There was panic in the palace. Justinian wanted to flee the capital. But it was his wife, Theodora, who took control. Procopius records a long speech in which she apologised for speaking up as a woman:

> *Whether a woman should speak boldly among men, or stir up those cringing with fear, is not a matter we have the luxury to discuss at the moment.* [64]

In other words – *it's not a woman who should be saying this but I'm going to do it.* She admonished her husband for wanting to run away, saying on the one hand she knew he could easily escape: 'If, now, it is your wish to save yourself, O Emperor, there is no difficulty. For we have much money, and there is the sea and here are the boats.'[65] We can just imagine her pointing to the ships moored in the palace's own private harbour. But she then reminded him of the ignominy of flight: 'However consider whether it will not come about after you have saved yourself that you would gladly exchange that safety for death. For as for myself, I approve a certain ancient saying that purple makes a fine burial shroud.'[66]

The last few words of this sentence 'purple makes a fine burial shroud' was a scholarly joke on Procopius' part since Theodora was quoting an ancient proverb. In fact, she misquoted the original which was '*tyranny* makes a fine burial shroud', a dangerously transparent reference to Justinian's reign being a tyranny, but one which he clearly thought Justinian and his ministers would not spot. As such it was presumably intended for a small audience of his classically educated friends. It's highly unlikely she actually said these words. Nevertheless, clearly some sort of intervention by Theodora did happen. It would change the entire course of Justinian's reign.

Meanwhile, the senators who opposed Justinian had not been idle. They had found a new emperor. This was Hypatius, Anastasius' cousin. As mentioned, fearing a palace coup, Justinian had sent him home. But this only made matters worse because the mob went to Hypatius' house and, together with Pompeius, Anastasius' other nephew, escorted him to the Forum of Constantine where he was crowned emperor with a golden necklace on his head, the best substitute that could be found for the imperial diadem. Procopius says Hypatius' wife, Mary, a very sensible woman according to him, begged the mob not to take her husband for she knew this would end in disaster. But she couldn't stop them dragging him away. Whether Hypatius was a willing accomplice remains unclear. Procopius suggests he overcame his initial hesitation to join the rebels but the *Paschale Chronicle* claims he was playing a double-game all along. According to him, when he was seated by the mob in the *kathisma* in the hippodrome, he secretly sent a messenger to the palace telling Justinian that he had lured his enemies into the hippodrome where he could now slaughter them.[67] Again according to the *Paschale Chronicle*, unfortunately for Hypatius, there was a misunderstanding and a messenger incorrectly told him Justinian had fled the capital.

Meanwhile, in the senate, they knew Justinian was in fact still in the palace. The senators debated what to do next. Should they storm the palace or wait for Justinian to flee? Procopius says a senator, Origenes, argued it would be too dangerous to march on the palace and they should wait for Justinian to go. But they hadn't expected Theodora's rallying call. For back in the palace, with his wife urging him to fight, Justinian turned to the only man who could save him. This was of course Belisarius.

Justinian unleashed the best general in the empire against his enemies. A plan was quickly devised, probably by Belisarius himself, to sow discord between the Blues and Greens by bribing some members of the Blue Faction to support Justinian. He sent Justinian's trusted steward, Narses (a remarkable man who was a eunuch and would later play a major role in the Italian wars), to slip out of the palace and talk to the mob. He was helped by Mundo, the general commanding the Heruli federate soldiers, who also was in the capital.

But Narses' and Mundo's activities were just a diversionary tactic designed to distract attention from the main assault led by Belisarius and directed against Hypatius. First, Belisarius tried to break into the *kathisma* directly from the palace and seize Hypatius (see Map 3). But his path was blocked by guardsmen unwilling to take sides for or against Justinian. According to Procopius, Belisarius returned to the palace and asked Justinian if he wanted him to continue with his aim of capturing Hypatius. He knew the answer 'yes' would mean taking on the mob and killing many of them. Justinian said yes.

Belisarius had no choice but to execute the plan, 'execute' being the operative word for what was about to happen. He led his heavily armed troops out of the palace through the mostly destroyed Bronze Gate, and into the north of the hippodrome, via the wrecked remains of the Baths of Zeuxippus. There he met an enormous group of rioters. It was impossible to get to Hypatius in the *kathisma* without dispersing them. We don't know how many soldiers Belisarius had with him. I suspect it was only a few hundred. But Belisarius' men were veterans. Trained killers who had defeated the Persian Immortals at the battle of Dara. A mob of civilians could not resist their onslaught, even if many of the young men in the Circus Factions thought they were tough. Narses had also bribed many of the Blue faction members to declare their support for Justinian and they were scuffling with the Green members. In short, it was chaos. Belisarius judged the moment was right to seize Hypatius. He drew his sword and commanded his soldiers to do the same, and they charged into the mob.

Procopius says 30,000 died that afternoon — an unbelievably large number and about 5 per cent of the entire population of some 600,000. The hippodrome must have been drenched in blood and gore. Belisarius' soldiers undoubtedly killed many, but it's quite likely others were trampled to death as panic seized the mob, and there was also fighting between the Factions themselves, particularly as the Blues were being paid by Narses to turn against the Greens. As the mob fled, Belisarius finally reached the *kathisma* and seized both Hypatius and Pompeius. He brought them back to Justinian. They wept and pleaded that they had been coerced against their will to rebel. The next day, on Monday 19 January, they were executed. Their bodies were flung to rot in the sea. Justinian arrested those senators who had led the revolt, although we have almost no details about them. Procopius, writing over ten years after the event, thought it unwise to raise such a sensitive subject.

The Nika riots came to within an inch of overthrowing Justinian. They reveal much about his inability to rule without the help of Belisarius and Theodora. First, he failed to emulate his predecessor, Anastasius, who had displayed such courage and charisma in talking the mob down without bloodshed. Second, it was Theodora who persuaded him not to flee. Third, it was Belisarius who saved the day. He stormed the hippodrome and did not flinch from perpetrating the greatest massacre of unarmed civilians in Roman history to save his master. Without Belisarius, Justinian would have been just another footnote in the history books.

24

The Eternal Humiliation

The Nika riots left the heart of Constantinople a burnt-out wreck with 30,000 dead on the streets. The anonymous author of the *Paschale Chronicle* described the shocked silence in the city on the day after the riots were crushed:

> *And on the 20th of January, a Tuesday, all of Constantinople was quiet, and no one dared to go out, but only the shops which provided food and drink for needy people were open. And business remained untransacted and Constantinople was without commerce for a number of days.*[68]

Justinian had survived, but only just and only thanks to Theodora and Belisarius. Without them he would almost certainly have been deposed. But now he was in a stronger position. Belisarius had presented him with a significant victory. His two major rivals for the purple, Anastasius' nephews, Hypatius and Pompeius, were both dead. The Green faction, containing Justinian's most vocal critics, was crushed. It had almost certainly suffered most of the

30,000 casualties. The Blue faction was cowed and no doubt regretting its actions. As for the rebellious senators, although we have frustratingly little information about them, we know 18 were exiled and their property confiscated.

But although Justinian had triumphed in the Nika riots, he was still afraid of arousing more unpopularity. He refrained from a wider purge of the senate. Even those members of the palace guard who had obstructed Belisarius' route into the hippodrome to arrest Hypatius were not publicly punished although I doubt their career prospects were helped. Instead, for once in his reign, Justinian held back from brutally imposing his will. He even began a charm offensive.

For example, he waited several months before reinstating his favourites who he'd dismissed at the mob's request. John the Cappadocian only returned to his position as chief finance minister in October 532, and Tribonian wasn't reinstated until November 533. His obsessive lawmaking stopped. He issued no new laws until October except for one rescinding an earlier instruction to reduce the bread rations to the poor of the city – another concession designed to curry favour with the mob.

Indeed, in 533, a year after the riots, he granted posthumous pardons to Hypatius and Pompeius. Hypatius was given his own small cenotaph, bearing an inscription that read: 'I am the tomb of Hypatius; but small as I am, I make no claim to cover the body of so great a champion of the Romans.'[69] In due course, he even restored the confiscated property of both Hypatius and Pompeius to their children and relatives and, according to Procopius, he did the same for the 18 exiled senators.

Another surprising concession was that extended to the Monophysites. As discussed in Chapter 10, before he became emperor, Justinian had carved an identity for himself as a staunch Chalcedonian. This stance undoubtedly helped him become emperor in the fiercely Chalcedonian city of Constantinople, but it hadn't helped him in the Nika riots, when most of the rioters were Chalcedonian but still opposed him. So, in 532, perhaps to win support in the eastern provinces, he sought to make concessions to the Monophysites by offering them a watered-down version of the Council of Chalcedon's ruling that Christ was both divine and human simultaneously (as opposed to the Monophysite view he was only divine). This was in effect the same sort of compromise the emperor Zeno had tried to secure with the *Henotikon* as discussed in Chapter 6. Although the Monophysite bishops were ready to accept this point of doctrine, which would have marked quite a victory for Justinian, they also wanted to reinstate 55 anti-Chalcedonian bishops who Justinian's uncle, the emperor Justin, had exiled. This was a deal-breaker. Justinian couldn't accept this and in the end no compromise was agreed. The 'conversations of 532' as they became known remained merely conversations. Justinian had achieved nothing.

But in 532, he made his biggest concession of all, and the one that was least justified – a humiliating peace with Persia. The origins of this lay with the shah Kavad's death in April 531. Because of this the Persians had broken off their offensive directed against Martyropolis. Kavad's death sparked a period of instability in Persian politics with his son and successor, Chosroes, facing stiff opposition internally.

To concentrate on these domestic problems, Chosroes made peace with the Romans. Therefore, soon after the Nika riots, in the spring of 532, the so-called 'Eternal Peace' was signed. A better name would have been the 'Eternal Humiliation' for this was a decidedly one-sided treaty. Justinian paid Chosroes the enormous sum of 11,000 pounds of gold to secure it and handed over two forts the Romans had taken from the Persians in Armenia, Bolon and Pharangion. In addition, he agreed to demilitarise Dara, the empire's major fortress opposite the Persian centre of military operations at Nisibis.

Why was Justinian so desperate? Eleven thousand pounds of gold was a vast sum and over five times the annual subsidy Theodosius II agreed to pay Attila in 447. And that was when Attila had led his army to the very walls of Constantinople. In contrast, in 532 the Persians and Romans were fairly evenly matched in terms of battles. Each side had won one and lost one. Belisarius had won the battle of Dara but lost at Callinicum. Persian casualties had probably been higher than Roman during the war, if Procopius' account was correct. The Romans had taken the two forts in Armenia which Justinian agreed to hand back. Admittedly, after Belisarius was dismissed to face court martial, the Persians seem to have put together a larger army to attack Martryropolis than the Romans could field, but the city had held out and the Persian army had withdrawn.

Justinian hid this utter humiliation behind the official line that the gold was payment for the Persian defences against the Huns in the Caucasus, an agreement long established to cover the joint cost of defending the Caucasus, and a very old excuse for Roman 'tribute' to the Persians. But this defence was paper thin, and the question remains why was Justinian so willing to buy the Persians off? Procopius is silent on this in the *Wars,* although in *The Secret History* he doesn't hold back from expressing his contempt for Justinian's huge payments of tribute: 'The barbarians have become in every respect the masters of the wealth of the Romans, either by receiving the money from the Emperor's hand, or by plundering the Roman realm.'[70]

Many historians[71] give Justinian the benefit of the doubt. This is because they are too easily convinced by Justinian's own propaganda justifying peace with Persia as necessary for his wars of reconquest in the west. However, as we will shortly discover, it was only after Belisarius achieved victory in the west that Justinian built his narrative of a long-held plan to reconquer the lost western empire. For example, it was not until 536, when Belisarius' wars were going well, that he made his first reference to it: 'We are inspired with the hope that God will grant us rule over the rest of what, subject to the ancient Romans to the limits of both seas, they later lost by their neglect.'[72]

Before 536, there was no mention of any such grand ambitions. Indeed, after the horror of the Nika riots Justinian was more than happy just to make a few quick wins to bolster his tarnished image. He was probably still counting his lucky stars that he'd survived at all and was only aiming for some modest success to stave off further criticism. As we will soon discover, his plans would now exceed his wildest expectations.

The Age of Conquest

25

Africa Revisited

In 533, Justinian's reign was about to be transformed. And the secret of his success was to be found where we started this book – with the Vandal kingdom of North Africa.

It would be no understatement to say the later Romans were obsessed with North Africa, and in particular their negligent loss of this wealthy part of the empire to a group of marauding Germans. This story is told in book three in this series, and we need do no more here than summarise it by saying it all began when a group of Vandals and other Germanic warriors crossed the frozen Rhine on a fateful night in December 406 to invade Gaul. Little did they realise that 33 years later they would end up sailing across the narrow strait of Gibraltar, and seizing control of the entire Roman province of North Africa, with its affluent capital of Carthage, the fourth largest and most prosperous city in the Roman world. I refer you to book three for the litany of errors, both strategic and tactical, which meant three Roman fleets in the fifth century failed to recover the province, with the most spectacular disaster being Leo's great expedition in 468, as already recounted.

Fast forward to the year 523, and things were looking very different for the Vandals. That year, Hilderic ascended the throne. Half Vandal but also half Roman, the son of Gaiseric's son, Huneric, and his Roman wife, the imperial princess, Eudocia, he represented the union of barbarian and Roman that his grandfather, the wily Vandal king Gaiseric, had sought for so long. But Gaiseric's dream that his grandson might inherit the Roman Empire had come to nothing, and when Hilderic finally ascended the Vandal throne, he was an old man in his sixties. He pursued a policy of rapprochement with the eastern empire. This centred on healing the religious divide that afflicted the Vandal kingdom. For like the Goths in Italy, the Vandals had never renounced their Arian faith. This was a source of conflict with the Roman population who were Catholic. Tension between the two churches was strong during the first 100 years of the kingdom's life but with Hilderic's ascension there was a clear step towards religious toleration. The Catholic Church of North Africa was allowed to function without impediment and even to hold its first council in two generations in Carthage (in 525).

Hilderic's more lenient religious stance was perhaps partly out of respect for his mother's faith but also because he wished to oppose the Ostrogothic kingdom of Italy which under Theodoric's rule had become the most powerful barbarian kingdom in the west. To counter Theodoric's growing power, he sought to ally with Constantinople and established a good relationship with Justinian. But luck was not on his side. During the 520s, the indigenous nomadic Berber tribes on the kingdom's southern borders had been growing in size, co-operating better and proving to be a more formidable opponent to the Vandals than ever before. Hilderic was not a strong military leader, and too old to lead his troops into battle. In late 529 or early 530, the Vandal army suffered a serious defeat in the province of Byzacenza. This provoked a rebellion against Hilderic in 530 by his younger royal cousin, Gelimer, who renewed the persecution of the Catholic Church.

Not surprisingly, Justinian was unhappy with this turn of events. His relationship with Hilderic had been politically valuable, and there seems to have been a genuine friendship between the two of them. So, he despatched messengers to Carthage to demand Hilderic's reinstatement. Gelimer ignored them. He inflamed the situation by replying to a second request from Justinian, telling him to mind his own business and focus instead on managing his own realm. This message arrived after the Nika riots and seems to have been a reference to them which stung Justinian. Procopius says it was then he decided to attack the Vandal state:

The emperor…upon receiving the letter, having been angry with Gelimer even before then, was now still more eager to punish him. And it seemed to him best to put an end to the Persian war as soon as possible and then to make an expedition to Libya (as Procopius called the Vandal kingdom); and since he was quick at forming a plan and prompt in carrying out his decisions, Belisarius, the General of the East, was summoned and came to him immediately.[73]

But this wasn't the only thing that encouraged Justinian to attack Carthage. A host of other reasons were preying on his mind. One was the enormous wealth said to exist in Carthage, amassed from the sack of Rome in 455, and added to by decades of prosperous trade under Vandal rule. The other was the attraction of a religious crusade. Procopius says Justinian was keen to display his piety by punishing the Arian Vandals for their persecution of the Catholic Church in North Africa. A story that Gelimer had ripped out the tongues of Catholic priests gripped Constantinople. These priests were banished to Constantinople, where they miraculously recovered the power of speech. Procopius, with his dry sense of humour, remarked that the miracle had only lasted until the African bishops were discovered consorting with prostitutes in the imperial capital, whereupon they lost their power of speech again.

But no one else shared Justinian's enthusiasm to attack the Vandals. The idea shocked the senate and they reminded Justinian of the disastrous outcome of the expedition in 468. The army was terrified by the prospect of a major new war in a distant foreign land and irked by the idea of a long sea journey. To quote Procopius:

> *The soldiers, also, who recently returned from a long, hard war (i.e. the Persian war) and had not yet tasted to the full the blessings of home, were in despair, because they were being led into a naval expedition, a thing they were ignorant about, and because they would be sent from the eastern front to the west in order to risk their lives against Vandals and Moors.*[74]

His trusted first minister, John the Cappadocian, recently restored to office, was the most vocal critic. He said the risks far outweighed the rewards, and pointed out, with good strategic understanding, that victory in North Africa would only lead to war with the Ostrogoths. Procopius says John swayed Justinian against the expedition until a bishop arrived at the palace determined to see the emperor. He told the emperor God had sent him a vision in which the expedition was victorious.

But in reality, Justinian was probably more influenced by news of revolts against Gelimer. The first one was at the extreme eastern end of the Vandal kingdom in Tripolitania (modern Libya), where a native African Roman nobleman, Pudentius, revolted against Gelimer and asked for support from Constantinople. Since there were few Vandals settled in this region, this didn't involve a meaningful military confrontation, and it provided Justinian with a convenient pretext to send troops to protect the local Roman population.

Then, much more importantly, at the other end of the Vandal domain on its most northerly edge, another revolt erupted, led by the governor of Sardinia, a Goth by birth who Gelimer had entrusted with the rule of the island. Like Pudentius, he also asked Justinian for support. With two rebellions distracting the Vandals, the prospects for involvement in North Africa looked interesting. And Justinian was nothing if not an opportunist. Even if he could only reinstate Hilderic, that would still give his prestige a much-needed boost. So, he turned to Mr Fix-it. The man who had saved him once already by crushing the Nika riots, and who he now desperately hoped could deliver another miracle. That man was, of course, Belisarius.

26

Belisarius' Armada

As you read Procopius' long account of the voyage you can almost smell the saltiness of the waves and hear the loud cries of the seagulls. He was a member of Belisarius' senior staff, probably his chief legal advisor, and has left us with a detailed history of the expedition that set out in 533.

To begin with, Justinian gave Belisarius supreme command and complete freedom to make all decisions without reference to him. Such was Justinian's trust in his general that, in Procopius' words, he 'gave him the authority of an emperor'.[75] This would prove essential in achieving victory.

The army that Belisarius put together was in effect a smaller version of the one that had won the battle of Dara, and many of the soldiers were the same. Fifteen thousand strong, it comprised 5,000 horsemen and 10,000 infantry. It mostly contained regular soldiers, and they were among the best, if not the best, in the Roman army. Of the cavalry, 4,000 were the elite armoured horse archers that were the 'panzers' of the new Roman army. As described by Procopius, these men were excellent horsemen, capable of shooting with deadly accuracy from the saddle, and engaging the enemy with spears and swords. Probably about a thousand of these were Belisarius' own household regiment, the *bucellarii*. There was also a thousand of the same auxiliary units that had fought at Dara with such deadly effect – 600 Massagetic Huns, the best light cavalry horse archers in the world – and 400 Heruli horsemen, noted for their speed and ferocity and who had caused the Persians such problems at Dara. The 10,000 infantry were all Roman regulars, the disciplined heavy infantry that had been at Dara but did little of the fighting, and who were the direct descendants, militarily speaking, of the Roman legionaries of old. Procopius also mentions an additional force of 400 soldiers specifically assigned to sail to Sardinia to help Godas' revolt on the island.

The fleet transporting this army comprised around 500 merchantmen and 92 warships called *dromons*, armed with a battering ram on their prows to sink enemy ships. Thirty thousand sailors from Greece and Egypt manned these boats, most of them oarsmen. All told, this force was probably less than half that despatched by Leo in 468. Since most of it was taken from the eastern front, this left the Roman army in Syria very depleted and dependent on Justinian's 'Eternal Peace' with Persia. As we will discover, the Persians had no intention of taking the word 'eternal' literally. But for now, there was peace in the east.

By late June 533, Belisarius' armada was ready to sail. Our sources say the soldiers were terrified by the prospect of a naval battle and determined to avoid it at all costs. Procopius confesses his own fear of putting to sea was only eased by a dream in which Belisarius appeared to be victorious.

When the fleet left port in Constantinople, the patriarch, Epiphanius, blessed Belisarius' ship and presented him with a newly baptised and converted soldier.

The initial progress was slow (see Map 5). The fleet stopped for five days in Heracleia in Thrace to take on board horses. Many more would later join the army in Sicily, courtesy of the Ostrogoths, who agreed to supply the expedition in a brief show of rapprochement between the two powers. Then a lack of wind delayed the ships' exit from the narrow straits of the Hellespont. Putting in at Abydos, there was a fight among the Huns, who were bored and got drunk. A man was killed. Belisarius acted decisively. He had the two men who committed the murder impaled on a hill, visible to everyone in the fleet.

He then addressed his troops, saying that if they did not maintain discipline they would not survive let alone triumph in this expedition. Procopius says the men listened in earnest and were so fearful of the coming conflict they heeded his words. Repeatedly, we hear from Procopius how Belisarius could deliver messages like this to his soldiers. He didn't deliver pep talks. Instead, he had an ability to tell his soldiers what they didn't want to hear and convince them they needed to up their game to succeed. This was one of the many qualities that marks him out as one of the greatest commanders in history.

Once in the open sea of the Aegean, the fleet made better progress. But Belisarius was worried some ships might go astray, so he made the three command ships containing him and his retinue more conspicuous by painting their sails with a red stripe, hanging lights on their prows at night, and using trumpets to announce when they were raising and dropping anchor. In this way, the large number of vessels kept together as they made their way round the treacherous Cape of Matapan in southern Greece, where storms could blow up at a moment's notice.

Belisarius was then forced to put in at Methone on the southern coast. A disaster had struck unexpectedly. Large numbers of men were ill because the main provisions in the form of hard biscuits had gone mouldy and were poisoning them. Procopius says it was John the Cappadocian's fault since he ordered biscuits which had been baked only once to save money on firewood instead of twice which was required to keep them fresh on a long journey. Belisarius was furious when, according to Procopius, 500 of his men died from poisoning. This seems a large number and there's just a possibility that Procopius exaggerated it to discredit John the Cappadocian who, as he described in *The Secret History*, was someone he particularly reviled. Whatever the truth, Belisarius purchased new rations for the army and sent a report to Justinian complaining about John the Cappadocian's potentially disastrous penny-pinching.

The next problem was to keep the water fresh. Procopius describes how the water taken on board at the island of Zakynthos spoiled by the time they reached Sicily because there was a lack of wind to propel the ships and the journey took 16 days, much longer than expected. He mentions Belisarius' wife, Antonina, who was travelling with him, had kept jars of water on their boat fresh by covering them with sand, thereby keeping them out of the sun, which she knew was what caused the water to spoil. This praise for her is surprising and noteworthy because Procopius was scathing about her in *The Secret History*, as we will hear in Chapter 48.

At this point, probably most contemporaries would not have given Belisarius' expedition much chance of success. But it was helped by two pieces of good luck. First, the Ostrogoths were hugely helpful to Belisarius' expedition by allowing him to use Sicily as a staging post and take on board large numbers of horses. As mentioned, the Ostrogothic Queen Amalasuentha was pursuing a pro-Roman policy at this moment for reasons we will cover in Chapter 32.

Second, Procopius says it was he himself who next discovered a game-changing piece of news: the Vandal fleet had sailed with 7,000 of its best troops to Sardinia to put down Godas' revolt. This revolt had been one reason Justinian thought it was a suitable moment to attack. And he was proven right. Procopius describes how Belisarius sent him to Syracuse, purportedly to purchase supplies for the fleet, but really to ask about the whereabouts of the Vandal fleet. There, he unexpectedly met a childhood friend from his home town of Caesarea in modern Gaza. This man was a merchant who had just returned from a trip to Carthage. And he had a vitally important piece of information. He'd just seen the Vandal fleet sailing away for Sardinia.

This was too good to be true. Belisarius was decisive. He immediately gave the orders to sound the trumpets for the Roman fleet's departure. The troops were told there was nothing to worry about since the Vandal fleet had gone. This was especially morale boosting since they'd long been terrified of a naval battle. Within two days, and after a brief stop at Malta, they beached on the headland of Caput Vada (now

Ras Kabudia) in the province of Byzacena. It had been about three months since they left Constantinople.

What now? Belisarius decided against a naval attack on Carthage. That had been Basiliscus' strategy in 468, when the Vandals had destroyed the Roman fleet with fire ships. Instead, he ordered his soldiers to build a fortified camp, in traditional Roman fashion, and prepare for a land march on Carthage. Next, he began a charm offensive to win the hearts and minds of the native Roman African population. To this end, he organised a public execution of looters who refused to pay for supplies. Officers were told to enforce strict instructions that all supplies must be fully paid for in cash and that the locals should be treated with great respect. To appeal to the pro-Vandal segment of the population, he spread the story that the army was only there to put Hilderic, the rightful Vandal king, back on the throne.

After three days of rest at Caput Vada, just long enough to bring the horses back into condition and for the troops to re-acclimatise to the land, Belisarius led the army north towards Carthage. Meanwhile, on the Vandal side there was panic. The Romans' arrival caught Gelimer off guard. He had just despatched the fleet to Sardinia and his troops were widely dispersed. Belisarius had also landed midway between his royal estates south of Carthage, where he was hunting, and Carthage itself. This meant he was cut off from Carthage. So, instead he sent messengers post-haste to his brother, Ammatas, who was in Carthage, instructing him to execute the unfortunate Hilderic, and to advance to meet Belisarius while his nephew, Gibimundus, gathered troops from the west to join him. Then he set out with all the troops he could gather, which seems to have been an enormous force although we have no numbers, to attack the Roman camp.

Belisarius' army was almost certainly heavily outnumbered. Was the disaster of 468 about to be repeated?

Figure 1: This mosaic of Justinian is the most famous depiction of him and has featured on the front covers of many books. It is part of a stunning collection of mosaics in San Vitale, Ravenna, which includes portrayals of his wife Theodora, Belisarius and Antonina as shown in the next figures. (Author's collection)

Figure 2: His wife, Theodora, looks imperious belying her past life as a prostitute. She and Justinian were one of the greatest 'power couples' in history. (Author's Collection)

Figure 3: Thought to be the face of Belisarius, he is depicted less as a great soldier than as a loyal servant of Justinian's. He was in fact both. (Author's Collection)

Figure 4: Considered to be Belisarius' wife, Antonina, this mosaic captures her forthright, captivating personality that made her husband devoted to her despite her infidelities. Together with Justinian and Theodora, she and Belisarius were the 'fab four' of late antiquity. (Author's Collection)

Figure 5: This bust of Belisarius, by Jean-Baptiste Stouf (1791), portrays the aged general as a beggar blinded by Justinian. A legend developed centuries after Justinian's reign that he had persecuted the man who brought him such great victories. This is completely false. Although Justinian became envious of Belisarius' success, and probably did accuse him of treason in 542, they were reconciled and Belisarius was allowed to retain most of his wealth. They both died in 565. (Wikimedia Commons, Public Domain)

Figure 6: Aqueducts brought water to several hundred cisterns in Constantinople. The Basilica Cistern in Istanbul, pictured here, was built by Justinian and was the largest in the city. (Author's Collection)

Figure 7: Marble columns in the Basilica cistern were taken from pagan temples, such as this head of Medusa. Superstitious Christians placed the heads of these pagan gods sideways or upside down to negate their power. (Author's Collection)

Figure 8: Hagia Sophia was Justinian's greatest architectural triumph. It was the largest Christian church in the world until it fell to the Turks in 1453 when it became a mosque. (Author's Collection)

Figure 9: Hagia Sophia's dome was the largest in the world for a thousand years until St Peter's in Rome surpassed it in the sixteenth century. (Author's Collection)

Figure 10: Theodosius I placed this obelisk of Thutmose III at the centre of the hippodrome in Constantinople in c. AD 390. It asserted Constantinople's position as 'New Rome', copying the tradition begun by Augustus of moving obelisks to the empire's capital. (Author's Collection)

Figure 11: The Theodosian walls of Constantinople (modern Istanbul). Comprising three walls, the tallest tower in this photo is part of the inner wall, which was larger than the first and second walls. No enemy breached these defences until 1453, when the Ottoman Turks used cannons. (Author's Collection)

Figure 12: Seventeenth-century portrayal of a biblical plague (La Peste d'Ashdod) by Nicolas Poussin, inspired by his experience of an outbreak of bubonic plague in Italy in 1629-31. This would have been similar to the Justinianic Plague. (Wikimedia Commons, Public Domain)

Figure 13: Plate depicting the Persian Shah Chosroes I, Justinian's most formidable enemy, who took advantage of the deployment of much of the Roman army to the west to sack Antioch in 540. Justinian resorted to paying Chosroes tribute so that the over-extended Roman army could concentrate on other fronts. (Wikimedia Commons, Public Domain)

Figure 14: Mosaic showing boats at Ravenna's port of Classe. It was a major military and commercial port in ancient times linking Ravenna with Constantinople but it has since silted up. (Author's Collection)

Figure 15: The Ostrogothic King Theodoric's mausoleum in Ravenna was made of Istrian stone and has a roof consisting of a single carved stone weighing 250 tons. Lifting this into place was an extraordinary feat of engineering and testimony to the wealth of the Ostrogoths. (Author's Collection)

Figure 16: Portrait of the Ostrogothic King Totila by Francesco Salviati, c. 1549. Totila was a fierce warrior who led an Ostrogothic resurgence in the 540s which undid most of Belisarius' conquests until he was defeated by Narses. (Wikimedia Commons, Public Domain)

Figure 17: Profile of Gelimer, the last King of the Vandals, on a silver coin. Gelimer was defeated by Belisarius and was said to have lamented his fall by playing the lyre. (Wikimedia Commons, Public Domain)

27

Lunch in Carthage

The Romans marched north for four days, and on 13 September, they reached the town of Ad Decimum. Belisarius had sent 300 of his armoured horse archers, under the command of John the Armenian, to reconnoitre the Vandal positions in front of Carthage. There they met Ammatas, as he advanced down the road from the city. But the Vandals were not in battle formation, instead advancing in groups of only 20–30 men. The Romans' horse archers shot them down and charged the survivors, in the process killing Ammatas himself but not before he'd fought valiantly and slain a dozen Romans, according to Procopius.

The next engagement happened about five miles inland when Gibimundus' cavalry, coming from the west, and probably several thousand strong, collided with the 600 Massagetic Huns who were covering the Roman left flank. It was the first time the Vandals had met Huns, and Procopius describes an initial stand-off between them in which the Vandals looked dumbfounded at these Asiatic steppe nomads, too afraid to attack them until the Hunnic leader declared the Vandals were a 'ready feast'. The tough Asians made quick work of the Vandals who Procopius says 'were all disgracefully destroyed'.[76]

Yet Procopius is adamant Gelimer could still have won the battle of Ad Decimum despite these two reverses. For he says he still had a huge number of cavalry with him although we have no precise details of numbers. Procopius says he was advancing towards Carthage on an inland road that ran parallel with the coast road the Roman army was taking. Both sides were unaware of each other until Gelimer realised Belisarius was almost right next to him, and he swung right to attack the Romans. Things started well for the Vandals. They easily won a skirmish for control of some hills that separated the two armies. Eight hundred of Belisarius' mounted archers retreated, and it looked as if the Vandals would crash into the Roman army and push it into the sea. Procopius says that 'so numerous appeared the force of the Vandals' they could easily have defeated the Romans.

But then something unexpected happened. The Vandals stopped. Procopius explains this was because Gelimer came across his dead brother's body and was overcome with grief. Both sides paused. The Vandals to carry away Ammatas' body and bury it. The Romans to re-group under Belisarius' command. Procopius points out that up to this point, Belisarius had not known about John the Armenian's successful dispersal of the Vandals advancing from Carthage, or of the Huns' destruction of the Vandals attacking from the west. But when Belisarius was in full possession of the facts, and realised he was in fact facing Gelimer's main army, he launched a ferocious attack on the Vandals who 'having already fallen into disorder and being now unprepared, did not withstand their onslaught but fled with all their might, losing many there, and the battle ended at night'.[77]

Procopius' account of this part of the battle is far too brief. Was the turning point really Gelimer's remorse about his dead brother? Did the Vandals really stop to bury him? Like Homer in the Iliad, Procopius was fond of making 'human' stories out of battles, in which an individual's moment of folly or bravery would decide the outcome. I favour a more purely military explanation. I suggest the missing link was the quality of Belisarius' mounted archers.

Let me explain. Throughout Procopius' account of the battles between the Vandals and Romans, one thing stands out like a sore thumb. Whenever the Vandal horsemen came into contact with the Roman cavalry, they were routed. For example, John the Armenian put them to flight in front of Carthage when he killed Gelimer's brother, the Huns regarded them as a 'ready feast', and Belisarius easily routed Gelimer's main army.

One thing we know is these were all cavalry battles. At no point were Roman or Vandal infantry involved. So, why were the Romans and Huns victorious every time? The key point I suggest is the Vandals had no horse archers. In contrast, every single one of the Roman and Hunnic cavalry was a mounted archer. Each battle represented the triumph of the horse archer over the old-fashioned Germanic warrior astride his horse, waving a sword or spear. The horse archers were the key to victory on the battlefield, just as tanks had been in the Second World War, and drones appear to be today.

Gelimer compounded the Vandal problems by making some spectacularly bad tactical mistakes. After his defeat at

Ad Decimum, he retreated west to the plain of Boulla and the road leading to Numidia rather than falling back on Carthage. It's possible he felt if he fell back on Carthage with his army, they would be trapped by the Romans. But equally, he missed the opportunity of using the city's strong Roman walls to his advantage.

The result was Belisarius headed straight for Carthage, with the Roman fleet moving in parallel along the coast. There was no resistance. The city's inhabitants opened the gates. The chain which protected the harbour was reeled in. Belisarius' fleet entered the harbour although most of it sailed to the nearby port of Stagnum since there were simply too many boats to dock in Carthage.

Procopius describes a tranquil scene as the Roman army reached the city in the evening: 'The Carthaginians opened the gates and burned lights everywhere and the city was brilliant with the illuminations that whole night, and those of the Vandals who had been left behind were sitting as suppliants in the sanctuaries.'[78] The next day, on 15 September 533, Belisarius made his formal entry into the city. He forbade any looting. He wanted the city's inhabitants to welcome his army not as conquerors but as liberators. And so they did. When he was satisfied the city was safe and that both his soldiers and its inhabitants were at peace with each other, he made his way to the Vandals' royal palace. There he sat on Gelimer's throne. Local merchants rushed in to complain that the Roman sailors had stolen their cargoes the night before. Belisarius promised them compensation and instructed the admiral of the fleet to provide this, something which Procopius says never in fact happened for the admiral, named Kalonymus, was a scoundrel.

Belisarius then invited his generals and senior officers to enjoy a lavish lunch which had been prepared by the palace staff for Gelimer. Procopius was there and enjoyed it as much as the rest of the Roman top brass: 'We feasted on that very food that the servants of Gelimer had prepared, and they poured the wine and waited upon us in every way.'[79] Belisarius was the hero of the hour. He had recaptured Carthage with very few losses, something which the emperors Majorian and Leo had only dreamed of. Procopius could put it no better when he said: 'It fell to the lot of Belisarius on that day to win such fame as not one of his contemporaries ever won nor indeed any men of ancient times.'[80]

But at that very moment, Gelimer was mustering his forces for one last showdown. The battle for Africa was not over yet.

28

The Last Vandal King

While Belisarius was enjoying lunch in Carthage, the Vandal king Gelimer retreated to the plain of Boulla, west of Carthage, to gather all the Vandal forces and prepare a counterattack. To help him, his brother Tzazo had defeated the rebel Godas in Sardinia, and returned with the Vandal fleet and the 7,000 troops he'd taken with him. Gelimer tried, in vain, to form a wider coalition against the Romans, appealing to the powerful Berber tribes, with whom he'd recently been in conflict, the Visigoths in Spain and also the native African Roman inhabitants, to come together and eject the eastern Romans. But the response he got was tepid indeed. The Berbers had little love for the Vandals and viewed the Romans as more legitimate rulers of Carthage. They were happy to wait and see who won the contest.

Meanwhile, the Visigoths had no interest whatsoever in getting involved in this war, and as for the native African Roman population, despite Gelimer offering a generous reward for every Roman soldier they killed, it was Belisarius who was winning their hearts and minds. When he captured Carthage, he treated its inhabitants with great respect and successfully leveraged his trump card – restoring the Catholic faith at the expense of the Arian. For example, he restored the Catholic priests to their historic positions and banished the Vandal-sponsored Arian clergy. Nowhere was this more apparent than in the main cathedral in Carthage, dedicated to a famous third-century African priest called Cyprian, which was restored to the Catholic faith, much to the approval of the city's population. Finally, Belisarius was generous to the Vandals trapped in the city and allowed them to stay, provided they accepted Roman rule. He also strengthened the city walls which he found had fallen into disrepair in places.

For three months, there was a sort of phoney war, with Gelimer waiting for the return of Tzazo from Sardinia and hoping that others would join his cause while Belisarius watched the Vandal movements from the safety of Carthage. Finally, in late 533, Gelimer advanced on the city. But he didn't feel confident enough to besiege it, so he merely cut the main aqueduct. He sent spies into the city offering the Huns money to swap sides which might have met with success, according to Procopius,[81] had Belisarius not become aware of it and lavishly entertained the Huns and promised them booty and a speedy ticket home should they defeat the Vandals. He also impaled one of the Roman inhabitants who was found liaising with the Vandals as a warning to anyone else thinking of doing the same.

With Gelimer threatening but still not committing to an assault on the city, Belisarius forced the issue and, on 15 December 533, he led his army out of Carthage towards the Vandals, camped about 30 miles away near to a place called Tricamarum. The Roman advance guard camped for the night a short distance from the Vandals. It comprised the bulk of the armoured horse archers under the command of John the Armenian, who had distinguished himself at the battle of Ad Decimum by killing Ammatas and routing his men. Meanwhile, Belisarius marched behind more slowly with the infantry and 500 of his elite horsemen. Belisarius also kept the Huns with him to keep an eye on them in case they switched sides. Procopius says they were waiting to see who would win the next battle before joining the winning side.

Procopius also narrates a strange omen that was seen in the Roman forward camp that night:

> *When it was well on in the night, the following prodigy occurred in the Roman camp. The tips of their spears shone with a bright fire and their points seemed to be burning most vigorously. This was not seen by many, but it filled the few who did see it with anxiety, not knowing how it would turn out. This happened to the Romans in Italy again at a much later time, but then they knew by experience that they could regard it as a sign of victory.*[82]

The next day, Gelimer came out of his fortified camp with a vast host of horsemen and confronted the Roman horse archers. What followed is not described in great detail by Procopius but seems to have involved the Roman cavalry making several sorties against the Vandals, showering them with arrows before galloping off in the typical Hunnic-style tactics the Roman army was now expert in. The purpose was to demoralise the Vandals as their horsemen died in a storm of arrows and encourage them to charge in a disorderly fashion. These tactics appear to have worked perfectly. The dispirited Vandals finally charged and battle was joined.

John the Armenian led the main Roman assault which broke the Vandal cavalry, killing Gelimer's brother, Tzazo, and in Procopius' words: 'many of the noblest Vandals fell'.[83] The Roman horsemen pushed the Vandals all the way back to their stockade. Procopius says only 50 Romans died while the Vandals lost 800 horsemen.

Meanwhile, when Belisarius reached the battlefield with the heavy infantry and the Huns, they weren't needed. At the sight of massed ranks of Roman infantry, Gelimer lost his nerve and retreated in panic. The entire Vandal army followed suit and fled the battlefield, taking as many of their women and children as they could. The Romans pursued them and cut many of them down.

But it was at the Vandal camp the Romans were stopped in their tracks. According to Procopius: 'They found in this camp a quantity of wealth such has never before been found, at least in one place. For the Vandals had plundered the Roman Empire for a long time and had transferred great amounts of money to Libya (as Procopius called the Vandal kingdom).'[84] But it was not just gold and silver they found. They also found a huge number of Vandal women and children, abandoned by their husbands. The women were, Procopius tells us 'young and extremely attractive'.[85] They were also long accustomed to being the aristocracy in Africa and getting what they wanted. They proved far more effective at stopping the Roman army than their husbands had been. With remarkable confidence, en masse they offered to marry the Roman soldiers. They then carried this out with remarkable efficiency. Procopius says most of the Roman soldiers were poor single young men overcome at meeting such women. Discipline collapsed as the soldiers paired off with them, totally preoccupied with their new companions: 'For neither did fear of the enemy nor respect for Belisarius occur to them, nor indeed anything else at all...'.[86]

Even Belisarius hadn't expected this. He was, according to Procopius, 'at a loss to know how to handle the situation'. The Vandal women did indeed become the wives of many, if not most of the army of occupation, and would continue to play an important role, as we will discover in Chapter 34.

The next day, with his love-struck army immobilised, Belisarius sent John the Armenian, his most trusted commander, with a group of soldiers to hunt Gelimer down. But Gelimer escaped because, Procopius tells us, of a tragic accident. When the Roman search party stopped for the night, one of John's best soldiers, Uliaris, a renowned horse archer but also a drinker, consumed too much wine, celebrating victory over the Vandals, in which he had played a brave and conspicuous part. Rebuked for being drunk, he jumped to his feet saying even if he was drunk he could still hit anything with his bow, and shot an arrow at a passing bird. Not only did he miss the bird, but the arrow happened to hit John the Armenian in the neck. John died in Uliaris' arms who was weeping with remorse for his foolishness. Before he died, John made his men swear they would tell Belisarius not to punish Uliaris since it had been an accident. When Belisarius caught up with them, according to Procopius, he wept over

John's death but reluctantly pardoned Uliaris out of respect for John's dying wish. Another source says that from that day, Uliaris gave up drink and became a monk to repent for his sins.[87]

Meanwhile, Gelimer had escaped but was in despair. The Vandal army had been shattered. The Vandal men were either dead or had been scattered. Most of the Vandal women were starting a new life with new partners. But rather than surrender, Gelimer fled to find refuge with some friendly Berbers on an inaccessible peak on Mount Papua in Numidia. There, Belisarius had no choice but to starve him out for no soldiers could climb the peak it was so high and well defended. After a couple of months of extreme hardship, in March 534, he agreed to surrender. Procopius tells us he asked for only three things in captivity – a loaf of bread to assuage his extreme hunger, a sponge to bathe an infected eye and a lyre to lament the fall of his kingdom.

His request for a lyre became famous and, although it sounds an unlikely story, he was apparently a skilled musician and harpist. Nevertheless, his wish to put the downfall of his kingdom to music might have reflected some sort of mental breakdown, especially since when he met Belisarius, apparently he fell at his feet and burst into a fit of hysterical laughter, which his attendants explained was his response to the extreme vicissitudes of life. However, Belisarius, always a man of honour and integrity, raised the stricken Vandal to his feet, shook his hand and reassured him he would always be treated as befitted a king.

So ended the reign of the last king of the Vandals.

29

Belisarius Triumphant

While Gelimer was starving on Mount Papua, Belisarius had not been idle. He mopped up the peripheral Vandal possessions around the western Mediterranean, occupying Sardinia to which he sent Tzazo's head as evidence of his victory, Corsica, the Balearic Islands, and the fortresses and towns around Gibraltar. He also seized Gelimer's royal treasury in Hippo Regius which was said to contain untold wealth. However, his attempt to occupy the Vandal fortress of Lillybaeum in Sicily was frustrated by the Ostrogoths who claimed it for themselves, an action that we will hear more about shortly.

All in all, Belisarius' achievements were nothing short of astonishing. His destruction of the Vandal kingdom within a year counts as one of the greatest victories in Rome's entire history. Meanwhile, back in Constantinople, Justinian wasn't slow to take the credit for himself. As he paced the long corridors of the Great Palace in the city's most eastern corner, for he seldom left the palace, he gave orders for the senate to award him the triumphal titles of *Alanicus*, *Vandalicus* and *Africanus*. After all, it had been his idea, hadn't it?

His insecurity was made worse, according to Procopius, by numerous jealous army officers and courtiers in the city who claimed to have information that Belisarius was looking to betray the emperor and set up his own kingdom in Africa. However, even Justinian, who could be paranoid and vengeful, saw these accusations for the lies they were. But just in case, he invited his general to return to Constantinople immediately.

Belisarius was keen to stamp out the rumours of his treachery and rushed back to the capital. But he needn't have worried for when the emperor met him, they quickly resumed their close and trusting relationship. Both Justinian and Theodora could show great generosity to their favourites and, on this occasion, Belisarius was treated as the emperor's best friend. He was the first Roman general to be awarded his own triumphal parade since the days of the Republic over 600 years before. In the imperial era, it had always been emperors like Titus and Trajan, who led the processions. And, in any case, for over 300 years, the dearth of Roman victories had meant there were no parades at all.

But this time it was different. A procession of Vandal captives who were 'very tall and fair of body'[88] was paraded through the streets, led by Gelimer and members of his family. Gelimer was allowed to wear purple garments to denote his rank. Throughout the proceedings he was said to repeat over and over again: 'Vanity of vanities, all is vanity' from the Old Testament, supporting the view of those who thought he had lost his mind.

A huge amount of captured gold and silver was paraded after him, including treasures from the temple of Solomon in Jerusalem, captured by the emperor Titus, some 450 years earlier. According to Procopius, when some Jews told Justinian that his victory was only because God wanted the Jewish treasures restored to Jerusalem, Justinian became fretful, and fearing some sort of divine retribution, he sent them to Jerusalem to be stored in Christian sanctuaries to appease both Jews and Christians.

Although the triumphal procession was in Belisarius' honour, Justinian ensured it was also an opportunity to make clear who was the boss. For example, when Gelimer reached the hippodrome and was brought before Justinian sitting in the imperial box, he was stripped of his royal clothes and prostrated before Justinian's feet. Even Belisarius had to prostrate himself before the emperor. How times change. Augustus would not have dreamed of so humiliating his great general, Marcus Agrippa. But Justinian's delight with the victory was such that he allowed Gelimer to live the rest of his days with his family in comfort on an estate in Galatia, and he was reputedly happy to make him a patrician if he renounced his Arian faith which he refused to do.

As for Belisarius, Justinian didn't deny him the honours he was due. On 1 January 535, he was made consul, the position which Justin had given Justinian himself before he became emperor, and he was allowed a second triumph, this time for him alone, and he was borne aloft by Vandal captives as he distributed some of the Vandal wealth to the people of the city.

Perhaps this was a calculated measure to make up for the slaughter inflicted in the Nika riots. Whatever the reason, Justinian felt he could be generous. The year 534 was a good one for him, perhaps the peak of his success. Not only had he achieved victory in Africa, but Tribonian also finished his legal code that year. And that was not all. After the Nika riots, he embarked on a building programme that would transform the capital, and for which he would be remembered long after his death. And it is to this that we will now turn.

30

'Solomon, I Have Outdone Thee!'

One of the main reasons for Justinian's fame to this day is his legacy of monumental buildings, in particular Hagia Sophia, which still dominates the skyline of modern Istanbul.

These began after the destruction of the Nika riots when the heart of the city had been wrecked. His top priority was to rebuild the church of Hagia Sophia, the city's effective cathedral, making it more splendid than it was before as a celebration of God's power and an entreaty for divine protection. He used the rebuilding programme to promote himself as the empire's chief healer by building a new heaven on earth, as the chronicler John Lydus described: '...just as if the Creator...were again calling forth the universe into light out of the formless matter by the mere power of his volition'.[89]

And it exceeded all expectations. In just five years and ten months, Hagia Sophia was rebuilt on a staggering scale and with such care and attention that it has survived to this day largely intact. Two architects, Anthemius of Tralles and Isidore of Miletus, were given the commission for the new building. Anthemius was a renowned mathematician, and it was his calculations that enabled a radical new church design. Instead of the traditional basilica structure with pitched roofs, widely used in churches in the late Roman Empire, such as the magnificent churches in Rome of St Peter and St Paul, Hagia Sophia had an enormous dome, more similar to the classical Roman Pantheon. Domes became the new fashion in the eastern Roman Empire and proved to be hugely influential in later centuries on Islamic mosques and Russian Orthodox churches.

Even before Hagia Sophia was built, Justinian had experimented with a mini-dome in the Church of Saints Sergius and Bacchus in Constantinople, which still stands today. But the dome of Hagia Sophia was breathtakingly large. The whole building was huge, some 90 metres long and 70 metres wide – probably the largest in the world at the time – and the scale and height of the dome remained unsurpassed for 1,000 years until the Renaissance version of Saint Peter's in Rome was built in the sixteenth century.

When Justinian dedicated the building on 27 December 537, he is said to have exclaimed, 'Solomon, I have outdone thee!' in reference to the grand temple Solomon built at Jerusalem. It immediately became synonymous not just with Justinian but with the power and authority of the eastern Roman Empire. Its spacious interior, with the light radiating through its topmost windows like a celestial beam, and its great beauty enhanced by sheets of wall-to-wall mosaics, together with its amazing acoustics, conspired successfully to make it the vision of heaven on earth Justinian hoped to create. Indeed, it was so breathtaking that, in the tenth century,

Viking visitors from the newly founded principality of Kyiv believed they had actually been to heaven when they entered the church and immediately converted to Christianity.

Justinian's rebuilding project didn't stop there. From 532 until 543, during the era of reconquest in North Africa and Italy, Justinian carried on building. Thirty-two more churches were constructed, six hospices and a host of public buildings were restored as well as new harbours dug for the city. After Hagia Sophia, the most impressive surviving church of Justinian's is the domed basilica church of Hagia Eirene, close to Hagia Sophia in modern Istanbul but often ignored by tourists in preference for its more splendid sibling. In addition, again close to Hagia Sophia, there's an enormous underground water cistern built by Justinian, called the 'Basilica Cistern' or, in Turkish the *Yerebatan Sarayi*, which is extremely well preserved, as described in Chapter 2.

Most of Justinian's other buildings have been lost over the centuries, including a restored Church of the Holy Apostles, Constantine's largest church, which was damaged in the Nika riots, and dozens of other smaller churches, the restored Baths of Zeuxippus, and the main entrance to the imperial palace called the Chalke or Bronze Gate, which was in effect a colossal triumphal arch.

Perhaps the most striking monument of all was in the *Augustaeon* square. This square was the heart of the city, a bit like Trafalgar Square in London, or Times Square in New York, and in 543, Justinian built an enormous column with a bronze statue of himself on horseback. It stood flanked by Hagia Sophia, the Baths of Zeuxippus and the Chalke Gate. The Turks pulled this down at some point after 1453 but our records of it are good, and at some 70 metres tall, it would have towered over Hagia Sophia itself.

Justinian's statue faced east, with one hand holding a globe with a cross upon it and the other stretched out, according to Procopius, as if he was commanding the world to stop and fall at his feet. By putting himself at the heart of both this vast rebuilding programme and imbuing it with a Christian message, Justinian behaved similarly to the emperor Constantine. Indeed, in the 530s, the city of Constantinople moved from being Constantine's city to Justinian's, and so it would remain until it fell to the Turks in 1453.

31

Meet the Goths

Let us now travel to Old Rome.

The spring sunshine reflects off Constantine's Arch beside the abandoned Flavian Amphitheatre, or Colosseum, as we know it today. The gladiatorial combat that so captivated the Romans of old is long forgotten. It is March, AD 500, and the inhabitants of the city that was once the centre of the Roman Empire, are preparing to meet their Gothic ruler, Theodoric the Great.

Should we call them Romans? I think not. As discussed in Chapter 2, centuries have elapsed since Rome was the centre of the Roman Empire. The city is now even outside the territories of New Rome. Nevertheless, these people treat Theodoric in the same way their ancestors would have done Diocletian, or any previous Roman emperor, although those emperors of old would have shuddered to see them bowing to a barbarian king. This time, however, not only are they paying homage to a barbarian king but their delegation is led by the Pope and not by the senate. Pope Symmachus is the most important person in the eternal city and he leads its inhabitants to meet Theodoric, with the senators following close behind, and behind them the mass of ordinary people.

Theodoric and his retinue come into sight on the Via Flaminia, the road from Ravenna to Rome. The Gothic horsemen are dressed in brightly coloured cloaks and gleaming chain mail. Theodoric himself is a tall man, a warrior first and foremost. His moustache marks him out as a Goth. No Roman would sport such facial hair. His first stop is St Peter's Basilica, where he pays his respects at the Apostle's grave. This is despite the fact Theodoric is an Arian, regarded as a heretic by the Roman Church, and in return, the Arian Church doesn't officially recognise Symmachus as bishop of Rome. This strange new Gothic-Roman world is full of contradictions.

Theodoric crosses the River Tiber on the Pons Aelius, built by Hadrian centuries before. From there, he passes along a route to the forum, through the triumphal arches of Constantine and Titus beside the colosseum, until finally he reaches the senate house, the Curia. There he addresses the senators in Latin. Theodoric is well acquainted with the Roman world, having spent ten years of his youth in Constantinople. He is also well aware of the cultural superiority of the Romans. In the past, he's famously said: 'The rich Goth wants to be Roman but only the poor Roman wants to be a Goth.'[90] But his comment is merely a convenient mask for the truth. The truth is that the Goths are the rulers of Rome.

This account of Theodoric's entry into Rome is not fictional. It is based on the writings of the biographer of Fulgentius, a Roman African prelate who was made a saint and travelled to Rome in the year 500 at exactly the moment Theodoric made his first visit to the eternal city.[91]

Theodoric only went to Rome once since, like Odoacer and most of the previous Roman emperors, he ruled from Ravenna not Rome. But in the year 500, he visited Rome for the first time to celebrate his 30 years of rule – his *tricenalia* – in the tradition of the Roman emperors going back to Diocletian, who had abandoned the eternal city as their capital. In fact, Theodoric had only been ruling Italy for seven years since 493, but his propaganda machine engineered the story that he had been a king ever since he killed his first royal victim, the Sarmatian king Babai, 30 years before.

Fulgentius' biographer gives us a fascinating insight into what Rome was like at this time. Its population had been in steady decline ever since Alaric's sack of the city in 410, and by 500 it had fallen to a fraction of its former size, from around half a million in 400 to probably some 50,000, at the very most 100,000. But that was still a large number for its time and made it the largest city in the western Mediterranean. The chronicler, Cassiodorus, who lived in the city, compared it to someone whose clothes have become too big for them. He marvelled at the size of the public buildings and walls: 'The vast expanses of the walls; the wide embrace for spectacles; the astonishing size of the baths; and that multitude of mills, which served specifically to provide food, attest to the throngs of its citizens [in the past].'[92] He described its inhabitants living in the shadows of the colossal monuments. Extensive areas of the city within its walls were now derelict and abandoned, with rubbish tips growing and land being used for small-scale cultivation. But it was still the residence of the senatorial classes, who maintained large houses, and whose revenues from their estates around Italy, still poured into Rome, bringing some wealth to its population.

There was also of course the Church. The bishop of Rome, or the Pope as he was now called, was the most powerful and wealthiest of the clerics in the west, and Rome had the largest Christian churches in the west; churches such as the old St Peter's (replaced by the modern St Peter's in the sixteenth century), and its sister church of St Paul Beyond the Walls, which still stands in a restored Roman construction.

So, how had this strange kingdom of the Ostrogoths been born?

In Chapter 6, we heard how in 488, Theodoric the Amal (later called the Great) had left the eastern empire and taken his Gothic followers west to Italy with the blessing of the emperor Zeno. There, he had personally slain Odoacer, the German warlord and self-proclaimed king of Italy, who had been responsible for bringing the western Roman Empire to an end when he deposed Romulus Augustulus in 476. Theodoric had killed Odoacer in Ravenna in 493, in direct contravention of a treaty the two had agreed for joint rule of Italy. The chronicler, John of Antioch, described how he tricked Odoacer into a peace treaty until one day two of Theodoric's men approached him as supplicants and grasped him by the hands so that he could not move or resist. Theodoric advanced upon the hapless German with his sword and with a single stroke, he allegedly clove him in two from the collarbone to the hip, saying: 'I always thought he hadn't got a bone in his body.'[93]

While this story was clearly embellished for effect, Theodoric wasn't a man to mess around with. He had a reputation as a great warrior, capable of killing his enemies with his own hands. In 471, at the tender age of 18, he is said to have killed his first royal victim, a Sarmatian king Babai, during a campaign he was leading. In 482, he killed a rival Gothic king, Recitach, after which he conquered Italy.

The kingdom he ruled kept the Goths and Romans quite separate from each other. For example, the Goths remained an entirely military society while the Italian population was completely excluded from any form of military service. Italians weren't even allowed to carry weapons other than those for hunting like daggers. This meant the Goths, with Theodoric as their king, were the undisputed masters of Italy with the military muscle to do whatever they wanted. At the same time, to buy the Goths' loyalty, Theodoric rewarded them with land taken from the Roman senatorial class.

So why did the Roman senators agree to give up their land and support Theodoric's imposition of Gothic rule? The answer was that they had little choice. While the western Roman army had ceased to exist during the course of the fifth century, and hence the Roman senate had no military power whatsoever, its senators remained in control of most of the land, despite a significant part (about a third) being given to Theodoric's Gothic followers. This meant they were still wealthy and were valuable to Theodoric as an efficient source of tax collection. For example, in the run-up to the formal abolition of the western empire in 476, most but not all of the senate seems to have supported German military leaders like Odoacer in exchange for their protection. Only a minority appear to have aimed for a restoration of the imperial regime. A good example of this occurred in 461 when the western emperor Majorian was murdered by the German warlord Ricimer who became the de facto king of Italy. Astonishingly, most of the senate actually supported Ricimer, a German warlord, against Majorian, an aristocratic Roman from a senatorial family because they preferred having a 'friendly' German ruler to paying higher taxes to fund an attempt to restore Roman rule.

Another astonishing aspect of the Gothic-Roman regime in Italy, similar to that of the Vandals in North Africa, was the duality in its religion. Theodoric and his Goths were Arians not Catholics. As discussed in Chapter 10, this argument about the true nature of Christ had divided Christians in the Roman Empire in the fourth century. The non-Arians (let's call them Catholics) triumphed. But because of the missionary work of Arian preachers, many of the barbarian invaders of the fifth century (if they were not pagans such as the *Alemanni*) were Arian, including principally the Goths and Vandals. Their conquest of most of the western empire made Arianism into a legitimate force again. This meant that in Italy, while almost all the estimated 6 million inhabitants were Catholic, the largely Germanic mercenary army that replaced the Italian legions, was Arian. A truly bizarre situation then developed with the de facto rulers of Italy belonging to a faith regarded as heretical by the vast majority of Italy's inhabitants.

But this didn't matter too much in the everyday life of the 6 million or so Roman population since most of the approximately 100,000 or so Goths lived in Northern Italy in a region of the Po Valley, stretching from Milan in the west to Verona and Ravenna in the east. Small Gothic garrisons existed in the principal towns and cities throughout the length and breadth of Italy, but even so, in some places in Italy, and especially in the south, it would have been rare to see a Goth.

Where Arianism did matter was in Ravenna which was the home of the Gothic court and the heart of the Gothic administration. Although in most of the rest of Italy, the churches and clergy were Catholic, in Ravenna Theodoric built several magnificent Arian churches. One of these has survived almost intact, the basilica of Sant'Apollinare Nuovo in the centre of the modern city. It contains stunning mosaics, made by Roman craftsmen but celebrating the Gothic court and king. It was next to Theodoric's palace which was another imposing construction, according to the Roman chronicler Cassiodorus: 'The marble surface shines with the same colour as gems…the gifts of mosaic work delineate the circling rows of stones; and the whole is adorned with marble hues where the waxen pictures are displayed.'[94]

The most striking of all Theodoric's buildings was his own mausoleum, perfectly preserved in modern Ravenna (see Figure 15). This is made of beautifully carved white Istrian stone, and has a dome fashioned from a single piece of stone, 10 metres in diameter and weighing a colossal 230 tonnes. Quite how it was raised and put in place remains a mystery, but it serves as testimony to the wealth of the Ostrogothic kingdom.

But this kingdom was deeply flawed. An edifice that was waiting to tumble down, as we shall now discover.

32

The Kingdom on the Edge

For centuries, many historians regarded Theodoric as an enlightened ruler who encouraged a multicultural and tolerant society. This view is now being challenged. A recent study by a German historian[95] suggests Theodoric was no visionary but a cynic who attempted to keep both peoples under his control through a policy of 'integration through separation'. As described in the last chapter, his Gothic regime was full of contradictions, unsustainable and towards the end of his reign the cracks were beginning to show.

The direct cause of this growing pressure came from Constantinople. This began when the eastern emperor Anastasius died in 518. Until then, Constantinople had tolerated the Gothic kingdom in Italy, partly out of sheer relief that the Goths had left the Balkans and were no longer threatening Constantinople itself, but also because there had been a rift between Rome and Constantinople over religion. The eastern emperor Anastasius was pro-Monophysite and therefore lukewarm towards the Pope who was fiercely Catholic, so there was little chance of a united western and eastern Roman front against Theodoric. This disunity had been a tremendous help to Theodoric's authority in Italy.

However, when Justin ascended the throne in 518, he was a Chalcedonian and pro-Catholic who looked to heal the rift between Rome and Constantinople. This presented a real threat to Theodoric. For one thing, it meant both the Roman senate and the Catholic Church began to view Constantinople as an ally. And that was when Theodoric's relations with his Italian subjects started to break down. First, a major ruction with the senate occurred in 523 when the highly respected senator and philosopher, Boethius, was accused of treason, condemned to death, and after a long imprisonment, executed in October 524. The cause of his alleged treason was Boethius' support for a senator named Albinus who was accused of illicitly corresponding with the eastern emperor Justin. When Boethius' own correspondence was examined, it was found he hoped 'Roman liberty' would be restored, a clearly treacherous thing to say. Albinus was executed, and later on so was Symmachus, another highly distinguished senator. The cosy honeymoon period of Gothic rule was well and truly over.

Incidentally, it's worth mentioning that during his imprisonment, Boethius wrote *The Consolation of Philosophy*, inspired by Plato, a well-known philosophical work both today and in the Middle Ages, when it was one of the few available Greek and Roman texts that survived the Dark Ages (most were brought to the west by the fleeing inhabitants of Constantinople after its fall to the Turks in 1453).

Back to Theodoric. He responded to the growing threat from Constantinople by adopting a more openly combative stance for the Arian faith. In 523, we know of an extraordinary incident from a source called the *Anonymous Valesianus*, a chronicle written in the sixth century by an unknown author, who some historians suspect was the bishop of Ravenna, Maximianus. This describes Theodoric ordering Pope John I to go to Constantinople, in either late 525 or early 526, to put the case to Justin for Arians to be tolerated in the eastern Roman Empire.

Not only is it astonishing that John agreed to undertake this mission in the first place – a sign he was put under considerable pressure by Theodoric – but his mission met with no success since, when he returned to Italy in May 526, he fell into disfavour again with Theodoric and died soon afterwards, with another source claiming he was actually imprisoned and martyred.[96] In the same year, a rumour circulated around Italy that Theodoric planned to persecute Catholics and forcibly convert them to Arianism.

If this is true, and unfortunately our sources are so limited we can't be completely sure of anything in this period, it was like putting petrol on a smouldering bonfire. Suddenly, the apparently friendly co-existence between Romans and Goths earlier in Theodoric's reign was going up in smoke. The truth was that, just as had been the case with the Vandals, Theodoric's kingdom was a deeply flawed attempt to keep a small governing elite in power.

Added to this was that Theodoric was very unlucky with his succession planning. He had no male heirs and only one daughter, Amalasuentha, with his Frankish wife (Audofleda). When, for whatever reasons, his wife bore him no more children, since he couldn't divorce her for political reasons (she was the sister of the Frankish king Clovis who had a reputation for splitting his enemies' heads with an axe), he turned to concubines but they only bore him more daughters. Now an old man, and knowing time was running out, he found a husband, Eutharic, for Amalasuentha who could be his successor. Bad luck struck again. Eutharic died early. But there was one consolation. Before her husband died, Amalasuentha gave birth to a boy named Athalaric (she also had a daughter). Finally, Theodoric had a grandson to pass his kingdom to.

However, the succession problem wasn't solved since Athalaric was barely ten years old when Theodoric died, aged 72, in 526. This left Amalasuentha as Queen of the Ostrogoths and regent for her son. It was not an ideal situation for a society in which a king was expected to lead his warriors into battle. Nevertheless, for about five years, Amalasuentha proved herself a ruthless and formidable ruler. She had the three nobles who most opposed her murdered, and she kept a ship loaded with treasure in Ravenna in case she needed to flee to Constantinople. This was when she negotiated the rapprochement with Justinian, allowing Belisarius to stop in Gothic-held Sicily, on his way to Carthage, to take on board provisions and, most important of all, horses, all of which were vital for the success of his African expedition as described in Chapter 26.

But, according to Procopius, matters came to a head when Amalasuentha disclosed her now-teenage son was learning to read and write, something which shocked the Gothic nobility who believed a boy only needed to be taught how to use a sword and spear, and should despise literacy, according to Procopius: 'For letters, they said, are far removed from manliness, and the teachings of old men results for the most part in a cowardly and submissive spirit.'[97]

Amalasuentha gave way to the nobles and allowed her son to be taken from his books to lead a more manly life, although Procopius says this actually consisted of nothing more than 'drunkenness and sex with women'.[98] Indeed, his life of debauchery resulted in his death in October 534 'at a drunken party that had no limits'.

This was disastrous for Amalasuentha. In desperation, she formed an alliance with a cousin of Theodoric's, named Theodahad, declaring him king and announcing their joint rule. But secretly, she was preparing to flee to Constantinople. When Belisarius tried to take the Vandal fortress of Lillibaeum in Sicily, she publicly protested but in private sent an urgent message to Justinian offering him the Ostrogothic kingdom if he would guarantee her a wealthy and safe retirement. She never got there. In April 535, Amalasuentha was found murdered in her bath by Theodahad's thugs.

Suddenly, Justinian was confronted with a situation similar to that in Vandal Africa. A foreign kingdom riven with internal conflict. And now with a letter on his desk from a murdered queen offering him her kingdom, he had the perfect pretext to invade Italy.

The wars of reconquest had only just begun.

33

Restoring the Roman Empire?

In the spring of 535, we can imagine Justinian, the sleepless emperor, staring out of his palace windows late at night, as he read and re-read Amalasuentha's letter. Staring into the dark waters of the Bosphorus, he was considering his destiny. Was this a God-given opportunity for him to restore the Roman Empire? He had secured victory in Africa. Was Italy to be next?

He sent an ambassador to Theodahad to protest at Amalasuentha's murder, hoping to open up discussions that might lead to some sort of peaceful reassertion of Roman authority in Italy. To achieve this, he sent one of his top diplomats, named Peter the Patrician, who Procopius admired as a silver-tongued negotiator, although noting in *The Secret History* he was a rogue not to be trusted.

In the magnificent Roman palace in Ravenna, where Theodoric had established the Gothic court, Peter ostensibly discussed with Theodahad the Roman rights to Lillybaeum in Sicily, a Vandal possession which he argued should be handed over to the Romans. But his real aim was much more significant than that – to persuade him of the merits of surrendering his entire kingdom to Justinian in exchange for a life of wealth and ease in Constantinople. However, Theodahad prevaricated, so to speed things up Justinian initiated some modest military pressure on the Ostrogoths.

In the Balkans, where there was a Roman army defending the Danube, he ordered its commander-in-chief, the Gepid general, Mundo, to advance into the western half of Illyria (modern Dalmatia) that belonged to the Ostrogoths, and to take the Gothic-held city of Salona on the Dalmatian coast. At the same time, Belisarius was still in Constantinople, having celebrated his triumph and equipping a small fleet with reinforcements to return to Africa where trouble was brewing with the local Berber tribesmen, as we will shortly discuss. This force comprised 4,000 regular infantry, 3,000 Isaurians and a few hundred others, including some of his household horse archers.

Frustrated with Peter's lack of progress in Ravenna, Justinian ordered Belisarius' small force to invade Sicily, presumably hoping that a Roman army landing on the island would frighten Theodahad and persuade him to surrender his kingdom rather than go to war. As usual, Belisarius exceeded expectations. He landed at Catania in Sicily, which immediately surrendered as did most of the other cities on the island. Only Panormus (modern Palermo) held out because of its solid walls, but it too surrendered when Belisarius put archers in the masts of his ships which could shoot down on the walls' defenders. On 31 December 535, he completed his blitzkrieg-like conquest of Sicily by taking Syracuse.

Back in Ravenna, Theodahad was nearly persuaded by Peter that resistance against the Romans, and Belisarius in particular, was pointless. He told him the invincible general had crushed the Vandals in less than a year and would do the same with the Ostrogoths. Theodahad was on the point of agreeing to abdicate in exchange for a comfortable retirement in Constantinople when news arrived from the Balkans. A Roman army led by Mundo, which had advanced into Dalmatia and taken the port of Salona, had retreated in disorder. The reason was not an actual defeat in battle but because Mundo himself had been killed. The story Procopius tells us is that Mundo's son, Mauricius, was killed in a skirmish which caused his father to launch a violent attack against the Ostrogoths. Although he defeated them, in his reckless pursuit of the enemy he was himself killed, and the dispirited Roman troops subsequently evacuated Salona and pulled back into Roman territory.

This was sufficient for Theodahad to change his mind. He put Peter in jail where he would languish for four years, and summoned his nobles to a council of war to decide the best course of action against the Romans. Meanwhile, Belisarius was still in Syracuse when he received a letter from Peter telling him to cross to Italy since Theodahad was about to abdicate. This letter was of course out of date. In an age when news travelled as fast as the fastest boat or horse could carry it, information was often dangerously out of date by the time it was received.

But as Belisarius was preparing for the Goths to capitulate, he received some terrible news from a totally unexpected source. This was from Solomon, the governor of North Africa who arrived by boat looking visibly shaken, and in the company of only six men including Procopius himself. Belisarius was astonished to see him and even more astonished when he was told that the army of occupation, which was the same one Belisarius had led to victory over the Vandals, was now in open revolt.

34

Mutiny in Africa

The story of the army's mutiny in Africa must rank as one of the strangest in the entire history of Justinian's reign. There is no doubt much of the blame lies with him. For after Gelimer surrendered in March 534, he installed a harsh new government. He made North Africa a province of the empire with its own Praetorian Prefect reporting to him and divided the province into seven areas, each with its own governor. Hundreds of administrative staff flooded into Carthage. They were mainly tax collectors but also lawyers and messengers. Justinian began in earnest the process of extracting as much tax from the new province as he could.

With the Vandals defeated it might have seemed easy, at least as a first step, to seize their property for the state. But there was one very significant problem. As narrated in Chapter 28, after the Battle of Tricamarum, a large group of Vandal women had married the invading Roman soldiers to save their lives, and those of their children, after their husbands had fled. These women were not to be underestimated. They had been the de facto aristocracy of Roman Africa and would not give up that position easily. Procopius explains that when the imperial authorities refused to restore the splendid houses and farms that these women had lived in with their Vandal husbands, they became hostile and urged their new husbands to rebel.

> *Each one of these women kept urging her husband to lay claim to possession of the lands that she had owned previously, saying that it was not right if, while living with the Vandals, they had enjoyed these lands, but after entering into marriage with their conquerors they were then to be deprived of their own possessions.*[99]

It was a powerful argument, and one which the Vandal women's new husbands were undoubtedly sympathetic to since they stood to gain from it considerably as well.

Other factors alienated the women, in particular the harsh treatment of the Arian clergy and their followers. With most of the African Roman population being Catholic, it wasn't surprising Belisarius' victory presented an opportunity for them to take revenge on the Arian church. The repressed Catholic Church sprang into action. It wasn't willing to compromise on anything and banned Arian church services, refusing to absorb any of the Arian clergy into its ranks, even if they recanted their Arian faith, and seizing the Arian churches.

This infuriated the Vandal women since they were all Arian. We don't have all the details and perhaps some were willing to be more pragmatic and embrace Catholicism especially if their new husbands were Catholic, but there was also a contingent of Belisarius' army, at least a thousand strong, who were themselves Arian since they were recruited from barbarian tribes like the Goths and Heruli who were Arian, and that made for an even stronger bond between the women and men who felt they were also being mistreated. To add fuel to the fire, Easter was the occasion when all rites of baptism took place, so the Vandal women with young children could not get them baptised at all unless they converted to Catholicism. Goaded by their wives, most of the Roman army rebelled.

The first act of rebellion was an attempt to kill the new Roman governor, Solomon, on 23 March 536, when he was attending the first day of the Easter celebrations in the cathedral at Carthage. On that day, a group of leading officers were waiting to kill him. But they failed to carry it out, as Procopius vividly describes:

> *When the appointed day came, Solomon was sitting in the sanctuary, utterly ignorant of the evils hanging over him. Those who had decided to kill the man went in and, urging one another with nods, grasped their swords but did nothing, either because they were filled with awe of the rites then being performed in the sanctuary, or because the fame of the general caused them to be ashamed, or perhaps some divine power prevented them.*[100]

However, this indecision didn't last long. The rebels gathered in the hippodrome in Carthage and, similar to how the Nika riots had begun, they chanted insults at Solomon and his officers. Solomon sent a senior officer to discuss their complaints, but he only ended up joining them. They then invaded the palace and began killing and plundering whoever didn't join them. Solomon, with Procopius, fled to the harbour and, with the help of an officer who had in fact sided with the rebels but obviously had mixed feelings about the matter, they escaped by boat to find Belisarius in Syracuse.

The insurrection was extended by Vandal men returning home after the Battle of Tricamarum. Quite what they made of their wives' behaviour is not recorded but it seems many of the disaffected Roman soldiers (perhaps those who were ethnically German) felt a common cause with them. Procopius has left with us with one extraordinary story about a bold group of Vandal men who found their way home from the other side of the Mediterranean. They had been shipped off to join the new regiments of Vandal-Roman cavalry on the Persian front. However, one group of 400 Vandals had seized control of their boat on the island of Lesbos in the Aegean and sailed all the way back to North Africa, where they landed and joined the rebellious soldiers who seem to have sympathised with their former enemies.

The mutiny was serious. Procopius says 8,000 of the Roman army of occupation, which probably numbered little more than 10,000, were in open revolt. Belisarius rushed back from Syracuse to Carthage with cash to bribe the soldiers and about a hundred of his own men. He used his money to recruit 2,000 soldiers to his standard and met the rebels who had gathered at Membresa, about 50 miles from Carthage. The rebels, perhaps now numbering around 10,000 since they were joined by a thousand or so Vandals and even slaves, lacked good leadership, and their nominal leader, a Roman soldier called Stotzas, could not prevent the group from fracturing and fleeing to Numidia when it met Belisarius' soldiers. It seems many of the Vandal women were abandoned for a second time.

Having put the rebellion down fairly easily, Belisarius returned to Syracuse. But he left a chaotic situation behind him with most of the army of occupation dispersed and still in revolt. The emperor's cousin, Germanus, was quickly despatched to Carthage to continue the task of restoring order. He was an able administrator and started to recruit the mutineers back, allowing them to return to their regiments on full pay with no questions asked. Meanwhile, Vandal men and women were deported. This worked well and Stotzas' rebel army dwindled away. He resorted to an alliance with Iudas, the Berber chieftain, who was still defying the Romans, but they were both defeated by Germanus in a small-scale battle near Scala Veteres outside Carthage.

Gradually order was restored, but it took a long time. In 539, when Belisarius was in the final stages of his long and difficult Italian campaign, mutinous soldiers were still being accepted back into the army. Solomon returned as governor and continued the process, in particular removing the last of the Vandal women who had been the original cause of the rebellion, although what ultimately happened to them is unknown.

35

The Invasion of Italy

Back in Sicily, Belisarius was a whirlwind of activity. Although Justinian's war against the Ostrogoths would become long and protracted, it began with a rapid advance into the Gothic kingdom in a way that only a general like Belisarius could achieve (see Map 5).

It is ironic that for his campaign against the Goths, who were stronger than the Vandals, he had an army half the size of the one he had taken to North Africa, only about 7,500 strong. Procopius tells us it comprised 4,000 Roman regulars, 3,000 Isaurians, 200 Huns and 300 Moors. The other striking feature was the lack of horsemen – there were only about a thousand of them – comprising the Huns and Moors and 500 regular Roman horse archers. This meant that it simply didn't have the offensive capacity of Belisarius' African expeditionary force which had 5,000 expert horse archers.

When, in the summer of 536, Belisarius heard the Gothic king Theodahad had broken off negotiations with Justinian and thrown the main Roman diplomat, Peter the Patrician, into gaol, he launched his invasion of the Italian mainland by crossing over the straits of Messina to Reggio in Southern Italy.

To the frustration of the Gothic nobles, Theodahad did nothing other than slowly gather Gothic forces at Ravenna to counter Belisarius' invasion. He was not a warrior and preferred reading Plato to warfare, probably the reason the unfortunate Amalasuentha had judged him more malleable than most Gothic noblemen when she chose him as king. However, her mistake had been to underestimate how easily such a weak character like him could be persuaded by the Gothic nobles to have her murdered. But those same nobles were still hesitant about doing the same with him. The result was paralysis at the top of the Gothic chain of command.

Belisarius took full advantage of this as he advanced into Southern Italy as a liberator not a conqueror. The towns welcomed him. As mentioned previously, the Goths lived mainly in Northern Italy in the Po Valley with small garrisons spread throughout the rest of Italy, and very few of them were in the south. The southern Italians felt no loyalty to the Goths and were happy to rejoin the Roman Empire. In addition, almost none of the towns had walls, so even if they'd wanted to resist, it would have been difficult. Even some Goths defected, including Theodahad's son-in-law, Ebrimuth. Belisarius celebrated his defection by sending him to Constantinople, where Justinian made him a patrician.

With no Gothic resistance, Belisarius' army swept through Calabria and headed north to Naples. But this town was different. It had large walls and was garrisoned by 800 Goths. The population was in a quandary what to do. Belisarius spoke with an emissary from the city and promised not to harm anyone if they would surrender. He offered the Gothic garrison free passage to the north if they surrendered.

But his peace offer was rejected. The Goths weren't going to budge, and this allowed two of the most prominent and pro-Gothic Neapolitans, Pastor and Asclepiodotus, to persuade the inhabitants to resist.

Belisarius had no choice but to attack. He cut the city's aqueduct but there were plenty of wells inside the city, so this had little effect. He launched several assaults on the city walls, but these were repulsed with not insignificant casualties. Weeks passed and Belisarius was getting frustrated, for he didn't want to waste his soldiers' lives, nor did he want to waste time while Theodahad was mustering the main Gothic army. Then Procopius tells us that one of the Isaurians – an ordinary soldier – found a tunnel in the aqueduct that led into the city. It was wide enough for a man to pass through, except for one point where it was blocked by masonry. When the man told his officer about it, they requested to see Belisarius, who was delighted with the information and promised them a significant reward if they could chisel the masonry down to make it passable. He then put a team of 400 soldiers together and, in the middle of the night, they proceeded down the tunnel holding lanterns. Since there was a tower above the aqueduct, he was worried the Goths manning it might hear the soldiers passing through the aqueduct, so he ordered one of his senior officers who was a Goth, Bessas, to shout in Gothic to the men in the tower offering them large bribes if they would surrender the tower. This started a slanging match between the two sets of Goths, and the Romans made their way through the tunnel undetected.

Yet when they were in the city, they ran into problems. First, they weren't sure where they were. Second, they weren't sure how to get down from the aqueduct, which, according to Procopius, was built on very tall arches. They walked along it until the tunnel roof ended and they could look over the edge. It was far too steep to jump down without injury, and Procopius vividly describes their finding a very tall olive tree which an intrepid soldier grasped onto and used to climb down onto the roof of a house. The house belonged to a poor old woman who was terrified at the sight of him but at sword point, she remained quiet as he threw a rope up to his comrades. The rest of the soldiers climbed down the rope and then rushed to the city walls to slaughter the Goths who were slumbering at their posts. They blew trumpets which was the pre-arranged signal for Belisarius' men outside the walls to storm in as they opened the gates.

The strategy was completely successful, and the Romans seized the city. Belisarius couldn't completely stop the ensuing slaughter and pillage, as the soldiers wanted revenge for their comrades killed in front of the walls. He was particularly angry with some of the Huns who killed people taking refuge in a church. But in the early hours of the morning, his officers restored discipline. He was keen to be generous to the Neapolitans to show his army was one of liberation not occupation. All the inhabitants his soldiers had seized were released and their property restored. As Procopius put it: 'Thus it came to pass for the Neapolitans that on that day they both became captives and regained their liberty.'[101]

But Procopius tells us the Neapolitans were not so generous with the two civic leaders who had encouraged them to resist Belisarius. They went to the house of one, Asclepiodotus, and 'killed him and tore his body into small bits'.[102] The other man, Pastor, died of apoplexy when he saw the city fall but the citizens took his body and impaled it in the main square.

Meanwhile, back in Ravenna, the news of the fall of Naples was too much for the Gothic nobility as they watched Theodahad dither indecisively. They gathered at Regata outside Ravenna and proclaimed a new king, Wittigis, who had won renown as a warrior when Theodoric was fighting the Gepids. On hearing this, Theodahad fled to Ravenna but Wittigis sent a young Goth called Optaris after him, who bore Theodahad a grudge since he had prevented him from marrying a beautiful young heiress who was also in love with him. Procopius says the king had prevented the love match to accept a bribe to betroth the woman to another man. Optaris rode night and day until he found Theodahad and 'slew him like a victim for sacrifice'.[103]

Unlike Theodahad, Wittigis flew into action. He marched down to Rome with 4,000 men and garrisoned the city before going back to Ravenna, with several senators in tow, to organise the main Gothic army and to negotiate an alliance with the Franks by giving them Gothic territory in southern Gaul. He also married Amalasuentha's daughter, Matasuentha, to establish a link with Theodoric's family although Procopius tells us she was not exactly a willing partner.

But if Wittigis was busy, Belisarius was busier. In forced marches, he rushed his small army towards Rome along the Via Appia, the ancient Roman road built over 900 years before in the early years of the Roman Republic, connecting Rome with Southern Italy. Procopius provides a fascinating description of how this road had survived the trials of time and was still in pristine condition, with the carefully laid stones providing a broad, flat surface to move on.

The senate sent Belisarius emissaries inviting him into Rome and promising to co-operate unlike the Neapolitans had done. The 4,000-strong Gothic garrison wondered what to do. Should they try to hold out with the city's inhabitants hostile to them and liable to open the gates at any time? The Gothic commander, Leuderis, decided not to. On 9 December 536, the Goths marched out of the northern city gate called Flaminia while Belisarius marched unopposed into the southern gate called Asinaria. Leuderis separated himself from his troops and surrendered to Belisarius, fearful that he would be executed for cowardice if he stayed with the Goths. Belisarius treated him honourably and sent him to Justinian carrying with him the keys to the city.

So, in this way, Procopius tells us, after 60 years, since the official end of the western empire in 476, Rome 'again became subject to the Romans'.[104] Belisarius had yet again achieved the impossible. He had reconquered Rome with a ridiculously small army and with almost no casualties. He was repeating the success of his victory in North Africa but with one major difference – he hadn't defeated the Goths in battle – and news soon arrived that the main Gothic army, 150,000 strong according to Procopius, and in reality probably numbering 20,000–30,000 against Belisarius' 6,000, was now ready to march from Ravenna to meet him.

The battle for Rome was about to begin.

36

The Siege of Rome

What should Belisarius do? He was vastly outnumbered. He had some reliable heavy infantry, but he didn't have the quantity of Roman horse archers that had brought him victory in Africa so he couldn't meet the Goths in a pitched battle. He had already sent messages to Justinian, begging for reinforcements, and the emperor had spent the last quarter of 536 mobilising all the troops he could spare from the eastern and Danube fronts, but he had to transport them to Italy and since it was midwinter, the weather made that difficult. An advance guard of 1,600 elite horse archers, commanded by Martinus and Valerian, had sailed from the east to Italy in late 536 but bad weather in Greece had held them up, and it would be weeks or months before they arrived, and by then the Gothic army would be at Rome.

Despite his lack of reinforcements, Belisarius chose to defend the city. It was one of the most courageous decisions of his life for he had barely enough men to man the 12- mile- long city walls that were crumbling in places. He also had no access to the sea to get provisions and reinforcements. Historical precedent was hardly reassuring since Rome had easily fallen to Alaric the Goth a century and a quarter before. Although the city's inhabitants had welcomed him, they were now distraught since they knew a siege would cause considerable hardship and suffering for them, and they begged him to leave. But Belisarius responded by setting them to work repairing the city's walls, collecting provisions from the countryside, and filling the city's water cisterns. He also arranged for a fleet of ships with grain to come from Sicily to provision the city.

Meanwhile, his troops seized the towns north of Rome which willingly joined the eastern Roman cause. Almost all the towns in Southern Italy also declared for Justinian. The news that his kingdom was slipping away from him, encouraged Wittigis to march post-haste down the Via Flaminia towards Rome. When he heard Belisarius only had 6,000 troops, he assumed he would retreat. But Procopius says he met a priest coming from Rome who told him Belisarius didn't know that word.

The Gothic army reached the Milvian Bridge on the River Tiber, where the emperor Constantine had famously defeated Maxentius over 200 years before (AD 312) and, so legend says, converted to Christianity in thanks for his victory.[105] Belisarius' soldiers were manning the tower guarding the bridge but when they saw the size of the Gothic host, they fled south in panic. This caused Belisarius a problem since he had brought up all his cavalry to stop the Goths from crossing. When they arrived, they found the Goths had crossed the Tiber. A furious battle ensued. Procopius says Belisarius fought in the front line, killing Goths with his own sword. The Goths fled but returned with thousands of infantry. This time the Romans had to retreat but the soldiers and civilians along the city walls kept the gates shut in case the Goths also pushed their way inside. Belisarius made a last furious charge against the enemy, pushing them back sufficiently for the city gates to be opened to let him and his men back in. It was now dark, and Belisarius ordered the citizens to light flaming torches and line the walls in case the Goths tried a surprise attack. Exhausted, he and his men settled down to rest.

That was only the first day of the siege of Rome. It would last for almost a year.

Procopius provides us with a vivid eyewitness account of the months that followed, making it the most notable record of any siege in late antiquity, and one worth reading for its excitement value alone. When Wittigis arrived with his entire army, the first thing he did was to cut the aqueducts that fed water into Rome. Belisarius responded by filling them with masonry to prevent their being used as a route into the city, just as the Goths had done at Naples. Wittigis then decided on a full-scale assault of the city. But to do this he needed siege engines, so the Goths spent weeks building a vast array of siege towers. Meanwhile, Belisarius was busy making wall artillery to fire at the Goths. The Roman specialties were *ballistae*, a sort of giant crossbow with a large arrow or bolt which could be fired with enormous force, and *onagers*, giant slings, which threw rocks at the enemy.

Finally, the Gothic assault took place. Procopius says when Belisarius saw the Gothic siege towers rumbling towards the walls, he burst out laughing. He saw they were all being dragged by oxen completely unprotected against arrows. Belisarius put an arrow to his bow and waited before giving the signal to shoot. When the oxen were within range, flurries of arrows shot out from the walls, killing all the unfortunate animals and many of the Goths.

Next, the Goths tried to storm the walls. Procopius' description reminds me of the film *Gladiator* when Russell Crowe famously said, 'unleash hell'. It must have been pretty much the same as the Romans unleashed a storm of arrows and ballista bolts against the oncoming Goths who weren't used to siege warfare, and advanced right up to the walls with ladders, leaving their siege engines stranded. The result was an unmitigated slaughter. Countless Goths were shot down in front of the walls, with Belisarius, who was himself an expert archer, picking off dozens of them, according to Procopius, who also describes the vivid image of a ballista bolt being fired at a Goth who tried to shoot back at the Romans from behind the cover of a tree: 'Passing through the breastplate and the body of the man, the arrow sank more than half its length into the tree [he was beside], pinning him to the spot where it entered the tree, and suspending his corpse there.'[106] Procopius says the Goths were so terrified by this spectacle, they retreated from that section of the walls.

Fierce fighting raged along the walls all day. Nowhere could the Goths break through. Belisarius was not content with shooting them down but rushed from gate to gate, giving orders to the defenders to sally out and burn the siege engines whenever he saw an opportunity. Soon the city was encircled with smoke rising from the smouldering wrecks. Meanwhile, there was fierce fighting at Hadrian's mausoleum, the modern Castel Sant'Angelo, which in the third century had been incorporated into the city walls by the emperor

Aurelian. Procopius describes how the defenders pushed the ancient statues on the top of this monument, 'representing men and horses, wonderfully made',[107] over the edge to crash onto the Goths below.

By the end of the day, Procopius says 30,000 Goths lay dead in front of the walls, undoubtedly an exaggeration and probably more like around 10 per cent of that number lost their lives. The Romans lined the walls, lighting the darkness with their torches, wildly singing victory songs and applauding Belisarius. On the Gothic side, the only sounds were the screams of the wounded and the laments for the dead.

It was one of Belisarius' finest moments. He'd stopped the Gothic army in its tracks. Wittigis was stunned at the ferocity of the Roman defence. But he didn't give up. If he couldn't storm the city, he would starve it out. So, the Goths made sure no supplies reached the city, especially by sea, as they occupied Rome's chief port, Portus, which had long replaced Ostia.

Belisarius sent more messages to Justinian asking for reinforcements. He ordered all the women, children and old men south to Naples to save the precious food in the city. Procopius says they could escape at night because the Goths couldn't patrol the entire circuit of the city walls and were also afraid of going out in small patrol groups since Belisarius sent groups of Berbers outside the city walls at night. These fierce North African tribesmen were adept at hiding and then jumping out and killing Gothic patrols. He recruited all the younger men in the city to join the army and guard the walls. He also detected a possible traitor in Pope Silverius, who was rumoured to be hoping to open negotiations of his own with the Goths, and sent him to Greece, replacing him with a new and more subservient Pope Vigilius.

But what really made the difference happened, finally, in early April 537, when the first of Justinian's reinforcements arrived. One thousand, six hundred horsemen, mainly Huns and some Roman regulars, under the command of Martinus and Valerian, joined the defenders. This transformed Belisarius' tactical options. He could now launch sorties through the city gates against the Goths. These were successful since the Roman and Hunnic horse archers would suddenly appear, pepper the Goths with arrows and disappear. The Roman advantage lay entirely with their horse archery as Procopius yet again emphasised: 'And the difference was this, that practically all the Romans and their allies, the Huns, are good mounted archers, but this fighting style was not practised among the Goths, whose horsemen are accustomed to use only spears and swords while their archers enter battle on foot and are shielded by their infantry.'[108]

But if Belisarius was winning at hit-and-run tactics, his army wasn't yet strong enough to defeat the Goths in a pitched battle. However, the starving city inhabitants persuaded him to try this, and he led all the cavalry out, supported by a phalanx of infantry made up of the citizen militia. This wasn't a good idea. In the ensuing battle, the citizens fled and Belisarius' horsemen had to retreat into the city. It was still a deadlock and food became so short that plague broke out in the city. In desperation, the inhabitants began to revive pagan traditions. For example, Procopius tells us that the bronze doors of the Temple of Janus in the forum were left open reviving the pagan tradition that they should always be left open when Rome was at war.

But in the fall of 537 everything changed.

Procopius tells us Belisarius had sent him and his wife, Antonina, who was with Belisarius throughout his African and Italian campaigns, to Naples to secure provisions for the city when, at long last, Justinian's promised reinforcements arrived. Ships had landed in Southern Italy with 3,000 Isaurian infantry, 800 cavalry from the Thracian field army and 1,500 horsemen from the eastern field army. At a stroke, Belisarius' army was almost doubled, and he had well over 2,000 expert horse archers. This was effectively the end of the siege of Rome, for Wittigis saw he had no chance now of taking the city and asked for peace talks.

Gothic ambassadors met Belisarius. Their initial suggestion was for the Romans to have Sicily and nothing more. According to Procopius, Belisarius laughed and joked if he got Sicily they could have Britain, which he reminded them also used to be part of the Roman Empire. They replied they might be amenable to giving more, including Naples, Southern Italy and tribute payments. Belisarius told them only Justinian could decide on this. Therefore, a three-month armistice was agreed to allow time for Gothic ambassadors to travel to Constantinople to discuss peace terms with Justinian.

But the negotiations were a trick. In the early of spring of 538, Wittigis broke the truce with a surprise attack on Rome through the aqueducts and an assault on the walls. Yet, it was a feeble attempt compared to the great assault he launched a year before with his siege engines. Belisarius easily defeated it.

Now it was his turn. He unleashed his horse archers, and the Gothic army poured back north towards Ravenna, harried by the Romans.

Belisarius' defence of Rome was one of his greatest victories. With an army a fraction of the size of the Goths, he had held onto the city and then sent the Goths fleeing. Wittigis was on the run and Belisarius' next objective was the complete defeat of the Goths.

37

The Sack of Milan

In March 538, the Gothic king Wittigis abandoned the siege of Rome and retreated towards Ravenna. It looked as if there might be a rapid end to the Gothic war, just as there had been to the Vandal one, and Belisarius would be rewarded with yet another triumph in Constantinople. But that was not to be. The Gothic campaign would drag on for another two years as divisions within the Roman high command delayed victory.

The first of these divisions emerged shortly after Wittigis broke the three-month truce and made his abortive surprise attack on Rome. Immediately afterwards, Belisarius sent his general, John, with 2,000 elite horse archers to harry the Gothic forces outside Rome. John was newly arrived in Italy, having landed at Otranto while Belisarius was holding out in Rome, and as mentioned, had brought with him some 1,800 horse archers among the other reinforcements which had transformed Belisarius' ability to hold on to Rome.

We know little about John except he was a nephew of Vitalian, the general who challenged the emperor Anastasius and was later murdered by Justinian, but despite this, Justinian seems to have liked him, and John later married the daughter of Justinian's cousin, Germanus, who was seen as the heir apparent to the imperial throne. Procopius describes him as brave and capable although I suspect there's a bit of flattery here since another source calls him John the Sanguinary,[109] or Bloody John, suggesting he had a reputation for brutality. The problem for Belisarius, as we will now hear, was that he proved too headstrong and keen to promote himself.

Initially, things went well for John. In the countryside, he destroyed a large Gothic force led by Wittigis' uncle, Ulitheus, killing him himself, according to Procopius.[110] His success caused the Goths to flee at the sight of his men, and finding no opposition to his advance, he became ever bolder and more ambitious. He headed straight towards Ravenna itself, hoping his threat to the Gothic capital would cause Wittigis to abandon the siege of Rome. But his strategy went against Belisarius' orders since he had been told not to bypass the Gothic strongholds in case they cut him off and trapped him. Ignoring this, he headed hell for leather straight towards Ravenna.

But Ravenna was heavily garrisoned and there was no possibility he could take it. However, this was not the case with Rimini, which was on the coast and a day's journey from Ravenna. There, in the absence of a Gothic garrison, its inhabitants threw open its gates. He occupied the town, still hoping to advance on Ravenna at some point. Procopius says he was encouraged in this by Wittigis' new wife, Matasuentha, the daughter of Theodoric's daughter Amalasuentha, who not only wanted revenge for her mother's murder in her bath, but also detested her new husband and offered herself to John instead: '[she] opened secret negotiations concerning marriage and the betrayal of the city'.[111]

At the same time, Wittigis withdrew from Rome. John wanted to take credit for this and claimed it was because he was threatening Ravenna. More likely is that Wittigis intended to withdraw anyway after his surprise attack failed. Belisarius took advantage of the Gothic withdrawal by attacking them as they retreated over the Milvian Bridge and inflicted heavy casualties. John felt Belisarius should be grateful to him. But in fact Belisarius was furious John had let himself be trapped behind enemy lines in Rimini. For the entire campaign now became about how to rescue him. Wittigis headed straight there to surround John, and to prevent a relief force from getting through to him, he strengthened the garrisons in the towns along the Via Flaminia, the main route to Rimini by putting 4,000 Goths in Osimo, 2,000 in Urbino, and smaller numbers garrisoned half a dozen other strongholds. Belisarius despatched a thousand horsemen, led by Hildiger and Martinus, to Rimini with orders to make contact with John and help him retreat to safety down the coast to Ancona, which was in Roman hands.

But when Hildiger broke through the Gothic lines and arrived in Rimini, John refused to move. This was an astonishing act of insubordination. He may have been motivated by Matasuentha's marriage proposal or the Gothic treasure that was apparently contained in Rimini. Perhaps he had a personal dislike of Belisarius. Only a few months previously, an officer had tried to assassinate Belisarius when told to hand over stolen property. He had been executed, which Procopius tells us was out of character for Belisarius and perhaps John thought he was becoming tyrannical.

Whatever John's motives, his decision left him stranded in Rimini and at Wittigis' mercy.

However, yet again, Wittigis proved inept. Even with overwhelming numerical superiority, he failed to take the city. Procopius tells us that just as happened at the siege of Rome, he made siege towers and rolled them towards the walls. Although this time he made sure there were no oxen pulling them, the towers came to a halt in front of a deep moat dug in front of the walls by John's men. The Goths couldn't get the towers anywhere near the walls, and as happened at Rome, they had to abandon them. The Goths swarmed up to the walls but couldn't break through. Procopius emphasises John fought heroically in defending the city. He may have been insubordinate, but he wasn't a coward.

Wittigis settled down to starve John out while strengthening his strongholds outside Rimini to prevent Belisarius from coming to his rescue. He increased the garrison at Osimo to 10,000 men, making it the main Gothic military base after Ravenna. There was a stalemate during the summer of 538, with Belisarius not strong enough to attack Osimo and Wittigis not strong enough to take Rimini. But Wittigis' blockade of Rimini was working, and John's men were getting close to starvation.

Just at that moment, an enormous group of Roman reinforcements landed at Fermo, further south from Ancona on the Adriatic coast. It comprised 7,000 soldiers, of which 5,000 were Roman regulars and 2,000 Herulian *foederati* under their own commanders, led by Narses, the general who had worked with Belisarius to crush the Nika riots and who was Justinian's chief treasurer. Narses was an unusual figure in Justinian's court. He was a eunuch, although we know nothing about his early life, and why this happened. But this was a distinct advantage in his relationship with Justinian since eunuchs didn't enjoy sufficient popular support to occupy the top positions of power, like those of consul and emperor. Therefore, he posed no threat whatsoever to Justinian unlike Belisarius who was popular. Indeed, that Justinian sent Narses to Italy at all was the first sign of his jealousy of his celebrated general. And there was certainly no doubt that at the top of Narses' personal agenda was a wish to discredit Belisarius.

The first problem Belisarius and Narses had to sort out was what to do about John. To make matters more difficult for Belisarius, Narses was a close friend of John's. At a council of war, Narses argued for an immediate advance on Rimini to save John. But Belisarius was worried the relief force would itself become trapped. He wanted to capture the Gothic strongholds of Urbino and Osimo one by one before rescuing John. Procopius tells us the other generals supported Belisarius, especially since they weren't impressed by John's antics, but Narses was adamant that they should go straight to Rimini.

Then a messenger arrived from Rimini, having got through the Gothic lines at night, to say John could last at best another week. This decided the matter. Circumstances forced Belisarius to rescue John. He quickly devised a three-pronged attack, with his own men advancing from the west while Narses' troops divided into two groups, one marching up the coast road from Fermo, and the other in ships led by Hildiger. Procopius delights in praising Belisarius' thoroughness and ingenuity. His primary concern was still that the Goths at Urbino and Osimo might join up with Wittigis' men at Rimini and surround his relief forces. So, he left 1,000 men camped right in front of Osimo as if they were about to launch an attack on the town. He instructed Narses' troops marching from the south to light more campfires than they needed when they got near Rimini to make the Roman army appear larger.

As usual, Belisarius' strategy worked. The Goths at Osimo stayed put, expecting they would be attacked. Meanwhile, those outside Rimini thought the number of Romans facing them was much larger than it actually was. Wittigis withdrew. The Romans had won. But the divisions in the Roman high command were only just beginning. When Belisarius met John in Rimini, looking painfully thin according to Procopius, and sarcastically told him he should thank Hildiger for rescuing him, John told him it was only thanks to Narses that he'd been rescued.

This put-down led to an open rift between them. Narses made a point of supporting John against Belisarius and challenged Belisarius' authority in every council of war, saying he had Justinian's trust and refused to take orders from Belisarius. In response, Procopius tells us Belisarius read out a letter Justinian had sent him confirming he was supreme commander of the Italian army despite Narses' arrival: 'We have not sent our steward Narses to Italy in order to command the army. We wish Belisarius alone to command the whole army in whatever manner seems best to him, and it is the duty of all of you to obey him in the interests of our republic.'[112]

This was to no avail. Narses seized upon the last words of the letter, saying Belisarius' orders were not 'in the interests of our republic', so he would oppose him. This was disastrous. Narses kept the 7,000 troops he'd brought with him under his command and refused to comply with Belisarius' instructions. John did the same with whatever troops he could get to follow him. There were now about 20,000 Roman troops in Italy, enough to defeat the Goths if properly led by Belisarius alone. But only about half of them reported directly to him. The rest obeyed Narses and John. Because of this there was complete paralysis in the Roman army in the last months of 538 and the first of 539.

The major victim of this was the city of Milan in Northern Italy. Belisarius had cleverly infiltrated a small garrison there, as well as in some of the other northern Italian towns, earlier in 538. However, Wittigis had persuaded the king of the Franks, Theodebert, to help him against the Romans despite Theodebert's pledge to Justinian he would be a friend of the Romans. But Theodebert was a double-dealer and sent 10,000 Burgundians to besiege the city, not to help the Goths, but to plunder the wealthy city. He told Wittigis he was coming to his rescue, while he told Justinian he was still a friend of the Romans, and he could not control his troublesome Burgundian subjects who were intent on plundering the city against his wishes.

Meanwhile, Belisarius' troops were busy besieging Urbino and Osimo, the main Gothic strongholds in front of Ravenna which Belisarius was determined to take before advancing on Ravenna. So, he ordered John, who had troops closest to Milan, to relieve the city, but he refused to move and Narses, who delighted in obstructing Belisarius' instructions, backed him up.

Procopius tells us Milan was the second largest city in Italy after Rome. It was still wealthy with long colonnaded streets, baths and powerful walls. But because of Narses' refusal to co-operate, Belisarius couldn't get reinforcements to it in time. The delay proved fatal. According to Procopius,[113] when the inhabitants had eaten all the dogs and mice in the city, they began to starve. The Roman garrison in the city surrendered on condition they would be released, which was honoured by the barbarians, but they left the city to its fate. The Burgundians, encouraged by the Goths, killed all the men and enslaved all the women and children. Procopius says 300,000 were killed, a huge exaggeration given the city probably had little more than 20,000 inhabitants. But Milan was left a ruin. For it, the dark ages had arrived.

Milan's destruction was sufficiently shocking for Belisarius to make a serious appeal to Justinian to remove Narses. We don't know precisely what he said, and Procopius is strangely silent on this subject, but I suspect he must have offered his resignation. Whatever it was, this time Justinian listened to his celebrated general and did as he wished. He recalled Narses to Constantinople and confirmed Belisarius as supreme commander. This was the first time Justinian had promoted a rival to challenge Belisarius, only for him to realise his mistake and reconfirm his support for him. It was not a good omen for the future.

38

The Frankish Invasions

Even with Narses out of the way, Belisarius still found it difficult to end the Gothic war. Urbino and Osimo were both hilltop towns protected by sturdy walls and almost impossible to storm. But for once, Belisarius got lucky. At Urbino, unknown to him, the Goths depended on a single well for water, which ran dry towards the end of 538. The Goths surrendered. But further problems arose. The 2,000 Heruli *foederati* brought by Narses, were unhappy with his recall to Constantinople, and deserted back to their homeland in the Balkans. Belisarius concentrated 11,000 of his troops against the fortress of Osimo, which contained 10,000 Goths. He also laid siege to another Gothic stronghold at Fiesole. But progress was slow and John was still stirring up trouble against Belisarius.

Then, in mid-539, a potential catastrophe occurred. The Franks struck. King Theodobert, enticed by the plunder from the sack of Milan, launched a full-scale invasion of Northern Italy. One hundred thousand Frankish warriors crossed the Alps. These were almost entirely infantry, armed with swords, spears and shields. Their specialty was a throwing axe – a solid double-edged weapon with a short handle which was hurled against their enemies before they engaged them with swords and spears. The Franks met the Goths at Ticinum beside the River Po in Northern Italy. The Goths welcomed them as friends and ferried them across the river. However, the moment enough of them had crossed, the Franks turned on the Goths, killing the men and abducting the women. Soon the River Po was heaving with the dead bodies of the Goths.

Procopius says the Franks, although officially recently converted to Christianity, were in fact still mostly pagan and delighted in making human sacrifices. They poured into the Po Valley, killing everyone in their path, and heading towards Ravenna. Horrified, both Goths and Romans fled before them. But they never made it to Ravenna. It wasn't the Goths, or even Belisarius that stopped them. Instead, they simply ran out of food.

The Franks had made no logistical plans whatsoever and Italy was suffering from harvest failure and famine at this time because of the volcanic eruptions of 536 which had lowered global temperatures significantly, a subject we will return to in Chapter 42, and consequently the Franks resorted to eating anything they could find and drinking contaminated water. The result was a severe outbreak of dysentery that killed one third of the invaders, according to Procopius. With losses on this scale, and with no other rewards for their invasion, the Franks fell to internal dissension and accused Theodebert of misleading his people. The survivors of this great host beat a retreat back over the Alps, and both the Goths and Romans heaved a tremendous sigh of relief.

Meanwhile, back in Ravenna, Wittigis was increasingly desperate. He looked for potential allies who might save him from Belisarius' slowly advancing armies but found none. The Franks had proved treacherous so they were of no use. In desperation, he looked further afield to Rome's greatest enemy: Persia. Communication between the Goths and Persians was almost impossible since the only practical route was through Roman territory. Cunningly, Wittigis bribed two Catholic priests who could pass unnoticed. They reached the Persian Shah Chosroe's court in Ctesiphon in mid-539, and passed to him Wittigis' message that Justinian's conquests in the west would increase Roman power to the detriment of Persia. They recommended breaking the Endless Peace and attacking the Romans now while Belisarius was engaged in the west.

Chosroes didn't need prompting. He'd been having the same thoughts. Although he wasn't quite ready to strike in 539, preparations were underway for a great offensive the following year. Justinian was also getting wise to this. The Italian war was dragging on for too long and he wanted Belisarius back in the east. He released the Gothic ambassadors held in captivity in Constantinople after Wittigis had treacherously broken the three-month armistice and sent them back to Ravenna with an offer for peace based on the partition of Italy, with the Goths keeping everything north of the River Po and the Romans everything south.

But before the peace delegation arrived in Italy, Belisarius was still keen to take Ravenna. The Gothic strongholds at Osimo and Fiesole were still holding out so he poisoned the water coming down from the mountains and stopped any food from getting into the town. When it was discovered that a Roman soldier, Burcentius, was treacherously passing messages from the garrison to Wittigis in Ravenna, he was burned alive in front of the city walls.

Finally, starvation forced the surrender of Fiesole in October 539, and Osimo in November. Belisarius was now free to advance on Ravenna. But no one had ever taken the city by storm since it was protected by impenetrable marshes on its land side and had good access to the sea. As described in Chapter 31, Theodoric the Great had only entered it by tricking the German warlord, Odoacer, into a peace treaty and afterwards treacherously slaying him. It was highly unlikely Belisarius could do something similar. So instead, he tried to starve Wittigis and his Goths into submission. And that would take time which he didn't have.

First, he needed to stop any reinforcements or provisions of food from reaching Ravenna. Procopius tells us the Goths had prepared a huge number of boats filled with grain on the River Po, ready to sail to Ravenna but, fortunately for Belisarius, there was a severe drought which caused the level of the river to fall to a point where the boats couldn't sail. He also bribed some of Ravenna's inhabitants to burn what grain was stored in the main warehouses in the city. Procopius tells us Wittigis' wife, Matasuentha, might have been complicit in this since she was still waging a secret war against her husband.

But Belisarius' most serious potential threat came, yet again, from the Franks. Rather surprisingly, King Theodebert had persuaded his followers to return to Italy after their disastrous expedition the previous year. Now he sent envoys to Wittigis, proposing an alliance against the Romans. Once they had been driven out, he wanted to split Italy between them. But Wittigis had seen the Franks' behaviour the previous summer and wasn't about to be duped a second time. He sent the Frankish envoys away empty-handed.

His only real hope lay with a Gothic relief force gathering in the Cottian Alps, which lie between modern France and Italy. Wittigis' nephew, Urais, had put together a small army of 4,000 and was ready to march east towards Ravenna to rescue his uncle. But John, Belisarius' insubordinate general, for once helped him by boldly attacking the Goths and, in a series of lightning raids, seized many of the Gothic women and children. He then offered to employ their husbands in the Roman army. Many of the Goths accepted this and joined the Romans. With his forces depleted, Urais couldn't do anything and stayed in Liguria (the area west of modern Genoa).

Despite this success, Belisarius was no nearer taking Ravenna when two senior senators, Domnicus and Maximin, arrived from Constantinople, with instructions to conclude a peace as soon as possible by offering Wittigis all the land north of the River Po, with the Romans keeping everything to the south. Why was Justinian so intent on a quick peace? The answer was he had no choice. He'd left the eastern and Danube frontiers under-manned and now he was paying the price for his poor strategy. In 539, the Bulgarian Huns, the descendants of Attila's Huns, launched a devastating raid across the Danube into the Balkans which we will consider in more detail in the next chapter.

Even more worryingly, Justinian was well aware that, goaded by the Gothic envoys sent to him by Wittigis, the

Persian Shah Chosroes was about to break the Eternal Peace he had signed with him. Justinian desperately needed Belisarius and his army to defend the east. And he needed it now. Indeed, by the time Domnicus and Maximin had reached Belisarius, it was already too late. The Persians had already attacked the Roman fortress of Sura.

But Belisarius was totally oblivious of these developments. It took time for news to travel in this age, and he hadn't heard about the problems on the Danube and eastern fronts. According to Procopius, Justinian's peace offer to the Goths threw him into despair. He wanted to finish the job in Italy. He felt five long years of warfare had been for nothing. But he couldn't prevent the embassy from going to Ravenna, where Wittigis, astonished by Justinian's generosity, accepted it. This sparked two extraordinary consequences – first, Belisarius refused to sign the peace agreement. It was his one and only act of insubordination in his entire career.

And second, it prompted an even more surprising counter-proposal from the Goths. Without his signature, they regarded the peace offer as worthless. Discontent was brewing among the Gothic nobility with Wittigis. After all, he'd achieved nothing other than misery for his nation. Meanwhile, their respect for Belisarius had grown. In the siege of Rome, he'd humiliated Wittigis' superior numbers using skill and ingenuity. So, they took a quite unprecedented step. They offered him the position of emperor of the west. The western empire was to be reborn, but this time led by Belisarius.

39

A Crown Refused

Procopius tells us the Gothic nobles communicated this secretly to Belisarius without telling Wittigis. But once he found out, he didn't object. Quite the opposite. He threw his support into the offer. This put Belisarius in an extraordinary position. Procopius says he harboured no wish to be emperor of the west. But he must have been flattered. A central question that has always puzzled historians is why Belisarius never tried to overthrow Justinian. Was he too loyal? Was he afraid of the civil war that might erupt? We'll never know the answer. But on this occasion, he played an intriguing game. He accepted the Gothic offer on condition they let him and his army into Ravenna in order to take on his new role. Resourceful as ever, Belisarius was about to play his most cunning trick.

But he had to be careful this didn't leak back to Justinian. So, he sent the insubordinate John, and some other senior officers who he didn't trust, away so that they weren't able to denounce him. It's not quite clear what he said to his own soldiers as they marched into Ravenna but Procopius tells us the Gothic women saw it as a sell-out: 'The women spat in the faces of their husbands for they had heard from them that the enemy were men of great size and too numerous to be counted; but now they had seen the entire army that had invested the city and, pointing with their hands to the victors, reviled them for their cowardice.'[114] But even the Gothic women's disgust with their men for bowing down to the Romans was placated when a Roman fleet also landed at Ravenna's port, Classe, loaded with grain for the starving Goths. The Goths were happy and now Belisarius sprang his trap.

Once inside Ravenna, he told his Gothic supporters he would never betray the emperor and they were now his captives. Or so Procopius tells us. Conspicuously absent from his narrative is a scene describing the reaction of the dumbfounded Goths. All he says is when they heard Belisarius had tricked them, most of them left Ravenna to gather at Pavia with Wittigis' nephew, Urais. Intriguingly, Belisarius made no attempt to stop or arrest them. Only Wittigis surrendered. He allowed Belisarius to seize the Gothic royal treasure which was said to be huge. It was a surprising capitulation. But Belisarius had sweetened the pill of defeat by offering him and his family a life of luxury in Constantinople.

It was a moment of triumph for Belisarius. He was the conqueror of two barbarian kings – the Vandal king Gelimer and now Wittigis. He had secured yet another unlikely triumph for Justinian. But what did Justinian make of it? Was he worried Belisarius might want to be emperor of the west? He recalled him to Constantinople. My sense is that the Goths' offer to Belisarius had unnerved him. After this incident, Justinian's behaviour towards his favourite general changed. The special relationship was over.

The other problem was that Belisarius was recalled before he'd finished the job. He had *not* destroyed the Goths as he had done the Vandals. Those nobles who had fled Ravenna to Pavia to join Urais eventually declared a new king of the Goths, Hildebad, despite Belisarius taking his children captive in Ravenna. Perhaps for this reason, before Belisarius left Italy, Hildebad and his supporters approached him one more time to offer him the western crown, which Belisarius again refused. The Goths had survived to fight another day.

And from every direction, the storm clouds were gathering over the empire. In late 539, the Danube front caved in completely when the Bulgarian Huns crossed the river and made a devastating raid through the Balkans.[115] Procopius describes 32 fortresses in Illyria falling to them, 120,000 captives being taken (almost certainly an exaggeration), raiding extending as far as the Adriatic Sea in the west to the suburbs of Constantinople and the Dardanelles in the east, and even south down to Thermopylae and Athens. This was a shocking breakdown of Roman defences on the Danube front which can only be attributed to one thing – Justinian had taken troops from this region to send to Belisarius in Italy and to North Africa where the Berber war was ongoing (which we will cover in Chapter 50).

Also in 539, an even greater threat was brewing in the east. Chosroes was preparing for war. In this light, it is little wonder Justinian was frustrated with Belisarius' inability to wrap up the Italian campaign where 20,000 of the best Roman troops were now concentrated. There was no triumphal procession on his return to Constantinople in the summer of 540. Procopius[116] tells us Justinian was satisfied to see him returning with Wittigis, Hildebad's children and some Gothic nobles together with the Gothic treasure, but there was no celebration and no recognition whatsoever awarded to Belisarius. All Justinian did was to display the treasure privately to members of the senate, claiming the honour of the victory for himself.

However, the rest of the city didn't share Justinian's view. Procopius highlights the inhabitants' frenzied excitement at seeing Belisarius return: '…everyone [in the city] was talking about Belisarius; to him were attributed two victories such as never before had fallen to the lot of one man to achieve…'.[117] Indeed, his popularity was such that crowds gathered simply to follow him around:

> *The people of Byzantion [Constantinople] took delight in watching Belisarius as he came out of his house every day and went to the forum…he had a fine figure and was tall and remarkably handsome.*[118]

This can only have irritated Justinian more, and made him feel increasingly wary of his general's popularity. And it wouldn't be long before Belisarius was arrested for treason. Even though he was pardoned, the magic had ended. And so too had the glorious age of conquest in the 530s. Now, the 540s would bring nothing but death and destruction to the empire.

PART IV

Apocalypse Now

40

Prelude to Disaster

By the time Belisarius was back in the capital in late 540, it was already too late.

Chosroes had inflicted the worst defeat on the Romans in the east since the third century AD when the Shah Shapur had defeated and captured the emperor Valerian.[119] This time, Chosroes had completely destroyed Antioch. It was the second city of the empire, home to over 100,000 people. He razed it to the ground and killed or enslaved most of its population. The question is not just how did such a catastrophe happen, but how did it happen when Justinian's Rome was supposedly at the height of its power?

To find the answer, we need to go back to 532, when Justinian signed the so-called Eternal Peace, a humiliating treaty for which he paid the Persians 11,000 pounds of gold. As discussed in Chapter 24, this was a knee-jerk reaction to the Nika riots that nearly toppled him from power. Justinian knew any defeat inflicted by the Shah Kavad would be the final straw and seal his fate. So, he welcomed peace at almost any cost.

According to Procopius, Chosroes spent the years of the Eternal Peace strengthening his own internal position.

A major weakness of the Persian monarchy in the fifth and early sixth centuries had been the power of the Persian nobles as discussed in Chapter 7. Chosroes' father, Kavad, had done much to restore monarchical power, and in the eight years in which the peace lasted, Chosroes developed this further.

He attacked the nobles' traditional power base which lay with four provincial governors called *marzbans,* who had the title of 'king' albeit supposedly reporting to Chosroes as the king of kings, the *shahanshah.* But the *marzbans* were powerful enough to challenge the shah and could act as kingmakers or breakers. Chosroes ingeniously undermined their authority by creating an additional layer of administration comprising military governors called *spahbedhs,* and civil governors called *padhospans.*

Chosroes gave increasing authority to the *spahbedhs* who could overrule the *marzbans* on military matters. He appointed his favourites as *spahbedhs.* In this way, Chosroes played the nobles off against each other and diluted their power. It was a return to the original Sasanian state, set up by Ardashir and his son Shapur, back in the third century AD, when Ardashir had crushed the rebellious nobles. It's worth noting that some historians think these structural reforms were a long, drawn-out process begun by Chosroes' father, Kavad rather than him, and he merely continued the process.[120]

But probably the main reason for Persia's growing threat to Rome in the sixth century came from the rapid decline of their chief enemy, the White Huns (sometimes referred to as the Hepthalites who were their ruling dynasty at the time). For example, in Kavad's reign, he was their vassal and had only initiated war with Rome with their approval, and with the express intention of paying them the tribute he extracted from the Romans. But by the middle of the sixth century,[121] the White Huns were coming under increasing pressure themselves from new enemies, such as the Avars and Turks. Because of this, their grip on Persia reduced during Chosroes' rule, allowing him to pursue a more independent and bellicose strategy towards Rome.

Chosroes' second war with Rome lasted a gruelling five years from 540 to 545. Procopius tells us it was borne out of Chosroes' jealousy of Justinian's success in the west. Embassies from both the Armenians and the Goths urged him to wage war on Justinian before it was too late and he had conquered so much territory that he became invincible. An Armenian embassy warned the shah of Justinian's ambition thus: 'The whole earth is not large enough for the man; it is too small a thing for him to conquer all people together. But he is even looking in the heavens and searching in the nooks and crannies beyond the Ocean, wishing to gain for himself some other world.'[122] In 539, as Belisarius closed in on Ravenna, a Gothic embassy arrived in the Persian capital, Ctesiphon, to plead with Chosroes to attack Rome.

Chosroes needed little persuading. By 539, he was tired of hearing of Justinian's success in the west and began preparing the army for war. Procopius says he instructed al-Mundhir, the leader of the pro-Persian Arab Lakhmids, to make up any complaint he could think of to break the peace.[123] Al-Mundhir duly complied by claiming the pro-Roman Arab Ghassanids had invaded his land. Procopius tells us the land in question, situated to the south of Petra in modern Jordan, was worthless. But it still served as a convenient pretext for war.

In 539, Chosroes sent an embassy to Constantinople to protest about two more reasons why the emperor was in breach of the Eternal Peace. First, the Persians claimed Justinian was conspiring to persuade the Huns in the Caucasus to attack Persia (probably true). Second, the Armenians were begging the shah to intervene to stop the Romans from overtaxing them (also probably true). Yet again, Justinian's overzealous tax strategy backfired on him.

Chosroes didn't even bother to wait for Justinian's reply. In the spring of 540, although we don't know the exact date, he marched west with a large army. Despite clear evidence war was brewing, Justinian had failed to strengthen the Roman army in Mesopotamia. Indeed, he'd done the exact opposite. Not only were the best troops in Italy with Belisarius, but in keeping with his policy of cutting military expenditure, he hadn't even paid some of the lower-quality garrison troops on the eastern frontier – the *limitanei*. For example, in 539, the garrison of the key Roman fortress of Dara, opposite the equally important Persian fortress of Nisibis, mutinied because they hadn't been paid.

In *The Secret History*, Procopius emphasised the disastrous consequences of Justinian's not paying the army. If he'd been diverting the money into a worthwhile project that would have been fine. But the truth was the soldiers' pay was almost certainly going into his vanity projects, such as his enormously extravagant building programme, of which Hagia Sophia was of course the main prize.

When Chosroes marched into Roman territory, he played a cunning game. He didn't head for the normal Persian target of Dara, where Belisarius had defeated him in 531. Instead, he followed the course of the Euphrates, about 200 miles south of Dara, into the heart of Syria (see Map 4). There was no Roman army to meet him. The towns were garrisoned but most of the field army troops were in Italy and North Africa. Justinian had been caught out.

Chosroes marched fast into the Roman interior. None of our sources say whether Antioch was his aim right from the beginning. But he was certainly going in the right direction to reach the empire's second most important city. He avoided the city of Callinicum, where Belisarius had suffered his only defeat, and stopped instead at the town of Sura. Procopius[124] says he chose Sura because as he passed it, his horse neighed and stamped the ground, which the magi (Persian priests) thought showed it would easily fall. But the magi had made a mistake. The first Persian assault was beaten back with heavy losses although the Roman commander, Arsakes, a brave soldier who led the defence and killed many Persians himself, was struck by an arrow and died. This panicked the inhabitants who begged their bishop to go to Chosroes and plead for their lives if they paid a large enough ransom.

When the bishop threw himself at the shah's feet, Chosroes concealed his anger at the losses his men had suffered and said he would happily comply with their request. But in reality, he was preparing a trick to take the town by storm. A ransom sum was agreed, and the bishop returned in jubilant mood, surrounded by Persian nobles who accompanied him to the town gate. Behind them came an advance guard of the

Persian army. The town's inhabitants watched the bishop and Persians embracing outside the gate, and in their joy at seeing what they thought was a peaceful solution, they opened the gate to let the bishop back in. Immediately, the Persians threw a block of wood into the gateway and stopped it from shutting as hundreds of soldiers rushed in.

The Persian army stormed the town, burned it to the ground and enslaved all its inhabitants, about 12,000 of them. Procopius says[125] it could have been worse had Chosroes not taken a liking to a pretty young captive called Euphemia, who he added to his many wives, and at her request, spared the inhabitants' lives. But the message was clear. Resist the king of kings at your peril.

41

The Sack of Antioch

There was panic across Syria.

The eastern field army wasn't there. Most of it had been sent to Italy or Africa. There were only unpaid garrison troops – *limitanei* – to resist the Persians. Chosroes led his army towards Hierapolis, a large and strongly walled city, on the road to Antioch. In Belisarius' absence, who was at that moment sailing back to Constantinople, Boutzes was the Roman commander-in-chief and was stationed at Hierapolis with what little existed of the eastern field army. We do not know its exact size but we can be sure it was a small force, probably only a few thousand strong. Procopius accuses him of cowardice,[126] saying he told the people of Hierapolis it would be better for him and his troops to go outside the walls where they could harry the Persians. He then literally disappeared: 'He chose the best part of the Roman army and was off. Where in the world he was neither any of the Romans in Hierapolis nor the hostile army was able to learn.'[127] Indeed, Boutzes fled so far away that he disappeared from the records of this campaign.

Not so another Roman commander, Justinian's cousin Germanus, who had returned from Africa where he'd been fighting the Berbers (see Chapter 50). Justinian despatched him post-haste from Constantinople to Antioch to take command of the defence of the city. But there was one problem. He only had 300 soldiers with him. Nevertheless, Germanus was a capable commander and immediately set about reviewing the city's defences. Although these were large and extended all around the city, which was also helpfully bordered by the Orontes River in places, he identified one point of weakness. This was on the northern side of the city where the ground rose steeply into the foothills of Mount Silpius, and there was a large, rocky outcrop at almost the same level as the walls themselves. Alarmingly, this provided a natural platform as good as any siege tower.

This deficiency was because Antioch had suffered two savage earthquakes, in 526 and 528, and the wall had not been repaired up to its original height. Germanus decided there was no time to build the walls higher or to extend them around the rocky outcrop which might have been the best solution. Instead, he directed the citizens to build a wooden platform behind the walls so that a mass of defenders could oppose the Persians on the rock. Procopius says this was a mistake, and in his view, the defenders should have occupied the rock and tried to defend it.

But Germanus was no fool. He knew the city's defences were too weak. He urgently called for reinforcements. In Boutzes' absence, the most he could summon were 6,000 *limitanei* from Palestine, a not inconsiderable force but nothing like the high-quality horse archers who had mostly been sent west. So, in desperation, he hoped to buy Chosroes off. He knew the Persian kings valued tribute from the

Romans almost more than victory in battle, so he sent an embassy to offer him peace terms including a large ransom.

Enter an important new character in our story. The leader of this embassy was the bishop of Beroia, Megas. Megas was a conspicuously brave man. He met Chosroes in front of the walls of Hierapolis which Chosroes was besieging. He offered him 2,000 pounds of silver to leave it and its surrounding countryside unmolested. He then offered the Persian king 1,000 pounds of gold to abandon his entire campaign and depart from Roman territory.

Chosroes was tempted. He seems to have been in two minds whether to sack Roman cities or leave them alone and just extract tribute from them. With Hierapolis, fortunately for its inhabitants, he accepted Megas' offer and left it alone. Megas then returned to Antioch to find the gold to pay him.

And the entire campaign might have ended there. Chosroes seemed to like Megas and trusted him, a little like Attila is said to have done when confronted by Pope Leo when he was on a similar mission to save Rome in 452.[128] Would Chosroes have kept to his word? Procopius seems unsure: 'He was the cleverest of all men at speaking untruths, concealing the truth, and blaming his victims for his own crimes; he was also ready to agree to everything and ratify the agreement with an oath, yet much more ready to completely forget what he had just agreed and sworn.'[129]

But whatever Chosroes' true intentions, it was Justinian who scuppered any hope for peace when his embassy arrived in Antioch to convey the unhelpful message that the emperor wouldn't pay the Persians. His instructions were to resist. This infuriated Germanus, who fell out with Justinian's embassy, and not long afterwards left the city clearly thinking it was a lost cause.

Meanwhile, Chosroes was still waiting at Beroia for Megas to return. The inhabitants had offered to pay the same ransom as Hierapolis, i.e. 2,000 pounds of silver. Chosroes insisted on double that. The inhabitants said they simply didn't have the cash ready. So, Chosroes prepared to assault the city. At night, its citizens retreated into the citadel. The next day, the Persians found the town deserted only to be shot at by the defenders from the walls. When they tried to storm the citadel, they were beaten off with heavy losses. But the Beroians had made a mistake. They had taken all their livestock into the citadel who drank the water well dry. Within a few days, they were so thirsty they had no choice but to surrender.

Just at that moment, the plucky Megas arrived back from Antioch. He found Chosroes furious that his thousand pounds of gold ransom money wasn't forthcoming. But Megas was far braver than any of the Roman commanders. He stood up to Chosroes and boldly protested the Persian king had also not kept to his side of the bargain by attacking Beroia while he was away. Procopius vividly describes the heated exchange between the two of them. Chosroes could have had Megas beheaded at any moment. But Megas lay on the ground and pleaded with the shah to allow his townsfolk to go free if they gave him all the money they could spare. When he wept for his people and told Chosroes it did not befit such a great king to kill innocent people, Chosroes relented. The king of kings respected a brave man when he met one. He said they could all go free and called Megas his friend.

Unfortunately, at this point Megas exits from our story and we never hear of him again. His bravery stands in stark contrast to the cowardly behaviour of the Roman high command. Back in Antioch, the commander-in-chief of the eastern army, Boutzes, had disappeared. And the city's new governor, Germanus, had fled the city.

The road to Antioch lay open.

Chosroes advanced right up to the city, where its inhabitants were crowded on the walls. His ambassador, Paulus, a highly regarded diplomat fluent in many languages, offered to leave them unharmed in return for a ransom of 1,000 pounds of gold. It was not an unreasonable offer. Chosroes expected them to beg for mercy. But in a strange display of almost childish petulance, they did the opposite. Procopius tells us: '[The inhabitants of Antioch] are not serious people but always engaged in disorderly jesting – and they heaped insults upon Chosroes from the battlements and taunted him with unseemly laughter.'[130] They even took potshots at Paulus, his respected ambassador.

Chosroes was a proud man. 'Boiling with anger' according to Procopius, he decided to spare no one. The Persian assault didn't last long. As Germanus had predicted, they broke through at the weak point in the walls beside Mount Silpius. The wooden platform, constructed to allow more defenders to resist the Persians, simply collapsed under their weight. Once the Persians were inside the walls, the 6,000 *limitanei* conducted a well-executed retreat through the south gate, which they had probably rehearsed expecting a Persian breakthrough. Most of them escaped, although Procopius says they trampled thousands of fleeing citizens to death as they went.

The city was at the mercy of the Persians. But they showed little mercy. They advanced down the ancient streets, killing all before them. The bravest of the defenders were the young men of the Blue and Green factions. They were the ones who had hurled insults at Chosroes. Now they lined up in the streets: 'some of them were in heavy armour but the majority were unarmed, using only stones as missiles. Pushing back the enemy they raised the paean [the Roman war-cry], and with shouts proclaimed the emperor Justinian triumphant, as if they had won the victory'. But their heroism was to no avail. The Persians slaughtered them in their thousands. The streets of Antioch ran red with blood. Procopius says the Persians killed everyone they came across, young or old, male or female, and women threw themselves into the Orontes River to avoid being raped.

Some inhabitants did escape with the retreating *limitanei*. But most were killed or enslaved. There is no reliable source for the numbers that died that day, but it must have been well over 50,000. Chosroes ordered the city to be burned to the ground, except for its cathedral. Then he sent messengers to Justinian saying he wanted not 1,000 pounds of gold to halt his offensive, but 5,000. And to celebrate his glorious victory, he did what no Persian shah had done for nearly 300 years.

He went to swim in the Mediterranean Sea.

42

The Little Ice Age

If you thought the Persian sack of Antioch was bad, worse was to come. The human catastrophe of the Persian war would soon be eclipsed by natural catastrophes that battered not just Rome but the entire world.

The most dramatic climatic event in human history since the end of the last Ice Age (some 12,000 years ago) began in the year 536, when people in the northern hemisphere, from Constantinople to China, noticed the sun was dimmer and the temperature was cooler. Writing that year in Constantinople, the puzzled Roman aristocrat Cassiodorus recorded: 'We see a kind of sea-coloured sun; we are puzzled that physical bodies lack shadows at midday and that [in summer] the strength of the sun's rays seem cool.'[131]

Procopius was in Africa in 536, where he was shocked: 'it came about during this year that a most dread portent took place. For the sun gave forth its light without brightness, like the moon, during the entire year, and it seemed exceedingly like the sun in eclipse, for the beams it shed were not such as it is accustomed to give out'.[132]

Another Roman writer, John Lydus, as mentioned earlier a civil servant and vociferous critic of John the Cappadocian, noted that the sun was dimmed by dark clouds in summer in a way he'd never seen before: 'so that it did not come into our sight or pierce this dense substance [the clouds]'.[133]

But it was not just the Romans who noticed this strange event. Across the entire northern hemisphere contemporary chroniclers recorded a weak sun, lower temperatures and most worrying of all, harvest failures and then famine. In Ireland, a lack of bread is recorded. In China, records say that yellow dust or ashes rained down from the sky and there were bitter, unseasonal frosts ruining crops. In Japan, a desperate record has been found saying: 'Food is the basis of empire. Yellow gold and ten thousand strings of cash cannot cure hunger. What avail a thousand boxes of pearls to him who is starving because of the cold?'[134]

So, what was causing this strange phenomenon?

Until 2015, the accepted view was either a meteorite strike or severe volcanic eruptions. However, in 2015, the volcanic explanation gained favour because ice core analysis showed significant sulphate deposits in the year 536 which most likely came from volcanic eruptions that year.[135] Although nothing is known for certain, using a mix of evidence from ice cores and tree rings, geologists now believe there was a 'volcanic winter' over 536–537, caused by an exceptional ring of volcanic eruptions around the globe, extending possibly from Papua New Guinea to Central America and to Iceland. Another major volcanic eruption followed this in 539 or 540. Together these made up the most spectacular period of volcanic activity over the last 2,000 years, much more significant than the last major volcanic eruption in modern times at Krakatoa in 1883.

Enormous amounts of dust and debris were thrown into the air creating a 'dust veil event' which blocked out the sun's light and warmth, in exactly the manner described by our Roman sources, and possibly causing summer temperatures in Europe to cool by as much as 2–3 degrees centigrade, with similar drops probably experienced elsewhere around the world.

It is now widely accepted the decade from 536 to 545 was the coldest in the last 2,000 years. Leaving Europe out of our discussion for a moment, historians have suggested it may have caused major societal changes across the globe. In North America, some archaeologists think the volcanic winter prompted mass migration and the emergence of new types of villages and settlements which formed the origin of the 'pueblo societies' that dominated much of the region until the advent of the European conquests in the modern age.[136] In Scandinavia, some think a major shift in religious culture took place, abandoning the traditional worship of the sun and moon (since the sun was waning) and replacing it with a new pantheon of deities more familiar to us today such as Thor, Odin and Freya.

But the volcanic winter, which might have lasted an entire decade from 536 to 545, was only the beginning. Recent scholarship[137] suggests another agent of global cooling accompanied it. For beryllium isotope records show a deep decline in solar heat for a century and a half, from the middle of the 530s to the 680s, which was probably the coldest period in the last 2,000 years. This period of cooling is also suggested by geological work that has identified a rapid advance in the Alpine glaciers in the seventh century, as temperatures remained low. What was the cause? Climatologists think it was increased sunspot activity.

Coinciding extreme volcanic activity and increased sunspot activity was unfortunate to say the least. Reduced heat from the sun extended the initial impact of the volcanic winter by a century and a half until the 680s. This period of global cooling has been termed the 'Late Antique Little Ice Age'. And it is interesting to note it was during this time that an unprecedented transformation of the world took place involving the rise of Islam, the destruction of Persia and the near destruction of the eastern Roman Empire.[138] Were these events linked? We will return to that important question in the next book in this series.

To return to Justinian's Rome, there is little doubt that, before the onset of the little ice age, the volcanic winter had profound implications. And most of them were very bad indeed. First, the cooler temperature caused harvest failures across the Roman Empire. Procopius has left us with a vivid description of the famine he witnessed in Italy in the late 530s, in the years after the 'dust veil event', when he was on campaign with Belisarius. He describes the villages and fields empty of people: so many had starved to death, stories of cannibalism he heard of, and the skeletal appearance of people reduced to eating grass. What he saw clearly shocked him profoundly:

I will now tell of the appearance they [the Italians starving to death] acquired and how they died, for I was an eyewitness. All of them first became lean and pale, for the flesh, lacking nourishment, 'turned in on itself' (to use the old expression) and the bile, taking over their bodies by its sheer excess, lent them its own appearance. As the evil developed, all moisture left them and their skin became so dry that it resembled leather more than anything else, giving the impression that it had been fastened upon their bones. They changed from a livid to a black colour, whereupon they came to resemble burned-out torches. Their faces always wore an expression of amazement, while they always had a dreadful sort of insane stare. Some died because of the lack of food and others by quickly eating too much. For all the warmth that nature kindled within them had died away, so whenever anyone fed them too much, and not little by little like newborn infants, the result was they died much more quickly because they were unable to digest the food.[139]

However, the colder temperatures weren't necessarily bad for everyone. One historian[140] has compiled evidence suggesting wide geographical variations in climate and agricultural experience. For example, while Northern Italy was struck by harvest failure and famine, as Procopius recorded, Sicily may have benefited from greater rainfall and actually delivered bumper wheat harvests. This was because, although it was colder everywhere, moisture accumulated more in mountainous areas leading to increased rainfall. Other examples are Southern Italy and Anatolia where more floods were recorded during the late 530s and 540s.

And sometimes, the changing climate had a mixed effect on agricultural production. For example, Anatolia seems to have been particularly wet which favoured its wheat production but, conversely, more frosts than normal killed off many of its olive trees which had been one of its farming staples.

Other areas were increasingly arid. The Sahara Desert seems to have continued to expand, reducing the breadbasket of North Africa, another worrying development for the late empire. It may also have prompted the Berbers to flee their increasingly arid homeland and raid more frequently into Roman territory, as we know they did in the 530s and 540s, which we will discuss in Chapter 50. We have records of serious droughts in Syria and Palestine. These may suggest[141] some of Justinian's building projects, such as his famous Basilica Cistern, which is now Istanbul's top tourist attraction, may have been a much-needed response to drier weather.

The colder and drier climate led to famine in many regions but it might also have helped to cause something far worse that was to rock Justinian's Rome and the whole of western Eurasia to its very core – plague. This would become the biggest killer of them all, and one that would change the entire history not just of the eastern empire but of the world. It is to this that we will now turn.

43

The Plague of Justinian

According to Procopius, the plague first appeared in the summer of 541 at the Egyptian port of Pelusium, where a canal connected the Mediterranean to the Red Sea. In the sixth century, no one knew what it was or where it came from and it was widely regarded as a sign of God's displeasure.

But today we know it was a bacterium – *Yersinia pestis* – identified as such in 1894 by Alexandre Yersin, a bacteriologist from the Pasteur Institute. This same bacterium was at work in both the Plague of Justinian and the Black Death in the Middle Ages. It can fatally infect the bloodstream of mammals, including humans, and can kill humans in just five to ten days. Over half of those who contract it are likely to die. Modern antibiotics, in particular Gentamicin and Ciprofloxacin, can kill it fairly rapidly, rendering it harmless in the modern world if treated quickly enough. But in the sixth century it was deadly. Symptoms included, and still do include, fever, headache, chills, weakness and most strikingly, swollen, painful lymph nodes typically in the armpit, neck or groin. These become black tumours or pustules known as 'bubos', the appearance of which gave it the medieval name

Black Death although the Romans never used that term. The bacterium still exists, and between 1970 and 2020, 496 cases were reported in the United States,[142] although today it is mainly confined to sub-Saharan Africa.

One crucial question is why did the first bubonic plague pandemic occur in the sixth century? There is no simple answer to this. Medical scientists are fairly certain that the origins of bubonic plague can be traced back a long time, at least around 7,000 years.[143] *Yersinia pestis* is thought to have split off from an ancient disease known as 'pseudo-tuberculosis', and by the Bronze Age there is evidence it was widespread in the rodent population of Central Asia. Transmission of the disease from rodents to other mammals, including humans, was most likely via fleas and other bloodsucking parasites. These were only too happy to jump from one host, such as a marmot or a rat, to another, especially if the original host had died of the disease. But it's not just fleas that spread the disease. It could also be transmitted through the atmosphere, via aerosol droplets, or by eating infected animals.

In the millennia after the Ice Age, the first humans to have been infected were almost certainly those in Central Asia where the infected rodents lived. These would have been steppe nomads. And we know steppe nomads loved to wear and sleep in animal skins especially those of marmots. Marmots are susceptible to the disease and the furs of these animals were particularly prized. So, this may have facilitated the first 'spillover' event whereby the disease moved from rodents to humans. Transmission to humans was also facilitated by the black rat (rattus rattus) which was widespread not just in Asia but prolific in the Mediterranean world, and especially in the

Roman Empire. This was because both the Romans and rats had a strong liking for grain. And therefore, rats were more than happy to inhabit the abundant Roman grain warehouses that existed throughout the empire.

But until 536, we have no record of the type of catastrophic outbreak of plague such as happened that year. This was probably because the disease found it more difficult to spread in the wide-open plains of Central Asia than in the densely populated cities of the Roman Empire. It was probably also because the steppe nomads had more time to develop immunity. Humans can resist the disease. The human body's ability to resist essentially depends on the strength of its immune system, and research into the medieval Black Death suggests survivors were often those who had genes which enabled them to resist it more effectively.

For example, a recent survey of medieval cemeteries around London in the United Kingdom[144] suggests Black Death survivors were helped by a gene called ERAP2 which ramps up the inflammatory response to *Yersinia pestis* and helps clear out the pathogen infection more quickly than normal. Survivors passed this gene onto their descendants improving human immunity to the disease and preventing its recurrence. The researchers also discovered a downside to this improved immunity. Apparently, those with this gene might also have a greater susceptibility to autoimmune disorders such as Crohn's. Indeed, the study suggests modern growth in autoimmune disorders has its origins in the two major outbreaks of bubonic plague in Justinian's reign and later in the fourteenth century.

Getting back to the Romans, the essential problem for them was that the teeming populations of the eastern empire had not developed the herd immunity of the steppe nomads in Asia. The crowded and insanitary cities of the late ancient world were the perfect places for *Yersinia pestis* to thrive.

But how did it get to Pelusium and why then? Most historians think it came from India. A booming trade network had long existed between Rome and India since the heyday of the classical empire, driven by the Romans' obsession with Chinese silk and Indian spices. The current scholarly consensus is that rats infected with the plague had found their way from Central Asia into parts of India where they travelled on board ships bound for the Mediterranean. Historians are unsure whether it travelled directly from India to Egypt or stopped elsewhere in Africa on the way.

The African theory[145] is based on the observations of a Roman doctor, Rufus of Ephesus, who encountered what sounds like something very similar to *Yersinis pestis* in the first century AD in North Africa (modern Libya). Other sources also refer to East Africa as a region with a similar disease. For example, the Ethiopian kingdom of Axum is mentioned as a source for the plague. It is known that Axum had a fair amount of contact with Constantinople since the Romans regarded it as a potential ally against the Persians. One historian[146] suggests even the faraway Congo rainforest in West Africa might have been a source for the disease since there was a major demographic collapse there at this time.

Whatever the route taken by the plague, another crucial question is whether the 'dust veil event' of the 530s was linked to its outbreak. Again, there is no simple answer to this. The closeness of the two events – the volcanic eruptions of 536 and 540 and the appearance of the plague in 541 – suggests there might have been a link. Common sense also suggests people on the edge of starvation would be more vulnerable to disease. But was there a more direct link?

One theory suggests there was.[147] The idea is that the global cooling event of the 530s caused poor harvests and a shortage of food which forced rats, accustomed to living off human produce stored in warehouses and outbuildings, to move closer to human habitations so that they could literally snatch food off the table. This not only exposed humans more directly to the rats, but also brought the plague-bearing fleas that fed on the starving rats to seek more succulent human hosts. We'll never know whether this was true but it seems plausible.

But whatever the true origins and course of the plague, by 541 there's no denying it was a deadly reality in the Roman Empire. In the summer of 541, the dead were piling up in Pelusium. It quickly spread east to Palestine and west to Alexandria, the empire's third most important city. By the spring of 542, it had reached Constantinople. The plague's deadly grasp was rapidly extending, like ink spreading out on blotting paper, to engulf Syria, Mesopotamia, Greece, Italy and North Africa. By 543, it had stretched out to the furthest extremities of Western Europe – Gaul and Britain – while in the east it rose up through Armenia into the Caucasus.

There was no escape from its clutches. Its deadly effect would transform everything. Warfare was curtailed. It effectively brought to an end the war between Rome and Persia, as we will cover in Chapter 46. Economic activity throughout the Mediterranean and the Middle East collapsed. In 542, even the emperor Justinian contracted the disease and, although he survived, it caused political instability and accusations of treachery against his great general, Belisarius. The plague was a turning point. The age of Justinian now entered a much darker phase.

44

The Plague Spreads

Unfortunately for the Romans, Pelusium was an excellent conduit for the spread of the disease (see Map 6) since it was a major port on the primary route from India to the Mediterranean. Its remains are sited near to the modern Suez Canal, and in ancient times it was close to its Roman equivalent, a canal linking the Nile to the Red Sea, first dug by the Pharaohs and later extended by the emperor Trajan.

Enter an important additional source for our knowledge of the plague – John, the bishop of Ephesus – whose descriptions of the plague are even more vivid than those of Procopius. John was in Egypt when the plague struck and he made his way from there to Constantinople literally in tandem with the route taken by the disease as it spread. Somehow he survived, and he collated an eyewitness account of the plague into a longer work of ecclesiastical history.[148] Unlike Procopius, who only saw the effect of the plague on Constantinople, John witnessed it spread like wildfire across the Roman Empire, and his account tells of devastation not just to cities but to the countryside, and even ships at sea found, when all their crew died, like a plague-induced version of the *Marie Celeste*.

John's account is a sobering and moving experience of the suffering caused by the plague, and I would recommend it to anyone interested in the history of pandemics. The overriding impression from his account is one of horror. Houses became family tombs: 'houses large and small, beautiful and desirable which suddenly became tombs for their inhabitants and in which servants and masters at the same time suddenly fell (dead), mingling their rottenness together in their bedrooms, and not one of them escaped who might remove their corpses out from within the house'.[149]

Streets were filled with dead bodies: '…others who perished falling in the streets to become a terrible and shocking spectacle for those who saw them, as their bellies were swollen and their mouths wide open, throwing up pus like torrents, their eyes inflamed and their hands stretched out upward, and (over) the corpses rotting and lying on corners and streets and in the porches of courtyards and in churches and *martyria* and everywhere, with nobody to bury [them]'.[150]

It was not just the cities and towns which were filled with the dead but John also describes a horrifying silence in the countryside with dead people lying rotting and untended livestock wandering about: 'Cattle abandoned and roaming scattered over the mountains with nobody to gather them – flocks of sheep, goats, oxen and pigs which had become like wild animals, having forgotten [life in] a cultivated land and the human voice which used to lead them.'[151]

The fields lay deserted with crops rotting: 'Fields in all the countries through which we passed from Syria to Thrace, abundant in grain but there was none to reap or gather it in.'[152]

John describes ships where all the crew were dead, drifting in the ocean: 'Ships in the midst of the sea whose sailors were suddenly attacked by [God's] wrath and [the ships] became tombs for their captains and they continued to drift on the waves carrying the corpses of their owners.'[153]

John ascribed the catastrophe to punishment by God for the sins of humankind:

At the sight of these things we had occasion also to recall what had previously been said by the blessed prophet when he prophesied saying: 'The earth shall be laid utterly waste and be utterly despoiled', and 'the earth shall be utterly stirred up and shall utterly totter and shall be utterly shaken and shall quiver like a hut, and its iniquity shall prevail over it', and, 'it shall be burned again like a terebinth or an oak, which fell out from its acorn cup;' all these things were completely fulfilled in our days, not over a long period but in a short time.[154]

When John reached Constantinople, his account is remarkably similar to that of Procopius. Both describe the city gripped by terror and death. Procopius emphasises the superstition of its inhabitants who believed demons were visiting them: 'Visions of demons taking every imaginable form were seen by many people, and those who encountered them believed that they were being struck on some part of their body by that man whom they met.'[155]

All commercial activity ceased, according to John: 'The entire city then came to a standstill as if it had perished, so that its food supply stopped. There was nobody to stand

and do his job, so food vanished from the markets and great tribulation ensued, especially for the people prostrate with exhaustion from illnesses. Only a few were strong [enough] to bring to any bazaar anything worth one obol, but if they wished they took a dinar for it. Thus everything ceased and stopped.'[156]

Procopius tells us people went mad, either because of the disease or because they became demented with suffering: 'Those gripped by the madness of dementia could not sleep and became delusional. Imagining that people were attacking them to kill them, they became hysterical and fled at a run, shouting loudly.'[157]

The plague was a random killer. Procopius says some who contracted it survived while others died. His confidence in the sixth-century medical profession was limited to say the least: 'The most eminent doctors predicted that many would die who shortly afterwards were unexpectedly freed of all their maladies, and they also claimed many would survive who perished almost immediately.'[158]

Procopius is explicit there was no cure: 'There was no cause behind this disease that any human reason could grasp, for in all cases the outcome made little sense. Some were saved by taking baths, others were harmed by it. Many who were neglected died but many others paradoxically survived. Likewise, the same treatment produced different results in different patients.'[159]

As for numbers, according to John, the plague: 'began (to assault) the class of the poor, who lay in the streets. It happened that 5,000 and 7,000, or even 12,000 and as many as 16,000 of them departed this world in a single day'.[160]

He says about half the population of Constantinople died – i.e. 300,000 or more people. The officials gave up counting once the number exceeded 230,000. This may have been an exaggeration but the numbers were certainly huge.

The most immediate problem was burying the dead. The plague struck so suddenly that there was chaos. There were simply too many dead to bury in the normal manner. Because entire households would die together, often no one was even left to bury their relatives. At first, corpses were taken to the seashore and dumped into the sea so that, according to John, the corpses: 'piled up on the entire seashore, like flotsam on great rivers, and the pus flowed, discharging itself into the sea'.[161]

The stench from the dead bodies was overpowering. Justinian had no choice but to take action. Both John and Procopius tell the same story. He appointed a highly competent and fearless administrator, Theodore, as a sort of emergency plague minister with absolute powers reporting directly to the emperor. John records Justinian instructed him 'to take and spend as much gold as was necessary'. His first step was to get the dead bodies out of the city. He had enormous pits dug, capable of taking 70,000 corpses each, across the Golden Horn in the neighbourhood of Sykai (the modern Galata). Officials paid the common people to take their dead in wheelbarrows and carts to the new graves, promising generous payment for each load of corpses. Highly paid teams of workmen scoured the city, removing corpses, often having to go into houses, according to John, where entire families lay rotting. Soon the city was rid of its dead and Procopius tells us: 'A foul stench wafted from Sykai to the city, bringing even more grief to its people.'[162] But at least the city was cleared of its dead. Procopius says the plague raged for four months before it abated.

John leaves us with the most moving scene when he describes the burial pits crowded with corpses flung pell-mell on top of each other, young and old, male and female, all crushed together like a 'wine-press of God's wrath', which is his favourite metaphor for the plague.

Meanwhile, back in Justinian's palace, John tells us it: 'was overwhelmed and overcome by sorrow. The emperor and the empress to whom myriads and thousands of commanders and the whole great senate had bowed and paid honour every day, (now) were miserable, and like everybody sank into grief, being served only by few'. Indeed, Procopius tells us even Justinian succumbed to the plague. But he survived, something which he seems to have ascribed to the medical saints, Cosmas and Damian. Others were less fortunate. Tribonian, architect of his legal reforms, died probably in 542.

Another key point is that the plague did not disappear after its outbreak in 541–543. Quite the opposite. Historians think it remained active in western Eurasia from 541 until as late as 749. Eight plague outbreaks have been recorded in Constantinople alone in this period. After the first in 542, it struck again in 558, 573, 586 and 599. In the seventh and eighth centuries, the incidence reduced but there were further outbreaks in 619 and 698, with the last in 747. The plague remained a killer for centuries after it first appeared in Pelusium.

45

The Economic Impact
of the Plague

The plague was clearly horrific for the people who lived through it but what was its true impact on the Roman Empire? Did it cause a lasting demographic and economic collapse and how much did it weaken the Roman state? Historians are still divided on this.

One of our best insights into its economic and social impact lies with the legislation and fiscal policies Justinian implemented after the plague struck. As mentioned in the last chapter, his first response was to appoint Theodore as plague minister, responsible for collecting and disposing of the dead bodies. After that, he had to deal with the problem of people dying intestate (i.e. without a will) as a result of the rapidity of the plague's spread. He instituted a method for property to be fairly distributed where the beneficiaries were all dead or not named.

He also enacted legislation to restrict 'blasphemy' recognising the widely held view that the plague was, as John said, the 'wine-press of God's wrath'. Procopius wryly describes how, when the plague first struck, 'people gave up the immorality of their lifestyles and became religious to an extreme degree', only to reverse this when they survived and 'became even worse than they had been before'.[163]

But the most important issue by far for Justinian was taxation. Common sense suggests the plague caused a massive fall in tax revenues. If we assume that between a quarter and a half of the empire's population was killed by the pandemic, tax revenues would have fallen by a similar or even greater amount as people were simply not there to pay tax, and the economic collapse meant even those who survived didn't have the means to pay their normal taxes.

The result was a fiscal crisis. And the evidence for this is supported by the state devaluing the currency for the first time since the third century AD. Procopius says Justinian instructed Peter Barsymes, the head of the treasury, and another corrupt and greedy bureaucrat according to Procopius, to strike 'light-weight' gold *solidi*. As mentioned before, the *solidus* was literally the gold standard of the Roman Empire. Introduced by Diocletian to stabilise the monetary system and reduce inflation, it was embraced by Constantine who issued large quantities of the new coin during his reign. These were not debased until Justinian reduced their weight to the equivalent of 20 silver coins (called *siliquae*) compared with the normal 24.[164] Our information on this is extremely limited, but it seems to have happened in direct response to the first outbreak of the plague in 542–3, or possibly a bit later in 547. And it was clearly done because there was simply not enough tax revenue to pay soldiers and civil servants. Fortunately for the Roman economy, it was a one-off, and Justinian quickly reverted back to the *solidus'* normal weight.

I say fortunate because the effects of debasing the coinage were always self-defeating, as the experience of the third century AD showed. Although nominal payments to soldiers and civil servants could be met more easily in the short term with debased coins, the longer-term result was always inflationary. People weren't fools and demanded more of the debased coins to reach a similar value to the old ones. And high inflation was always bad. It crippled commerce and trade which required a stable currency and prices to ensure profit margins could be maintained.

Inflation was also caused by the high death toll of the plague. Fewer labourers meant they could demand more for their work. This phenomenon was repeated during the fourteenth-century Black Death. In Justinian's reign we can track this by measuring the exchange rate between copper coins and gold coins since, in the Roman monetary system, there was no fixed number of bronze coins, called *folles*, required to buy a *solidus*. Labourers were paid in bronze coins and not gold, and the number they were paid fluctuated according to the demand for labour. In the decade following the plague's first outbreak (542–550) the number of *folles* per *solidus* halved from some 360 to 180,[165] meaning labourers' wages doubled in terms of their value in gold. Justinian tried to control this by imposing wage controls such as Diocletian had done in the third century. But as Diocletian experienced, this probably achieved little since people paid whatever the true market price was by resorting to private black-market deals.

Another consequence of the high death toll of the plague was the abandonment of agricultural land since there weren't enough people to work it. This caused taxes to fall. Controversially, Justinian assigned abandoned agricultural land to neighbouring landowners or communities and made them liable for the associated taxes. Not surprisingly, this was deeply resented.

In conclusion, we still don't know how many people died in the Justinianic plague and how much the economy was impacted. Some historians[166] have speculated the effects of the plague were not as disastrous as those of the Black Death in the fourteenth century which radically changed medieval European society. The evidence for this lies with archaeological work that suggests most of the cities and towns in the eastern provinces of the empire were still functioning in the early seventh century, on the eve of the great war with Persia which saw many of them destroyed. For example, excavations at Ephesus and Sardis have revealed these cities changed beyond all recognition *after* the Persian/Arab conquests but not before.

But this view is increasingly open to question. It now looks more likely that, while these cities continued to function after the plague, they were much smaller than before. Common sense suggests if around a quarter to a half of the population of the Roman Empire died in the plague, this would have been an economic catastrophe.[167] This view is supported by Justinian's chronic shortage of cash and inability to balance his budget from the 540s onwards. In short, it seems highly likely the Justinianic Plague was a turning point in the history of not just the Roman Empire but of the whole of the ancient world.

46

The Return of Belisarius

As mentioned in Chapter 41, Chosroes celebrated the destruction of Rome's second city by going for a swim in the Mediterranean Sea, the first time a Persian king had done that for 300 years.

Once he'd dried himself off, envoys arrived from Justinian to negotiate a peace. Chosroes drove a hard bargain. He wanted 5,000 pounds of gold, five times the amount he had originally demanded to spare Antioch, as well as 500 pounds of gold annually. The Roman envoys sped back to Constantinople to see if Justinian was willing to pay this huge sum. Meanwhile, the Persians agreed to wait for his reply and suspend hostilities.

But, as Procopius was keen to point out, Chosroes was not a man to be trusted. Despite agreeing to a truce, he didn't honour it. Indeed, he wanted a bit more fun at Justinian's expense. So, he advanced south from the smoking wreck that was Antioch to the town of Apameia. There he demanded and received 1,000 pounds of silver to spare the city and organised a chariot race in which he ensured the Greens won against the Blues, since he knew Justinian was famously a Blue supporter. Procopius also tells us[168] he also nearly walked off with a portion of the True Cross, which was the town's main religious relic, but probably not realising its significance, he let the town keep it.

He then started the journey back to Persia, but at a conspicuously leisurely pace that allowed him to stop off at the Roman cities along the way to demand tribute. After Apameia, came Chalcis which paid him 200 pounds of gold. Then Edessa paid another 200 pounds of gold for him to leave, not, Procopius tells us, because its inhabitants were afraid the Persians would storm their tall walls, but because they wanted them to leave their crops in the countryside alone. At this point, envoys arrived back from Justinian to say he agreed to the payment of 5,000 pounds of gold.

But it seems Chosroes didn't trust Justinian to come up with the gold, for he continued to break the truce and set about besieging Dara, the hugely powerful fortress the emperor Anastasius had built to oppose the Persian stronghold of Nisibis. But the sturdy walls kept the Persians out. Their efforts to tunnel underneath them were skilfully defeated by the Romans when they dug an opposing tunnel to meet the Persians underground. Procopius tells us this was organised by a clever engineer called Theodore. In fierce underground fighting, he sent the Persians fleeing. In the winter of 540, Chosroes gave up and accepted 1,000 pounds of silver to depart from Roman territory.

Perhaps he should have simply accepted the promised 5,000 pounds of gold without attacking every Roman city he passed, since Justinian refused to pay him anything when he heard what had happened. This left him with a considerably smaller sum – 2,000 pounds of silver and 400 pounds of gold – collected after the sack of Antioch.

But whether Chosroes had in fact short-changed himself or not, it was still an utter humiliation for Justinian. Procopius was so shocked by the sack of Antioch, he wrote: 'I become dizzy as I write about such a great calamity.'[169] Justinian had mismanaged his eastern frontier shockingly. But Roman hopes were soon revived. For by the fall of 540, Belisarius was back in Constantinople, mustering an army.

In the spring of 541, just months before the plague hit Pelusium in Egypt, Belisarius marched from Constantinople to meet the Persians. But his army was small, emphasising yet again how Justinian had run down the eastern field army. Procopius says he only had his own *bucellarii*, including a contingent of Goths from Italy who returned with Wittigis and would prove their worth against the Persians, together with the *limitanei* on garrison duty in the east and a force of Arab allies led by al-Harith. Procopius is scathing about these troops who presumably included the 6,000 *limitanei* who had abandoned Antioch to its fate the previous year, describing them as: 'for the most part without either arms or armour and in terror of the name of the Persians'.[170]

Justinian urged Belisarius to take revenge for the sack of Antioch by advancing on the Persian stronghold of Nisibis. This audacious move was prompted by the false information he'd received that Chosroes and the main Persian army were far away in the east dealing with an attack by the White Huns. In fact, they were in Lazica (see Map 4) in the western Caucasus, where Chosroes' attention had been attracted by its inhabitants' appeals for Persian help against a corrupt Roman commander, Peter, who had monopolised imports of grain and salt to sell them at extortionate prices. This racketeering had occurred when Justinian strengthened Roman defences in this region in the 530s, building a powerful fortress at a place on the Black Sea coast called Petra (not to be confused with the Nabatean Petra in modern Jordan).

Procopius tells us Chosroes led a large army into Lazica, spreading the false rumour that he was away fighting the White Huns, so that he could launch a surprise attack on Petra. Despite his deception, the first assault on the Roman stronghold was so disastrous that, according to Procopius,[171] Chosroes had the general in charge impaled as a punishment. But a second attempt, which mined underneath the town's walls and caused a tower to collapse, was more successful, and the town was taken with Chosroes displaying uncharacteristic mercy by sparing the lives of the defenders in return for their quick surrender.

Meanwhile, back in Mesopotamia, Justinian was still urging Belisarius to avenge the sack of Antioch by attacking Nisibis. However, Belisarius was more cautious. He had little confidence in his motley army and he knew Nisibis was held by a highly competent Persian general, Nabedes. Procopius narrates an intriguing story in which Belisarius, ever the wise commander, had to rein in the enthusiasm of overconfident Roman officers who wanted to attack Nisibis. When one of them disregarded orders and was routed in a skirmish with the Persians, Belisarius intervened with his Gothic cavalry and put the Persians to flight.

One senses Belisarius' increasing frustration with Justinian's inability to give him sufficient resources to get the job done. This had been the case in Italy and it was even more so now on the eastern front. But resourcefulness was Belisarius' middle name. He abandoned the siege of Nisibis in search of easier prey. He found a Persian fortress nearby, Sisauranon, garrisoned by 800 elite Persian cavalrymen but a much softer target than Nisibis. Although his first assault failed, he let loose his Arab allies on the Persian countryside, and they returned with prisoners who said the Persian garrison was running out of provisions. With his gift for diplomacy, Belisarius negotiated a surrender, promising the Persians they would receive excellent pay if they switched sides to join the Roman army. This they did, and the town was occupied securing a small Roman victory.

Towards the end of 541, he called off the campaign. Procopius tells us he had little choice since not only had his Arab allies deserted to gather booty[172] but a disease he ascribes to the severe heat also suddenly afflicted a third of the Roman soldiers. This doesn't seem to have been the Justinianic plague, which would come later, and instead it was probably dysentery or something similar. In *The Secret History*, Procopius also alleges Belisarius was desperate to join his wife, Antonina, to sort out a serious domestic dispute that had arisen – a subject we'll cover in the next chapter. But for the moment, the second year of war with Chosroes was over. It was essentially a draw between the two sides. The Persians had taken Petra in Lazica and Belisarius had taken Sisauranon in Mesopotamia. He returned to Constantinople for the winter. He hadn't avenged the sack of Antioch, but at least he'd stabilised the frontier.

The year 542 was extraordinary by any standards. Not only did the plague work its way up to Constantinople by the summer, but in spring, Chosroes launched yet another major invasion of Mesopotamia with an army probably similar in size to that with which he had taken Antioch. His target seems to have been Jerusalem. His route was the same as in 540, along the Euphrates. First stop was the city of Sergioupolis which successfully resisted the Persian hordes and was fortunate enough, Procopius tells us,[173] for the enemy to run out of water and to have to move on.

Meanwhile, Belisarius had arrived in Syria and taken command of the army of the east. This time, he seems to have had additional reinforcements although none of our sources gives any detail on the numbers involved on either side. He set up camp near Europeum, further up the Euphrates (see Map 4), ready to intercept the Persians. But Chosroes never got there. The Persian army retreated back the way it had come.

Why did Chosroes retreat? Procopius provides us with a rather imaginative explanation. He claims it was Belisarius' resourcefulness that once again saved the day. The story goes that Chosroes sent his royal secretary, Abandanes, to the Roman camp to demand the 5,000 pounds of gold he'd been promised after the sack of Antioch. Procopius says Belisarius wanted to trick him by making his army look larger and more intimidating than it really was. So, he spread it out over a huge area. Then he surrounded himself with '…six thousand men of tall stature and especially fine physique'.[174] These were men picked from various Roman regiments, including native troops like Thracians and Illyrians, but also a large contingent of Goths and Vandals now serving in the Roman army. They were told to look as if they hadn't a care in the world, certainly no fear of the Persian army close by. 'Each one had his horse whip, and for weapons one had a sword, another an axe, yet another an uncovered bow. All gave the impression they were in a hurry to be off on a hunt with no other concern in mind.'[175]

Procopius says this display of confidence had the desired effect. The Persian envoy returned to tell Chosroes: '…he had met a general who in manliness and wisdom surpassed all other men, and soldiers such as he, at least, had never seen'.[176]

But most historians think another explanation is more likely. The plague was now raging throughout Constantinople and the rest of the empire. Our records provide almost no detail about its effect on Persia although Procopius is clear that its ravages were also felt there. Chosroes' army may well have been suffering its effects even though Belisarius' troops seem to have been spared, at least for the time being. Even if neither army was directly affected, both sides knew something much bigger was happening and it would be unwise to risk a titanic battle. Perhaps, another reason was Chosroes' fear of Belisarius. For his reputation was now at its height.

Chosroes retreated to Persian territory although he stopped on the way to burn Callinicum which the Romans were in the middle of refortifying and had left mostly deserted apart from a group of farmers who, Procopius tells us,[177] found themselves in the wrong place at the wrong time and were hauled away by the Persians as prisoners.

The war in Mesopotamia was nearly over. In 543, Chosroes launched his last attack, targeting Edessa. This was a powerful fortress. Procopius has left us with a very detailed account of the two-month siege. The Roman general

Martinus put up a determined resistance. Repeated Persian attacks on the walls were beaten off. Procopius describes boiling oil poured onto the Persians as they scaled the walls. When they tried to build up an artificial hill against the walls using tree trunks, stones and earth, the Romans sallied out and poured more oil onto the wood and set it alight so that the smoke, according to Procopius, could be seen 50 miles away.[178] Eventually, Chosroes abandoned the siege for the payment of 500 pounds of gold and returned to Persia.

But by that time Belisarius was back in Constantinople. His recall had come as a surprise. He was not congratulated for halting Chosroes' offensive. He was arrested for treason.

47

Belisarius and Antonina

The new dome of Hagia Sophia gleams in the midday sun. Belisarius and his general, Boutzes, can see it as they take the boat from Chalcedon across the choppy water.

When they land at the harbour, a group of soldiers meets them. Leading them is Narses, Justinian's first minister. Belisarius' heart misses a beat. He knows something's up. Narses is his sworn enemy. They haven't spoken since the emperor recalled him from Italy for refusing to obey Belisarius' orders. Now he has a nasty feeling the tables are about to be turned against him.

A rope is thrown to the soldiers who tow the boat to the steps beside the harbour wall. As they get closer, Belisarius can see Narses is smiling. *Prepare for the worst*, he tells himself. But not even he expected the sneering welcome Justinian's most trusted minister greets him with: 'Resistance is impossible. You are both under arrest.'

We have two versions of Belisarius' arrest from Procopius. In the first, it didn't happen. His narrative in the *Wars* is silent about the incident. But in *The Secret History*, he sets out a revelatory story that when Justinian himself was struck down by the plague in 542, and was expected to die, Belisarius and Boutzes were overheard saying they didn't like the emperor and would never serve under someone like him again. This was reported back to Justinian who, when he recovered, had them arrested for treason.

Procopius' version of events doesn't stop there. He explains it was Theodora who told Justinian and then after Belisarius was arrested, she pleaded with Justinian to release him. Why? Because it was part of a subterfuge to save Belisarius' and Antonina's marriage by making Belisarius think it was Antonina who had secured Justinian's reprieve.

If you think this story sounds more like a soap opera than the gritty tale of war and politics we have become accustomed to, you have my sympathy. Many historians have dismissed it as fantasy. But there are good reasons to believe it. Let me explain.

First, Belisarius was definitely summoned to Constantinople in late 542 and did not leave until 18 months later, in the spring of 544, when he led a new expedition to Italy. During this time, another source from Procopius, the Chronicle of Marcellinus Comes, says he was in disgrace: 'Belisarius was summoned from the east and, although running into enmity and serious danger and being exposed to envy, he was again sent back to Italy.'[179]

So, what really happened?

Let's start with *The Secret History*, Procopius' short and vitriolic record, which provides some of our best insights into this period. *The Secret History* actually starts with Belisarius. And you're in for a shock. The hero of Procopius' *Wars* is described as a fool, cuckolded by his scheming wife. Is this the same Belisarius who Procopius repeatedly assures us is not just the greatest soldier of his age but a man of brilliant intelligence? And with his wife, are they not the perfect couple as Procopius wrote in the *Wars*? – '…he never touched any woman other than his wife. Although he took captive so many women from both the Vandals and the Goths, and such beautiful women as no man in the world, I suppose, has ever seen, he refused to allow any of them to come into his presence or meet him in any way.'[180]

Well, I'm sorry to disappoint you, but in *The Secret History*, Procopius reveals a very different side to Belisarius, his wife and their marriage. He says before Antonina met Belisarius, she had 'lived a profligate life' and 'given birth to one child after another'. He says her mother '…had been one of the theatre tarts'. But none of this stopped Belisarius from being devoted to her. According to Procopius, he was far too devoted: 'she had her husband wrapped around her little finger'.

Procopius' allegations are scandalous, to say the least. He reveals in *The Secret History* that Antonina was having an affair with her adopted son, Theodosius. The background to this is that Belisarius and Antonina had no biological son. They only had one child – a daughter named Ioannina – although she also had one legitimate child from a previous marriage, called Photius, and an unnamed daughter.

Because they had no son, they adopted a promising young man to be Belisarius' heir, named Theodosius, who was already serving in his household. Then the problems began. He was a handsome young man and Procopius alleges Antonina fell in love with him. She always accompanied

Belisarius on campaign, which gave her the opportunity to form an adulterous relationship with him during the Vandal campaign of 533, completely unknown to Belisarius. Procopius says this shocked her natural son, Photius, who forced Theodosius to flee to a monastery and told Belisarius the truth about his wife's misdemeanours. Not surprisingly, this caused their hitherto happy marriage to fall apart.

At this point in Procopius' story, the empress Theodora tried to save her friend Antonina's marriage by first imprisoning Photius and then planning a way for Antonina to be reconciled with Belisarius. An idea came to her when Justinian himself was struck down by the plague in 542 and was expected to die. Not surprisingly, this sent the rumour mill into overdrive. Who would succeed Justinian? Belisarius was of course an obvious candidate. So, for her to concoct the story told by Procopius is plausible.

Her next step was to prove true her boast that she could wrap her husband around her little finger, by persuading Justinian to drop all charges against Belisarius and reinstate him. This she did and then told Belisarius, who was living in fear for his life in Constantinople, that Antonina had persuaded her and Justinian to reinstate him, and he should therefore forgive his wife. Procopius says Belisarius threw himself at his wife's feet, forgave her for her infidelity: 'raining kisses on each ankle in turn, he declared that he owed his life entirely to her'. Rather conveniently, Theodosius, the cause of their dispute, mysteriously died at this point as well. Procopius hints Theodora may have poisoned him. The couple were reunited and lived happily ever after.

So, what are we to make of Procopius' story? Many scholars dismiss it as being a fantasy. I disagree with this. There's normally some truth in all of the allegations Procopius made in *The Secret History*. And I don't find any contradiction in Belisarius being both one of the greatest generals in Rome's history, and also having a very difficult wife who was probably unfaithful to him.

So, to return to our earlier narrative, by the end of 543, Justinian forgave Belisarius and restored him to his former position. With the plague now affecting Persia as well as the eastern Roman Empire, the war in Mesopotamia fizzled out and, although he kept the bulk of the Roman army on the eastern front to guard against any possible repeat of the sack of Antioch, Justinian decided he could spare his best general to sort out the problems in Italy where the Gothic king Totila was running amok.

So, in the spring of 544, Belisarius sailed to Italy for his second campaign against the Goths. But by this time, the empire didn't have the resources to send more than a token force with him. Justinian seems to have hoped Belisarius would magically conjure up victory from nothing, as he had done before.

48

Totila

Enter a new and important character in our story: Totila.

Since Belisarius hadn't completely defeated the Goths, there were still thousands of Gothic warriors and their families living freely in the Po Valley, north of Ravenna, which had been the traditional heartland of the Gothic kingdom. As I mentioned earlier, the Gothic nobles who fled Belisarius' occupation of Ravenna, had turned first to Wittigis' nephew, Urais, and then, at his suggestion, to Hildebad, who was proclaimed king. But this partnership didn't last long since, according to Procopius, their respective wives fell out when they visited the baths. When they'd insulted each other over who was the more important, their husbands became even more incensed and Hildebad murdered Urais. Hildebad was then himself murdered by the Gothic nobles who were fed up with his conduct. Procopius has left us with a vivid description of his assassination – his head was cut off so suddenly at a dinner party that his hand was still holding the food he was about to eat when his head hit the ground.[181]

The next royal candidate was the leader of the Rugi, a Germanic tribe subject to Gothic rule, whose leader Eraric was a highly regarded warrior and well liked by the Gothic nobles. But he only lasted for five months before he too was assassinated for secretly conspiring to surrender the Gothic kingdom to Justinian in exchange for a comfortable life in Constantinople. Finally, in late 541, the Goths found their man. This was Hildebad's nephew, Totila.

Over the next 11 years, Totila proved to be an exceptional leader. Well-connected within Gothic aristocratic circles, he also had connections with the Visigothic royal family in Spain. But his main qualification was his martial prowess. He was a brave and skilful warrior as Procopius described when, before a battle, he advanced up to the Roman lines to display his skills: 'He wheeled his horse around in a circle and then turned him again to the other side and so made him run round and round. As he rode, he hurled his javelin into the air and caught it again as it quivered above him...'.[182]

To help Totila, the Roman administration in Italy imploded after Belisarius left. The moment Belisarius was on the boat home, Justinian sent in the tax collectors, led by a notoriously harsh and corrupt administrator called Alexander 'Snips' because he would snip gold and silver from the edges of coins to keep for himself. Alexander alienated the Italian population by imposing higher taxes than they had paid under the Goths. He also targeted those who had prospered under the Gothic administration requiring them to pay special taxes to make up for their ill-gotten gains, thereby antagonising many of the wealthiest and most influential Italian senators.

But his most damaging action was to reduce or even stop the pay to the army of occupation. Justinian had done this in North Africa with disastrous consequences when, as we covered in Chapter 34, the Roman army in Africa mutinied. Not only was it a very short-sighted tactic to reduce the pay of soldiers who had fought hard and well, but Justinian had clearly learned nothing from the North African experience. In short, he caused morale to plummet.

Into this cauldron of discontent, Justinian threw one more disastrous ingredient. After Belisarius' departure, there were 11 Roman generals in Italy, all of equal rank, with no commander-in-chief. Justinian's strategy to divide and rule in this way was presumably prompted by fears the Goths would repeat the imperial offer they made to Belisarius to one of his successors. So, better to keep them divided. In this, he succeeded. But the cost was a confused and incompetent Roman high command, as became immediately apparent in the Romans' first engagement with Totila's forces.

In the spring of 542, a Roman force of 12,000 men, led by the 11 generals, marched out of Ravenna to take the Gothic-held Verona. A local inhabitant bribed some of the Goths guarding the walls to let a small Roman advance party into the city, who opened the southern gates. The Gothic garrison fled, but they returned when they discovered the main Roman army had stopped a few miles from the city, with the 11 different commanders arguing over how to divide the plunder they expected to take from the city. The Goths locked the gates and the Roman advance guard had to jump from the walls, many of them to their deaths.

Meanwhile, Totila had been shadowing the Roman army

with a force of 5,000 Goths. At Faenza, he offered battle. He outmanoeuvred the larger Roman force, which lacked cohesion, by sending 300 cavalry to attack the Romans in the rear. The Romans panicked and fled in different directions following their various generals. The same happened outside Florence, which Totila's army was besieging. A Roman relief force, including John, Belisarius' previously insubordinate general, as well as some of the other generals, attacked the Goths. Procopius says John's forces attacked first and were doing well until one of his guards was killed right next to him. This caused a panic among John's men who thought John himself had been killed. They retreated, and the sight of this confusion caused the other Roman generals to retreat. The Goths sallied forth in pursuit and the retreat turned into a rout in which many Romans were killed.

The demoralised Roman army dispersed under its various generals to garrison the towns Belisarius had occupied, hoping reinforcements would arrive from the east. This break-up of the Roman army made Totila's offensive easier since he could pick the Roman garrisons off one by one. He marched south, taking the Roman strongholds individually, sometimes by offering generous terms to the defenders who had often not been paid and were willing to join the Goths. Totila was not just a good soldier, he was also a clever diplomat. Generosity and restraint became the hallmark of his campaign of reconquest. He stopped his soldiers from looting and treated the Italian inhabitants well. Belisarius himself could not have done it better.

He bypassed Rome and brought most of Southern Italy back under Gothic control. The only real resistance the Romans offered was at Naples, just as Belisarius had experienced. He besieged it for several months before it too fell in the spring of 543. For once, Totila exacted revenge not on its inhabitants, to whom he was conspicuously lenient, but on its governor, who had delighted in shouting personal insults to Totila from the walls. He cut out his tongue and chopped off his hands.

Totila undid nearly all of Belisarius' Italian conquests in less than two years. It was now up to Belisarius to restore the situation.

49

The Lost Years

In early 544, Belisarius returned to Italy to find a rapidly deteriorating situation there. Procopius tells us that the Roman army was not only retreating from the Goths, but it had lost its discipline and was now more of a menace to the Italian population than the Goths:

> *…the commanders of the Roman army together with the soldiers were plundering the possessions of their subjects, and they did not shrink from any act of insolence and licentiousness whatsoever: the officers were cavorting with mistresses inside the fortresses, while the soldiers, showing themselves more and more insubordinate to their commanders, were falling into every form of lawlessness.*[183]

Meanwhile, Procopius, who was no longer Belisarius' legal secretary, and was writing this last section of his long *History of the Wars* from the safety of Constantinople, seems to sympathise more with the Goths than the Romans. This is an interesting step in his own personal development, discernible in his writings, from being an admirer of Belisarius to one of general disillusionment with everyone in Justinian's government. For example, in contrast to the disorderly conduct of the Roman soldiers, he describes the Gothic king meting out punishment to a Gothic soldier accused of raping a young Italian maiden: '…he executed the man…and gave to the raped girl all the money that belonged to him'.[184]

It was now up to Belisarius to restore the situation. But the legendary soldier had one major problem. He had almost no soldiers. This was because there were none to spare for the Italian campaign. After the sack of Antioch in 540, the bulk of the Roman army was concentrated in the east to prevent another Persian incursion.

In Justinian's defence, it must be said the empire's overall position was made far worse by the plague that ravaged it in 541–543, as discussed in Chapter 45. Tax revenues had probably at least halved. Indeed, it's astonishing Belisarius agreed to go to Italy at all. In the *Wars*, Procopius says Justinian gave him some money, but in his more honest *The Secret History*, he tells us Belisarius promised the emperor: '… he would never ask him for money during the campaign but would himself pay for all the necessary equipment out of his own pocket'.[185] It was an extraordinarily generous offer from Belisarius, even if he was reputed to have enormous wealth. The only explanation can be his wish to restore good relations with Justinian after falling out with him so badly in 543.

But not even Belisarius' wealth could finance an entire field army. And that was what was needed in Italy. Considering this, it's hard to see what Justinian expected Belisarius to do. He recruited and trained 4,000 troops in Thrace but this was hardly going to make a dent in the Gothic recovery. He led the small force to Salona on the Adriatic coast to cross to Ravenna which was still in Roman hands. When he got there, he found an almost impossible military situation. The Goths were in control of most of Italy with the Romans only holding onto a handful of fortified towns, including the principal cities of Ravenna and Rome. He resorted to playing a game of cat and mouse, trying to stem the Gothic reconquest by strengthening the garrisons of the places being besieged.

Meanwhile, Totila was forcing the Roman strongholds to capitulate one by one. Belisarius stopped him from taking Bologna and Osimo but couldn't launch any sort of counterattack. In desperation, he despatched John, the commander who had been insubordinate in his first campaign, to Constantinople to beg Justinian for reinforcements. Procopius tells us[186] Belisarius complained that even those troops bravely holding out in Italy were not being paid. John was an unexpected choice for Belisarius since the two had been at loggerheads in the first Italian campaign. However, in *The Secret History*, Procopius explains a sub-plot existed with John sweet-talking Belisarius to get him on his side to further his chances of marrying the daughter of Germanus, Justinian's cousin.

In short, John achieved nothing in Constantinople to help Belisarius, although he did achieve his personal objective aim of marrying Germanus' daughter. Meanwhile, back in Italy, Totila was winning the war. He took a series of Roman fortified towns in 544 and 545, including Spoleto, Assisi, Firmum, Asculum, Clusum and Auximum. By the end of 545, he was ready to attack Rome itself. Control of the eternal city now took centre stage in the contest between Totila and Belisarius. The latter put 3,000 of his best troops into the city, determined to hold it at all costs. But landlocked Rome was always vulnerable to being starved into surrender and, although the Romans still held onto its port, Portus, which could get some provisions into the city from the sea, soon the garrison's supplies ran dangerously low.

Belisarius repeatedly tried to break through the Gothic defences to relieve the city, but to no avail. Finally, always the master of ingenuity, he came up with a daring plan. He put the entire cargo of grain from a large Sicilian grain fleet into 200 river transports. The idea was to sail these 15 miles up the River Tiber and into Rome. Opposing them were a series of obstacles: Gothic forces on the riverbank, a great iron chain laid across the river and, most terrifying of all, a fortified bridge with Gothic bowmen ready to shoot at anything that moved underneath.

But Belisarius relished challenges like this. He put together a commando-style raid. First, he armoured his transport ships with wooden panels punctuated with holes to shoot through so that his men could pick off the Goths on the riverbanks. Then to deal with the fortified bridge, he constructed a sort of fire ship by lashing transports together and placing on them a tower as tall as the bridge and loading it with flammable material.

Belisarius personally led the Roman attack force upriver. Everything went well. His archers cleared the riverbanks. His soldiers sortied out from the transport ships and dragged the great chain away. Then, most amazingly, his strategy with the fortified bridge worked. When his 'fire ship' made contact with it, the Romans lit it and it exploded into flame, killing 200 Goths inside, including, Procopius tells us, a highly regarded Gothic commander, Osda.

The Goths fell back, astonished by the ferocity of Belisarius' attack. But then disaster struck. Roman horsemen arrived saying Portus was under attack by the Goths and the Roman commander, Isaac, had been captured. This was true but in fact Portus wasn't in danger of being occupied and its defenders had beaten off the Gothic attack. However, according to Procopius, Belisarius panicked because his wife, Antonina, was in Portus. Procopius criticised Belisarius for being overprotective towards his wife. Fearing for her safety, he called off the attack, and the boats returned home. Defeat was snatched from the jaws of victory. But worse than that, Procopius says Belisarius' distress was such that he had a fit of aphasia, meaning he temporarily lost the ability to talk, something that sometimes happens when someone has a stroke. He returned to Portus to find his wife was safe, but even so, he fell ill with a fever, which Procopius says nearly killed him.

As Procopius repeats frequently, fate was against Belisarius in his second Italian campaign. Things went from bad to worse. On 17 December 546, almost exactly ten years after Belisarius had captured Rome, the city fell to Totila. The Gothic king bribed a group of Isaurian soldiers to open the Asinarian gate. He let the Roman garrison exit by the opposite gate, and in much the same way that Belisarius had first taken Rome without bloodshed, so Totila retook it with, according to Procopius, the deaths of only 26 soldiers and 60 civilians.

But the Goths' reconquest of Rome was not the prelude to their recovery of Italy. It was not even a turning point in the war. Totila felt he didn't have enough troops to defend the city so he considered burning it to the ground. According to Procopius, when Belisarius recovered from his illness, he sent a message to Totila begging him to spare it, saying: 'Among all the cities under the sun, Rome is agreed to be the greatest and most noteworthy.'[187] Totila relented, but he demolished about a third of the walls and removed the city gates to make it indefensible if the Romans reoccupied it.

Knowing his resources were limited, Totila was desperate to make peace. With Rome back in Gothic hands, he thought he might use it as a bargaining chip. He sent Pelagius, a papal deacon, to Constantinople to ask for the restitution of the old peace between Goths and Romans, such as had existed in the days of Theodoric and Anastasius. According to Procopius, Justinian was not interested. He said Totila should negotiate with Belisarius, reiterating the same faith he had in his general as in the old days: '[he said] he had made Belisarius supreme commander in the war and that he, then, had full power to make any settlement with Totila that he wished'.[188]

But Justinian's support for Belisarius didn't extend to sending him reinforcements. So, the increasingly ridiculous war of cat and mouse between the Romans and Goths continued for another two years. If Belisarius was short of troops, so too was Totila. He didn't have enough to defend Rome which was largely deserted by now, with only a few hundred inhabitants. In April 547, Belisarius, who had fully recovered from his stroke, walked straight back into the city through its undefended gates. It must have seemed like a ghost town. But holding Rome at least carried some kudos. And Totila, criticised by his nobles for letting Rome be recaptured, was stung into action. He led his army south to retake the city but Belisarius, in his most valiant encounter of his whole second Italian campaign, used his horse archers to shoot down the Gothic cavalry. Procopius described the defeated Goths retreating to camp, peppered with arrows stuck in their shields and embedded in their bodies.[189]

Belisarius' heroism allowed him to hold onto Rome but there was no hope of defeating the Goths. He begged Justinian for reinforcements but the few soldiers he sent to Italy weren't remotely sufficient to mount a proper campaign. In desperation, he sent Antonina to Constantinople to use her influence with Theodora. But when she arrived in early July 548, she found Justinian and the court in mourning. Theodora had died on June 28 548, at around the age of 48, probably from cancer. This must have been an enormous blow to Justinian. Theodora had been the love of his life. He never remarried or took a mistress that we know of. Instead, his life became even more austere. He was increasingly withdrawn and devoted himself to religion, probably hoping to win back the divine favour he seemed to have lost. Antonina had also lost her most powerful friend. There was nothing more she could do to help her husband. The days of the fab four were over.

Meanwhile, back in Italy, things went from bad to worse for Belisarius. He left Rome to join reinforcements arriving in Taranto in Southern Italy. These were the most Justinian had sent him so far and included 2,000 horsemen from the Armenian field army. Taking 900 of his best men from Rome, including 700 horse archers, he set sail from Rome rather than risk the arduous march overland. But a storm blew his ships off-course to land at Crotone, where they were ambushed by the Goths. His 700 horse archers were killed almost to a man. This had a devastating effect on Belisarius. For once, his morale was broken. He wrote to Justinian, asking to be relieved of his command. In the winter of 548–9, he was on the boat back to Constantinople. It was the end of his career as a general. But it would not be the last of Belisarius.

50

War with the Berbers

Why was Belisarius deprived of the resources needed to defeat Totila in his second Italian campaign?

A host of reasons come to mind. The state's coffers were clearly empty, drained by the wars of reconquest, Justinian's grandiose building programme and the dire consequences of the plague. The Roman army was also overstretched, fighting on three fronts – Persia, Italy and the Danube. But there was another reason seldom mentioned in histories of this time. This was the existence of a fourth front in Africa. For after Belisarius' quick victory over the Vandals, there was an important but largely forgotten war, that raged from 534 to 548, against the Berbers.

Back in the 520s, when the Vandals ruled North Africa, the Berber tribes had started to become stronger. Historians[190] have speculated whether this was because the Vandal military presence guarding the borders was less effective than that of the old Roman garrison troops – the *limitanei*. Another school of thought is that the Vandals paid them too much gold to keep quiet, enriching some Berber groups who then sought to extend their dominion over poorer tribes, thereby encouraging a process of tribal consolidation which created larger and more dangerous Berber groups. Whatever the reasons, Berber power was growing and, in around 530, they inflicted a defeat on Hilderic which cost him the throne and kick-started the entire process of Roman intervention.

When Belisarius invaded, the Berbers stood on the sidelines, waiting to see who won. After he left, they wanted to test the strength of the new Roman administration. As Belisarius sailed for Constantinople in the summer of 534, the new Praetorian Prefect, Solomon, suddenly faced a substantial escalation in Berber raiding. Four Berber tribes formed a coalition and started to raid the civilised province of Byzacena.

Since Procopius was there with Solomon, before joining Belisarius in Italy, we have an excellent first-hand account of the first two years of the Berber war, which I will summarise. It began with Solomon sending 500 of the elite Roman horse archers to patrol the border land, under the command of two of Belisarius' most respected commanders, Aigan and Rufinus, who had distinguished themselves in the Vandal war. But Procopius[191] tells us that after they ambushed a Berber raiding party in a narrow mountain pass, they were themselves trapped in the mountain by thousands of Berbers. After shooting many of them down, they ran out of arrows and were overwhelmed. Aigan and Rufinus were both killed, and according to Procopius, one of the Berber chieftains sent Rufinus' head to his wife in triumph.

Solomon acted decisively, marching the Roman army of occupation out of Carthage and into the African interior. This was essentially the same army as Belisarius' expeditionary force, less those with Belisarius in Sicily and those occupying Sardinia, Gibraltar and other Vandal strongholds. There, he came up against the Berber confederation's main army which numbered tens of thousands, and could according to Procopius, put 50,000 warriors into the field. The Berbers were lightly armed and should have been easy prey for the Romans but they had enormous numbers of camels which scared the Roman horses.

The Berbers surrounded their encampment with camels, 12 deep, to serve as a horse deterrent since horses were scared of them. A Roman cavalry charge against the camels broke up with the horses plunging and rearing. So, Solomon came up with a new plan of attack. He ordered his infantry to assault the camp to distract the Berbers, while his horsemen dismounted and went to the back of the Berber camel circle where they attacked the unfortunate animals, and slaughtered so many they broke through into the Berber camp. Attacked on both sides, the Berbers fled, leaving 10,000 dead on the battlefield according to Procopius, and allowing the Romans to take captive most of the women and children and a huge number of camels.

But the war was far from over. When Solomon returned in triumph to Carthage, he heard the Berbers had summoned every warrior and formed an even larger army to raid the land around Carthage. So, he gathered his troops again and marched back into the African interior to Mount Bourgaon where the enemy was camped. Procopius says the Berbers were now too afraid to meet the Romans in battle on the open plain, but they were confident they could repel any attacks on their positions halfway up this mountainous peak.

The result was a stand-off with the Romans not wanting to fight their way uphill.

But Solomon, showing resourcefulness worthy of Belisarius himself, sent 1,000 infantry who were good at rock climbing, up the eastern side of the mountain at night which the Berbers had left undefended. The next morning, these men raised their standards, blew their horns and showered arrows down on the Berbers while the rest of the Roman army advanced uphill. The result was complete panic on the part of the Berbers who tried to flee into a gorge so thick with dead horses and men most of them couldn't escape. Procopius[192] tells us 50,000 died for not one dead Roman. So many prisoners were taken that a Berber boy would sell for the price of a sheep in the Carthage slave market.

But despite this decisive victory, it was still not the end of the campaign. One of the Berber chieftains, named Iaudas, was still raiding Roman territory. Confronted by a Roman general named Althias, Iaudas offered him single combat and was nearly killed but fled into the Aures plateau, a rugged mountainous region in the foothills of the Atlas Mountains. Solomon pursued him there with some Berber allies, but after weeks of marching around in the scorching sun, he achieved nothing and withdrew as he was increasingly worried his so-called allies were leading him into a trap.

After this, the Roman army of occupation mutinied, as described in Chapter 34. In addition, Procopius left Africa to join Belisarius' Italian campaign. The loss of our only reliable eyewitness means the Berber war was thereafter poorly recorded. This lack of source material has led some historians to largely ignore it. This is a mistake since I contend that, in the 540s, the war intensified, pinning down large numbers of Roman troops, and diverting them from other fronts where they were desperately needed, like Italy. In 544, Solomon was killed and his army defeated, apparently overwhelmed by superior numbers of Berbers. It's hard to know why the Roman army lost control in these years but it could have been due to a rebellion by a general, Guntharis, who seems to have tried to seize power, leading to a civil war, only to be murdered.

Matters improved dramatically for the Romans in 546 when an experienced soldier, John Troglita, who had been part of Belisarius' invasion force in 533, was made *magister militum* for North Africa. In 548, he inflicted an overwhelming defeat on a huge Berber army on the Plains of Cato. Seventeen Berber chieftains were killed, and the Berbers never again posed a critical threat to the Romans. Procopius tells us: 'Thus it came to pass that the Libyans who survived, few as they were in number and extremely poor, at long last and just barely managed to find some peace.'[193]

It had taken 15 years to achieve peace in North Africa after Belisarius destroyed the Vandal kingdom in less than a year. The need to divert troops there in the 540s was one of the reasons Belisarius did not have the resources to defeat Totila. North Africa was not the pot of gold Justinian initially thought.

51

Expect the Unexpected

The second half of Justinian's reign was not just deeply troubled, it was catastrophic.

Famine and plague killed a significant proportion of the eastern Roman population, especially in the cities. Persia resumed hostilities. Antioch was sacked. New enemies appeared on the neglected Danube front and wrought havoc in Illyria and Thrace. War dragged on in Africa for nearly 15 years after Belisarius' victory over the Vandals. Meanwhile, in Italy, the Gothic king Totila undid almost all of Belisarius' conquests. Belisarius himself was so disillusioned by 549 that he asked to be relieved of his command. Rome's best general was gone, and, as Procopius put it: 'At this point in the war, the barbarians became unquestionably masters of the whole West.'[194]

But as always in history, expect the unexpected. As Justinian's empire seemed to teeter on the brink of collapse, it still had the capacity to surprise.

So, let's rejoin our narrative where we left off, with Belisarius sailing back to Constantinople for the last time. With the news of his departure, Totila's hopes of restoring the Ostrogothic kingdom of Italy rose, and he advanced for the third time to the walls of Rome. But Belisarius had left the former capital of the Roman Empire well defended, with 3,000 of his best troops under the command of one of his most capable lieutenants, Diogenes. The Goths' attempts to storm the walls were beaten off and Totila resigned himself to a long blockade. Finally, in January 550, just as had happened in his last siege of the city, it was a group of treacherous Isaurians who opened the city gates – discontented because they had not been paid for years and remembering the large rewards Totila had given those who opened them last time.

The Roman defenders fled the city, including their commander, Diogenes, except for 400 of Belisarius' elite horse archers who chose to stay and fight. They occupied the fortress that had been constructed out of Hadrian's Mausoleum (later developed in the Middle Ages into the Castel Sant'Angelo). For two days, they resisted the entire Gothic army. But they had no food. They thought of eating their horses but could not bring themselves to kill their faithful companions. So, instead, they decided on a heroic death. They would ride out to meet the Goths and die together in battle.

But as these brave men were embracing each other and saying their last farewells, Totila was watching them and realised their plan. Thinking that, as Procopius says, these fierce warriors '…intent on death and with no hope for safety would inflict irreparable harm upon the Goths',[195] he quickly sent messengers to them offering unbelievably generous terms. If they took an oath never to fight the Goths again, he promised to let them go free with their horses and possessions and either pay for their transport to Constantinople, or allow them to join the Gothic army on completely equal terms with the Gothic warriors. Belisarius' men were astonished by this and signalled they would accept. Totila was true to his word. Although the Romans said they wanted to be reunited with their wives and children, they feared retribution from the emperor, and almost all of them joined the Goths. Yet again, Justinian's incompetent financial management had backfired on him.

Totila sent an envoy to Justinian offering a peace treaty with the Goths keeping most of Italy. This was in effect asking the emperor to recognise Gothic victory. Justinian felt too insulted to even see him. But he was in a quandary. He and Belisarius had clearly fallen out over the lack of resourcing for the Italian campaign. Either Belisarius had refused to have anything more to do with Justinian's government or the emperor had sacked him. The answer was probably a bit of both. But who to appoint to succeed Belisarius? And what to do about Italy? Justinian was indecisive. First, he selected Germanus, his cousin, but then for reasons that have never become clear, he chose Liberius, a Roman senator. Meanwhile, Totila took advantage of Justinian's hesitation. He conquered what remained of Southern Italy still in Roman hands, taking Rhegium (modern Regio Calabria), on the coast opposite Sicily, in May 550. Then he crossed over to Sicily itself and, not showing the restraint extended to Italian inhabitants on the mainland, he began a campaign of retribution against the Sicilians for the help they had given Belisarius 15 years before. The war in Italy had reached its lowest point. It looked as if the Goths would now triumph.

But as mentioned earlier, always expect the unexpected.

We have reached a pivotal moment in the Italian war. For five years, Belisarius had been denied the resources to fight. Procopius summed it up neatly: 'The emperor Justinian had indeed conducted this war negligently in the past, but he made the most notable preparation for it at last.'[196] Having let down his best general for five years, Justinian began to allocate troops back to the Italian front.

So, what had changed?

I suggest three things. First, Justinian was confronted with the genuine possibility of complete defeat in Italy and the loss of all of Belisarius' conquests. This would have been an utter humiliation. Second, fighting on the eastern front with Persia had eased. We will cover this in Chapter 54 but suffice to say fighting in Mesopotamia had ceased in 545 when Justinian had agreed another costly peace with Chosroes in this region although the Romans and Persians continued to fight over Lazica. Third is a subject about which we have very little information but which I suspect was hugely important: the population and economy had started to recover from the devastation of the plague.

Although historians still have a wide range of opinions about the scale of loss caused by the Justinianic plague, as we discussed in Chapter 45, I suggest its similarity to the fourteenth-century European Black Death, suggests it was a truly seismic event, causing tax revenues to fall by over a half and a severe manpower shortage. This was one of the main reasons why Belisarius failed in Italy. Not even his military genius could win a war with only a handful of unpaid troops.

In contrast, by 550, the economic and demographic situation was much improved. The treasury's coffers were fuller. Young men who had been children when the plague struck were now of fighting age. The Roman army was once again able to recruit soldiers in adequate numbers.

However, victory was delayed by some unfortunate events. Justinian's indecisiveness led to confusion about who would replace Belisarius. At first, Justinian chose his cousin, Germanus, but then replaced him with Liberius, only to reinstate Germanus. Germanus was in a powerful position. He had crushed Stotza's revolt in North Africa in 537, and despite his rather embarrassing exit from Antioch in 540 when he fled before the Persian army, he was widely regarded as capable and the probable heir to the throne. Theodora's death in 548 also improved his prospects since she had taken a strong disliking to him. But this was no longer a concern.

However, we all know random events can play a decisive role in history. Just as Germanus was mustering a large army in Illyria, ready to invade Italy from the east, he died. The cause of death has never been identified. The best we have is Procopius' comment that: 'By some chance he fell sick and abruptly reached the term of his life.'[197] He was probably around 45 years old. This was a serious blow to Justinian's plans. Added to it were fairly continual invasions by the newly arrived Slav tribes and Kutrigur Huns north of the Danube. Troops were continually being diverted to meet their attacks which formed a much greater menace to the empire than did the Goths. We will cover this in Chapter 53. With Germanus dead, John, Belisarius' former insubordinate officer, took temporary command of the western armies. But he wasn't regarded as suitable to be Belisarius' long-term successor, probably because his arrogance had earned him too many enemies. Instead, Justinian made an unexpected choice. This was Narses, his chief minister and a eunuch, who had, like John, fallen out with Belisarius previously. What made it especially surprising was that Narses was not a soldier. He was instead an excellent politician and administrator. This meant almost everyone liked him except of course the now discredited Belisarius. John, in particular, was a close friend, and his appointment was almost certainly the result of his lobbying.

Meanwhile, Totila, now aware the Romans were mustering their forces, did his best to seize control of all of Italy. Only a handful of fortresses remained in Roman hands. Ravenna and Ancona, both on the Adriatic coast, were the principal ones. He focused on Ancona and used the Gothic fleet to blockade the port. But John sailed from Salona on the Dalmatian coast to relieve the city. Ships from Ravenna joined him so that a Roman fleet of 50 warships faced 47 Gothic ones. In the autumn of 551, near the coastal village of Sena Gallica, the Goths intercepted the Romans but their maritime skills were completely inadequate compared with those of the Romans whose ships were manned by skilled Greek sailors. The Roman ships sailed through the Gothic formation, as soldiers raked the Gothic boats with arrows, boarded them and set them on fire. Thirty-six Gothic vessels were sent to the bottom with a great number of Gothic warriors, including, Procopius tells us, many of their best. It was a spectacular victory and a severe blow to Gothic resources and morale.

In the spring of 552, Narses was at last ready to march against the Goths. Justinian had opened the purse strings and the largest Roman army in his entire reign had been put together. The core of it was the regular Roman horse archers and heavy infantry, taken from across the Roman frontiers, especially from nearby Thrace and Illyria, but it also included units from Armenia to Mesopotamia and maybe some reinforcements from North Africa. Perhaps there were some 15,000 to 20,000 Roman regulars. In addition, there was a very significant auxiliary force, comprising 5,500 Lombards, 3,000 Heruli, 400 Gepids and contingents of Huns. There was also a regiment of Persian deserters. In total, there were probably some 30,000 troops, more than twice the number Belisarius took to Carthage and four times the number he originally took to Italy. If these resources had been given to him, we can only guess what might have happened. Perhaps Justinian's empire would have stretched to Gaul.

<h1 style="text-align:center">52</h1>

A Sort of Victory

Narses advanced to the top of the Adriatic and then down to Ravenna which he reached by 6 June. He hugged the coast to avoid the Franks who had occupied most of Northern Italy at the Goths' invitation. Meanwhile, Totila marched north to meet him. The two armies met at Busta Gallorum in the Apennine hills, about 40 miles west of Ancona.

Procopius has left us with a vivid account of the great battle derived from an eyewitness, since, unlike most of Belisarius' battles, he was not present. Totila delayed the battle by a day, in order to let Gothic reinforcements arrive, by arranging single combat between a Gothic and Roman champion. To the Romans' delight, the Goth was killed. Then to use up more time, he displayed his own equestrian skills, performing a ritualised horseback war dance the Goths had learned from the Huns, throwing a javelin in the air and catching it, as described in Chapter 48.

The next day, battle was joined. Narses positioned the Lombards and Heruli in the centre of the Roman army. On either flank, he positioned the Roman cavalry, almost all horse archers supported by 4,000 infantry archers. Although

Narses is credited with this battle formation, I suggest it was probably devised by John, by far the most experienced Roman general present, who had first-hand experience of Belisarius' tactics. Against this, Totila made a terrible mistake. Ignoring the Romans' archery skills, he instructed his soldiers to: '… use neither bows nor any other weapon in this battle except their spears'.[198] He placed his entire cavalry in the centre, with his infantry behind them. His aim was to smash the Roman formations with a massed frontal charge.

The result was the Gothic cavalry charge became like that of the Light Brigade in the Crimean War. Instead of cannon, they were raked by thousands of arrows. Horses and riders were shot down in their hundreds. Their charge lost its impact. The Lombards and Heruli held their line and the Roman cavalry closed in on the flanks. The Goths were forced back and finally fled, leaving 6,000 dead on the battlefield, and many more were killed as the Romans pursued them. According to Procopius, Totila was killed as he fled. His bodyguards buried him at a distance from the battlefield in an unmarked grave. However, an old woman was watching and when she told the Romans, they dug him up to make sure the king of the Goths was truly dead.

It was a glorious Roman victory, as worthy as any of those of Belisarius. But the war wasn't over yet. One of Totila's commanders, Teias, was raised on a shield and proclaimed king. Deciding that a glorious death was better than surrender, he executed all the senators Totila had taken hostage and slaughtered 300 boys from senatorial families. There would be no redemption after this. It was now war to the death. He hoped to persuade the Franks to join the

Goths in a Germanic crusade against the Romans, but they did nothing more than extend their occupation of the Po Valley at the Goths' expense.

Meanwhile, Narses advanced on Rome. The Goths made a stand in the fortress that used to be Hadrian's Mausoleum, just as Belisarius' horsemen had done two years before. But to no avail. Surrounded and cut off, they rapidly surrendered on condition their lives would be spared, and for the fifth and final time during this long war, Rome was captured.

Attention now shifted to the coastal fortress of Cumae in Campania in southern Italy, near to Naples, where the Goths had stored their treasure. Teias hoped to use this to bribe the Franks to come to his help. But first he had to defend it from Narses' advancing armies. Narses' advance through Central Italy was relatively easy since many of the supposedly Gothic garrisons in the principal towns were actually former Roman soldiers willing to rejoin the army. Narses copied Belisarius' policy of generously waiving any punishment and welcoming them back to the Roman colours which they did almost to a man.

Teias also led his Gothic warriors towards Cumae and the two armies met at the base of Mount Vesuvius. They opposed each other across the river Draco (the modern Sarno) for nearly two months through September and October 552 without engaging. But in the end, the Roman navy cut off their supplies from the sea and, as Procopius says: 'The Goths were driven to be courageous through despair.'[199] Teias led them en masse towards the Roman lines at Mons Lactaris, literally Milk Mountain in Latin, in the foothills of Mount Vesuvius.

The Goths left their horses behind and advanced on foot to meet the Romans. Teias exhibited the bravery expected of a Gothic king. He led his men at the front, holding up his shield to ward off the Roman javelins. However, once the Romans realised who he was, he became the target for every Roman lancer and javelin thrower. Twelve Roman javelins quickly pierced his shield, making it so heavy, he called to his shield bearer for a replacement. Just as he was transferring shields, and for a moment exposed his chest, a 13th javelin pierced through his chest, killing him instantly. The Romans rushed to cut his head off and put it on a pole to intimidate the Goths.

But the Goths would not give up. They fought until nightfall, and, according to Procopius, the next day they lined up at dawn: '…with the fury of wild beasts… knowing they were fighting their last battle'.[200]

Having fought off the Romans for another day, they sent a delegation to Narses asking for peace and permission to travel north of the Alps as free men on the promise they would never invade Roman lands again. Procopius says Narses wanted to crush them completely, but it was John who argued the Goths should be spared, saying: 'Victory is enough for the wise. To want more might be a mistake.'[201]

Thus ended the Gothic war. It had taken 16 years to conclude after Belisarius had first taken Rome in 536. But even now peace wasn't restored in Italy. The Goths were defeated but in 553, a huge Frankish army invaded Italy from the north. This was the one Teias had hoped would save him. Led by two brothers, Butilinus and Leutharis, it mainly comprised Alemanni, who had been conquered by the

Franks. Unlike the Franks, these Germans were still pagan and had no scruples about pillaging and raping everywhere they went. By this time, Procopius had ceased writing his history. Instead, we have a detailed account from the pen of the Greek historian, Agathias. Yet again, the poor Italian population was subjected to brutal treatment as the Franks and Germans advanced down the entire length of Italy even reaching the Straits of Messina. The larger towns and cities held out, but Narses could only pin down one half of the invaders at Capua.

There, in October 554, the Roman army achieved one of its greatest victories. Things began inauspiciously, when the Heruli auxiliaries deserted the Romans because Narses had executed their commander for killing a servant. However, the new Heruli leader promised Narses he would return and Narses left a gap in the Roman front line ready for them. Heruli deserters rushed to the Frankish leader, Butilinus, and persuaded him to attack immediately, heading for this gap.

The Franks and Alemanni, numbering about 30,000 according to Agathias, streamed towards the Roman lines, where they were met by Roman heavy infantry in the centre and thousands of horse archers on both flanks. In a textbook repeat of one of Belisarius' battles, the barbarians' supposed advantage was turned to disadvantage. Advancing into the gap left by the Heruli, they were contained by the Roman heavy infantry on either side and then surrounded by the horse archers who attacked from the rear. It was carnage. Agathias says only five of 30,000 Franks and Alemanni survived. Butilinus was killed. Roman casualties were minor.

Although most historians ascribe this – and the other victories over the Goths – to Narses, I disagree. Narses was a politician in Justinian's court, not a soldier. I suspect the chief architect of Narses' victories was in fact John, Belisarius' insubordinate commander who'd caused so much trouble in his first Italian campaign but was also a ruthlessly efficient soldier who'd learned his trade from Belisarius.

Meanwhile, the rest of the Frankish force, led by Leutharis, retreated to the Po Valley where they became the victim of disease, probably malaria, such as had destroyed Frankish armies in the past. Agathias delights in telling us that Leutharis developed insane fits and died miserably.[202]

At long last, Italy was at peace.

But at what cost?

Italy was left a wreck. Its population had probably fallen by well over 50 per cent. In the city of Rome, it was far worse. The Goths had cut its magnificent aqueducts in the first siege of the city. They were never restored. Its inhabitants had to draw water from the Tiber or from wells. The excellent supply of pure running water, which had distinguished the city as a place of luxury, replete with its astonishing baths, was gone. For example, the Baths of Caracalla, which were still in use up to this point, were abandoned, the many statues there only to be rediscovered again in the Renaissance. It must have been a peculiar experience to walk through its great public buildings, its enormous forums, all of them empty and desolate. Perhaps its poorer and less educated inhabitants stared up into the lofty arches of the Colosseum and wondered who had created this.

Procopius is at least conspicuously clear on this point. For him, victory in Italy was the hollowest of all Justinian's achievements. Even in the *Wars*, he's not afraid to describe how Justinian's Italian wars were a disaster for the Italian population and the Roman senate: 'This victory turned out to be for the Roman senate and people a cause of far greater destruction.'[203]

In 554, Justinian issued an edict known as the 'Pragmatic Sanction' setting out the future rule of Italy. All laws and tax requirements would in future be decided in Constantinople and not in Rome. The senate, or what little was left of it, was stripped of all its powers. Any idea of a western emperor was firmly banished. Only one person was deemed worthy of respect. This was the bishop of Rome, better known as the Pope. Henceforth, he was to be the spokesman for the city and 'all known inhabitants of the west'[204] subject of course to the authority of the emperor in Constantinople.

It stands as one of history's greatest ironies that Italy, and Rome in particular, the former heart of the Roman Empire, suffered far greater destruction in Justinian's wars of reconquest than they ever did under barbarian rule.

53

The Wolves from the North

Going back to the days of classical Rome, the Danube had always been one of its three most important frontiers alongside the Rhine and Mesopotamia. For example, in the third century AD, the emperor Decius died fighting the Goths who broke through the Danube defences to plunder the Balkans. In the 440s, Attila's empire north of the Danube posed the greatest threat to the eastern empire since the Battle of Adrianople in 378. As discussed in Chapter 3, this proved to be a turning point. For the eastern Roman army was expanded and reorganised, with two praesental field armies added to its existing three field armies – two of which were already in the Balkans (the Illyrian and Thracian). This meant that in effect four out of the five field armies were defending the Danube.

As discussed in previous chapters, we have no record of what happened to the praesental field armies in Justinian's reign. It seems fairly certain they were simply sent wherever they were needed. First, they fought with the army of the east, and then they were sent to North Africa and Italy. They were integrated into Justinian's new military organisation which developed out of his conquests. To the existing three field armies for Thrace, Illyria and the East, he added new ones for North Africa, Italy and Armenia. But Justinian was no Diocletian. He didn't increase the size of the army even if he increased the number of its field armies. Instead, an overstretched army was left to defend frontiers that required many more troops than were available. The result was disastrous. In 540, Chosroes sacked Antioch. What would happen on the Danube frontier was just as bad.

To understand the situation facing Rome along the Danube, we need to go back over half a century to the year 488 when the Ostrogoths left the Balkans for Italy, as discussed in Chapter 5. For many years, this stabilised the Balkans with two German tribes co-existing north of the Danube: the Gepids to the east and the Lombards to the west (occupying roughly modern Hungary and western Romania). To the east of the Gepids, and still with a toehold on the Danube delta joining the Black Sea, were the remnants of Attila's Huns, forming two groupings: the Kutrigur and Utigurs. Procopius says these nations were led by two Hunnic kings – Kutrigur and Utigur – hence their names. Another people, the Slavs, existed to the north of these in Central and Eastern Europe (modern Poland and Ukraine). The Slavs comprised many small, separate tribes, some of which were migrating south towards the Danube, where they became vassals of the Lombards and Gepids.

With this web of barbarian tribes north of the Danube, Roman diplomacy was simple: play the barbarians off against each other. Using bribes, the Romans allied first with the Gepids against the Lombards, and the Kutrigurs against the

Utigurs, and then reversed these when their allies became too powerful. This worked reasonably well while there was also a Roman army guarding the Danube frontier. But when the army was reduced, real trouble began. The first sign of this was in 539, when Justinian sent a significant detachment of troops from the Balkans to help Belisarius in Italy.

The result was a large Kutrigur raid across the Danube. As mentioned in Chapter 39, Procopius tells us this raid was devastating. The Kutrigur captured 32 fortified centres and carried home reportedly 120,000 prisoners. They even briefly crossed over to Asia Minor from the Chersonesus. This was like one of Attila's raids, albeit on a smaller scale. What stands out like a sore thumb is that there was no Roman field army to oppose the Kutrigurs. Although, unfortunately, for this period, we have no detailed records about the Roman army similar to those of the fifth-century *Notitia Dignitatum*, we can be fairly sure that most of it was in North Africa and Italy.

The Kutrigur raid of 539 stung Justinian into action, but not in the right direction. Instead of increasing the army so that it could defend the empire's extended frontiers, he just tried harder to play his enemies off against each other. So, he paid the other Hunnic group further east – the Utigurs – to attack their cousins. This policy worked for a time, but it still left the Balkan provinces exposed to another enemy – the Slavs.

Little is known about the origins of the Slavs who would play a significant role in European history. In ancient times, they inhabited the region located in modern Poland and Belorussia on the northern and eastern edges of the vast area known as ancient Germania. They migrated south towards the Danube when the Huns pushed the Germans out of this area.

In the early 530s, Procopius tells us Justinian appointed an able general, Chilboudius, *magister militum* of the Thracian field army. At first, he defended the Danube frontier well but in around 533, he was defeated and killed. The Slavs remained in the area north of the Danube and posed a continual threat to the Romans.

Procopius described them comprising many tribes who lived a basic life, believing in a god of lightning to whom they made sacrifices. In battle, they were poorly equipped 'the majority of them go against their enemy on foot carrying little shields and javelins in their hands but they never wear breastplates'.[205] They lived in: 'pitiful hovels', but they were tall and strong: '…they are all exceptionally tall and hardy men'.

The politics of the Slavs is obscure. Politically, the tribes were fragmented, and surprisingly democratic, according to Procopius: '…[they live] under a democracy, and consequently everything that involves their welfare, whether for good or ill, is a matter of common concern'.[206] They didn't have the centralised government of the German tribes or the Huns, and probably some paid allegiance to the Gepids, Lombards, Kutrigurs and Utigurs, and may have served in their armies.

However, worryingly for the Romans, it seems there was consolidation among the tribes so that by the late 540s, they were making larger and more effective raids. For example, when Justinian was building up his army in Illyria to fight Totila in 549, Procopius says there was a significant raid of 3,000 Slavs, which seems a relatively small number but which the Romans nevertheless found hard to contain. The Slavs avoided pitched battles and preferred ambushes and hit-and-run tactics.

Germanus was told to crush them, but his unexpected death meant the Romans did little. According to Procopius, the Slavs pillaged far and wide in Thrace. Trickery was their speciality. At the largest town they tried to take, Topirus in Thrace, Procopius says they tricked the garrison into coming out of the town thinking they were quite a small force, only to ambush them and take the town by storm, where they killed all the men and enslaved the women and children. According to Procopius, they were brutal in their treatment of captives and enjoyed impaling them: 'They killed their victims not with sword or spear, not in any familiar way, but by planting stakes very firmly in the earth, having made them extremely sharp, and, by impaling the poor wretches upon them with great force, drove the point of the stake between the buttocks and pushed it up into the intestines.'[207] Not even the Huns seem to have been as vicious.

In 552, as Narses was defeating the Goths, the Slavs struck again. This time, it may have been the Gepids who put them up to it, since Procopius tells us they charged the Slavs one gold coin per man to ferry them across the Danube.[208] The Roman defences were again inadequate. It was only Justinian's offer to pay the Gepids that stopped the Slav incursions. I cannot help thinking the Gepids had calculated they could double their money, first taking it from the Slavs, and then from the Romans.

But if the Slavs were making an unwelcome entry onto the Roman stage, even more significant events were taking place far away on the distant plains of Asia. In the second volume in this series, we discussed how in the fourth century AD a severe drought in Central Asia caused a group of Huns to migrate westward towards Europe, putting pressure on the German tribes to invade Roman territory to escape from this fierce new enemy. This triggered the fall of the western empire.

In the sixth century, it happened again. This time it wasn't the Huns but another group of steppe nomads called the Avars. The reason for their migration seems to have been the same: drought. Recent research by palaeoclimatologists[209] looking at millennia-old juniper tree-ring records suggest there was a severe drought on the eastern Asian steppes after the great cooling event of 536. This drove both the Avars and the Turks – the two main nomadic groups in Asia living around the Chinese borders – to migrate westwards (see Map 7). The Avars fled from the Turks who seem to have gained the upper hand between the two groups.

The first contact with Rome occurred in 558 when, according to the chronicler Menander Protector, the Avars sent a delegation to Justinian:

One Kandikh…was chosen to be the first envoy of the Avars, and when he came to the palace he told the emperor [Justinian] of the arrival of the greatest and most powerful of the tribes. The Avars were invincible and could easily crush and destroy all who stood in their path. The emperor should make an alliance with them and enjoy their efficient protection. But they would only be well disposed to the Roman state in exchange for the most valuable gifts, yearly payments, and very fertile lands to inhabit.[210]

Justinian's response was to pay the Avars tribute. According to Menander, unusually for him, he referred the matter to the senate in Constantinople. Perhaps he was aware of the growing resentment at the amount of money being paid to Rome's enemies. But no senators were brave enough to voice their disapproval. We don't know the amount of tribute he sent north but it was probably substantial. In the short term, and for Justinian's lifetime, it worked. The Avars conveniently subjugated both the Utigurs and Kutrigurs in 562 and stopped them from raiding Roman territory. Just before this, in 559, the Kutrigurs raided almost to the walls of Constantinople, and Justinian called Belisarius out of retirement to deal with them – which he did with extraordinary success, as we will cover in Chapter 56. But the Avars made sure this was never repeated. The Slavs and Gepids also fell under their control.

During Justinian's life, his alliance with the Avars appeared successful. But in reality he was only nurturing a problem for his successors. For, just as happened with the Huns, the Avars pushed the Germans into imperial territory, and were responsible for the Lombard invasion of Italy soon after Justinian's death. Thereafter they came to pose as great a threat to the Romans on their Danube front as Attila had done.

It is worth telling the story of the Avars' rise to power in brief. After Justinian's death, they defeated the easternmost Frankish king, Sigibert in 566. In 567, they helped the Lombards to defeat the Gepids, and the Lombard king Alboin made the skull of his Gepid counterpart, king Cunimund, into a drinking cup.[211] The Avars expanded into the space north of the Danube where the Gepids had been.

Seeing they were next on the Avar menu, the Lombards didn't want to stick around. Alboin knew it wouldn't be long before the Avars made his own skull into a drinking cup. In 568, the Lombards left the middle Danube, and similar to the Ostrogoths 80 years before, they headed en masse to Northern Italy. There they would shatter the frail Roman control of the region, undoing the Roman conquest for a second time (the first time was due to Totila).

Meanwhile, the Avars had become the dominant power in the Balkans. When Justinian's successor, Justin II, cancelled the Avar tribute, his successor, Tiberius II, had to reinstate it pretty quickly. Justinian's payment of tribute to the Avars may have worked temporarily in his own lifetime but in the longer term he only succeeded in strengthening an Avar kingdom that would pose a major threat to Roman security in the Balkans for the next century.

He had been feeding the wolves from the north, not pacifying them.

54

A Window on the Black Sea

Let us now turn our attention back to the Sasanians who were also the recipients of Justinian's tribute. In Chapter 46, we left the Persian Shah Chosroes before the walls of Edessa in 543. He couldn't take the town, and its inhabitants paid him 500 pounds of gold to go away. By this time, both the armies of Rome and Persia were weakened by the plague. Chosroes saw little more to gain in Mesopotamia now that Roman forces had been redirected there. In 545, he agreed to a five-year truce with Justinian in exchange for 2,000 pounds of gold and the loan of the physician, Tribounus, who had allegedly saved Justinian from the plague.

Two years later, Chosroes' attention returned to Lazica (modern Georgia in the Caucasus – see Map 4), where he'd secured the port of Petra as a window on the Black Sea. His aim was to build a fleet and perhaps to attack Constantinople itself. But according to Procopius, the timber he assembled to build the ships was torched by lightning but more likely by sabotage. Chosroes' ambitions were also undermined by the logistical difficulties of supplying a Persian army in a mountainous, densely wooded region.

In contrast, the Romans had much shorter supply lines and could invade with greater ease. The indigenous Lazi supported the Romans, and combined Roman-Lazi forces defeated the Persians in 548 and 549 and put Petra under siege. Chosroes devoted enormous resources to fighting the Romans in Lazica, but he was always at a logistical disadvantage. In 551, the Roman general Bessas, one of Belisarius' lieutenants and now in his seventies, besieged Petra. The Persian defenders fought back valiantly. Procopius[212] tells us they built wooden towers on top of the city's walls so they could drop incendiary bombs onto the Roman battering rams. But one day the Persians were unlucky, and a high wind blew the incendiary bombs onto the wooden structures, setting them alight. In the ensuing chaos, the Romans forced their way into the city. At last, Petra was back in Roman hands and Chosroes' window on the Black Sea had been firmly shut.

Chosroes made one last attempt to achieve his dream. In 556, according this time to Agathias now that Procopius had put down his pen, a huge Persian army of 60,000 advanced into Lazica. But yet again, the Romans repelled it. A Roman-Lazi force, led by Martinus, another of Belisarius' generals, prevented the Persians from advancing further than Phasis. The next year, Chosroes, now an old man, and increasingly preoccupied with the appearance of the Turks on Persia's north-eastern frontiers, agreed a peace with the equally aged Justinian. Despite the Roman victory in Lazica over superior Persian forces, Justinian yet again kowtowed to the Persian shah and bought peace by paying tribute. In 557, Chosroes demanded 400 pounds of gold per annum for five years. Justinian paid it up front, 2,000 pounds of gold, apparently thinking a one-off payment looked less like tribute than annual payments. In 562, this was renewed as a peace for 50 years, yet again with the Romans paying 400 pounds of gold a year. This time, the first seven years were paid up front.

Some historians regard Justinian's policy of paying tribute to the Persians and Avars as clever diplomacy. After all, didn't he secure peace at less cost than fighting a war? I think the opposite was true. Buying his enemies off was certainly cheaper and easier than defeating them in battle but it solved nothing in the longer term. The long-term solution was to increase the size of the army so it could defend the borders. Justinian completely failed to do this, as contemporaries, such as the chronicler Agathias, tell us:

> *The Roman armies had not in fact remained at the desired level attained by the earlier Emperors but had dwindled to a fraction of what they had been and were no longer adequate to the requirements of a vast empire. And whereas there should have been a total effective fighting force of six hundred and forty-five thousand men, the number had dropped during this period to barely one hundred and fifty thousand. Some of these, moreover, were stationed in Italy, others in Africa, others in Spain, others in Lazica, and others still in Alexandria and Egyptian Thebes.*[213]

Quite where Agathias got the figure of 645,000 from is unclear – presumably he was thinking of the Roman army as it had been in the time of Diocletian and Constantine – but most historians agree 150,000 was probably about the right size for the sixth-century Roman army before Justinian's conquests (see Chapter 3). The problem was that this needed to be increased to defend his enlarged empire. And Justinian failed to do this.

Instead of increasing the army, he paid both the Avars and Persians tribute. This simply passed military dominance to the empire's two major enemies and gravely weakened its longer-term security. In 626, 61 years after Justinian's death, Constantinople was faced with a combined siege by the Avars in the west and the Persians in the east. I suggest the origins of this catastrophe lay with Justinian.

55

The Secret in the Sands

Their long shadows walk together under the warm December sun.

The year is 1896, and the place is Egypt, about 120 miles south of Cairo, in the site of the ancient city of Oxyrhynchus. Two young English classical scholars, Grenfell and Hunt, are walking towards what appears to be a huge rubbish mound. Their faces are downcast. They have had little luck. Hoping to find papyri or artefacts that would throw light on the origins of Christianity, their search has been fruitless. The remains of the Roman buildings have been demolished for their stone. No treasures lie buried here. Oxyrhynchus is no Pompeii.

Then, almost in despair they try one last thing. Hiring local labour, they dig through the centuries of sands and debris to find out what lies at the heart of these strange mounds that surround this ancient city. What they discovered has added immensely to our understanding of antiquity. Buried under the sand were an estimated half a million papyri documents. Mostly in fragments, the two Englishmen collected the pieces and put them into boxes and sent them home.

Most of this book has so far been devoted to the political and military history of Justinian's reign. Although I have mentioned economic and social history, this has mostly been from a top-down view, based on what few insights chroniclers have left us. In this chapter, I would like to discuss the extraordinary archaeological treasure-trove in the form of papyri documents that was discovered at the turn of the last century by British and French archaeologists.

In the hundred and more years since Grenfell and Hunt's discovery, some of their papyri fragments have been painstakingly pieced back together. So far, only about 5,000 papyri, or 1 per cent of the total number, have been restored to a condition where they can be read. However, just these have provided us with some unknown works by Plato, the playwright Menander and the poet Pindar and many other less well-known ancient authors. Christian and Jewish texts are also abundant, with some of the earliest known copies of the Old and New Testaments.

Over 90 per cent comprise what appear to be mundane and dull everyday transactions such as legal petitions, court records, sales, leases, wills, accounts, inventories, codes, edicts, registers and private correspondence. But these are invaluable to the historian. And a great number relate to the sixth and seventh centuries AD. These provide us with a unique insight into the social and economic condition of Egypt in the age of Justinian.

So, what do they tell us?

The first point is society was dominated by the big landowners. They had estates cultivated by agricultural labourers, legally designated not as slaves but as *coloni adscripticii.* These were free men and women but ones who were essentially tied to the estates of the rich. They were paid for their labour, and in return paid rent for their board and lodging. The fragmentary papyri show some of them left to find a better life. Others lived beyond their means and fell into debt, whereupon the estate managers were ruthless in punishing and fining them.

It's worth mentioning at this point that Egypt was by far the wealthiest province in the eastern empire. Indeed, this had always been the case ever since it was annexed to the Roman Empire in the days of Julius Caesar. And in the age of Justinian, this was more true than ever before. Indeed, historians think nearly 40 per cent of all the eastern empire's tax revenues came from Egypt[214] as we will discuss in more detail in Chapter 57. The Nile region was one of the most fertile on the planet, providing a huge wheat harvest which supplied Constantinople. But Egypt's wealth extended far beyond just grain; it also exported textiles, papyrus, highly prized utensils and a menagerie of exotic animals such as camels and African birds.

The papyri from Oxyrhynchus, as well as from another site, Aphrodito, illustrate vividly the three-way conflict between the big landowners, peasants and the state. They tell us about both the rich and the poor. On the one hand, they throw light on a family that was one of the richest in the eastern empire, and on the other, on that of a small-town hero, a lawyer who devoted his career to protecting the poor against the rich.

Let's begin with the landowners. The Oxyrhynchus papyri provide copious information about a family called the Apions. They are a perfect example of the type of landed aristocracy that became powerful in the late Roman Empire in both east and west. Because of their wealth, they mostly lived in Constantinople and were absentee landlords. One member of the family was even elected to consul in 497. Their web of business activity was wide and prominent. For example, the emperor Anastasius appointed one of them – Flavius Apion – to supply the Roman army with grain during the Persian war of 502–506. He is mentioned by Procopius as being: 'an extremely efficient man of eminence among the patricians'.[215]

The Apion family seem to have fallen in and out of imperial favour. The Flavius Apion who supplied Anastasius' army was subsequently exiled so maybe he was guilty of embezzling government money? But he made his peace with Anastasius' successor, Justin, and even recanted his Monophysite beliefs in Justinian's reign, presumably to appease Justinian who was anti-Monophysite. His descendants continued their lively interaction with the Roman emperors until the family disappears from history in 626 when the Persians conquered Egypt.

Much scholarly ink has been spilled over what the relationship between the great landowners and state was really like. Did they co-operate or were they at loggerheads? In Chapter 9, we discussed how Anastasius fought the landowners for control of the tax system, appointing *vindices* to collect tax for the state rather than allowing the landowners to collect it on behalf of the state.

However, the papyri records suggest Egypt was rather different. There seems to have been more co-operation between the big landowners and the state. Indeed, the landowners still often collected tax from their estate workers to be sent to Constantinople in a practice termed *autopragia*. The landowners claimed this worked well. But a set of papyri documents discovered in the ancient settlement of Aphrodito suggests otherwise. They show the landowners were corrupt and exploited their workers, keeping much of the tax raised for themselves.

This is revealed in a fascinating set of papyri concerning the life of an Egyptian small-town lawyer, Dioscorus, originally born into a lowly peasant family but who, showing that social mobility existed at least for some, escaped the drudgery of agricultural life to gain an education and probably studied law in Alexandria. We are fortunate to have an extensive number of papyri fragments detailing his legal contracts, letters, accounts of proceedings and even poems written by him in his spare time (which one historian has commented were some of the worst poems he has ever read).[216] But Dioscorus was a better lawyer than poet, and he was also a very brave man. For he worked to protect the poor from the demands of the rich. In particular, he resisted some brutish landowners, named Theodosius and Julian, who he accused of pocketing the tax collected from the peasants.

His endeavours were rewarded when he even came into contact with Justinian himself. This occurred when he took one of his cases on appeal to Constantinople. The case was a truly nasty one of exploitation, even involving murder. The emperor listened to him and supported the humble lawyer. In 551, in response to a second trip by the indefatigable Dioscorus, Justinian wrote to the governor of Egypt praising the lawyer and ordering a full investigation into the matter. Our last papyri concerning Dioscorus show him, now an old man, still fighting the rich on behalf of the poor. Dioscorus was a local hero, a man who truly stood up for what he believed in. It is a very human story that has emerged from the Egyptian rubbish tips 1,500 years ago, but it also provides us with a vital insight into why the eastern empire survived and thrived while its western half collapsed.

The difference lay with taxation. The eastern Roman state had a very good tax system. It was not a 'feudal' state in which the rich landowners refused to pay tax to the central government. In contrast, in the fifth century, the western Roman government was unable to raise sufficient tax to maintain a standing army. Not only did it lose half its territory to barbarian invaders, but what remained in Italy and Africa was dominated by a selfish, blinkered senatorial elite who put their own wealth ahead of the interests of the state. Tax evasion was so ingrained in the minds of the Roman senators they even connived in the murder of the last emperor who tried to save the empire, Majorian, in 461.[217]

The eastern Roman state was different. This was partly because the rule of law was still respected. Men like Dioscorus lived in a society where corruption cases could still be taken to the emperor. Civilisation had survived. The question was for how much longer?

56

Three Hundred Heroes

Belisarius may have retired from public life in 548 but ten years later he still achieved one last triumph. He saved Constantinople from a Hunnic attack.

As discussed in Chapter 53, Justinian left the Danube front weakly defended. In late 558, a group of Huns, called the Kutrigurs led by Zabergan, crossed the river into the Balkans and defeated the Thracian field army under the command of the Roman general Sergios. By March 559, they had reached the Long Walls in Thrace, 20 miles from Constantinople itself. In panic, the aged Justinian turned to his old general to save the city. Our principal source is no longer Procopius, who probably died a few years earlier in around 555. Instead, Agathias provides us with a vivid description of Belisarius, now around 55 years old – no longer the dashing young general in his twenties who won the Battle of Dara – donning his armour and mustering an army to face the barbarians. He says he could only find 300 veterans to fight with him – although this might also be a poetic reference to the famous 300 Spartans who fought at Thermopylae – and so he recruited a large group of civilians to join him and gave them some basic military training. Repeating the tactics he used to defeat the Persians at Dara, nearly 30 years before, he got the citizens to dig a trench to attract a frontal assault by the Kutrigurs while he concealed his 300 veterans – all armoured horse archers – behind a hill.

The Kutrigurs fell into the trap. They sent an advance guard of 2,000 horsemen to probe this new Roman army. Seeing the infantry in their trench blocking their way, they charged them only to be attacked in the flank by the concealed veterans. Agathias says 400 of the Kutrigurs fell but not a single Roman. To add to the Kutrigurs' panic, Malalas adds Belisarius had ordered some citizens to cut down trees behind the trench and drag them around, blowing up a large cloud of dust, to make it look as if a much greater Roman army was moving up. This persuaded Zabergan to retreat all the way back to the Danube. Agathias praises Belisarius just as Procopius might have done: 'by this feat of arms, which was to be the last in his life, he [Belisarius] won as great a measure of glory as he had done by his earlier victories over the Vandals and the Goths'.[218]

This is our only mention of Belisarius after his recall from Italy apart from two brief incidents. One is an ecclesiastical record which mentions his involvement in negotiations in 552–3 to persuade Pope Vigilius to make concessions to the Monophysite Church. The other is ten years later in 562, when he was implicated in a plot against Justinian. This was an attempt to murder the emperor orchestrated by a banker who had some grudge (which has never been made clear). Belisarius' alleged involvement seems to have been unfounded. Our only source, Malalas, tells us that seven months after being stripped of his titles, Belisarius was reprieved and had his titles restored. He died two years later, in March 565. Justinian, then around 83 years old, survived him by only six months.

The albeit brief punishment meted out to Belisarius seems to have been the basis for a popular legend that he, the ever-loyal general, was betrayed and blinded by a vindictive emperor. There is no contemporary evidence for this whatsoever, but in the tenth century, it became a popular story in medieval Byzantium mentioned in a text called the *Patria of Constantinople*.[219] Its popularity spawned several literary and artistic works in the early modern period, from a medieval Greek story called the *Novel of Belisarius*, to an influential eighteenth-century French novel called *Belisaire*, written by Jean-François Marmontel. The famous painter, Jacques-Louis David (1748–1825), depicted Belisarius in old age, blind and a beggar, in a picture entitled *Belisarius Begging for Alms*. The sculptor, Jean-Baptiste Stouf (1742–1826), made a striking bust of Belisarius, again blind and emaciated (see Figure 5).

More recently, in the twentieth century, Robert Graves, author of the famous *I, Claudius* novels, wrote about Belisarius and Justinian in a historical novel called *Count Belisarius*, in which he portrayed the general as a loyal soldier tragically mistreated by the scheming Justinian. However, Graves is clear Justinian never actually blinded him.

Unfortunately, we will never know the full truth about the relationship between Justinian and Belisarius, but I think it's safe to say it was complicated. Early in his reign, Belisarius enjoyed Justinian's complete confidence. His loyalty was unquestioned, and his advice and actions valued more than those of any others except Theodora herself. His quelling of the Nika riots saved Justinian. For that, he was rewarded with absolute authority over the army sent to reconquer North Africa. He delivered beyond all expectations. But his very success became a threat to Justinian's authority, and it would have been quite normal for any emperor to be suspicious of such a popular general.

So, what did Belisarius really think? Did he ever want to overthrow Justinian? Procopius thinks not. Indeed, he explicitly says when he pretended to accept the position of emperor of the west from the Goths, he had no intention of rebelling. In *The Secret History*, he repeats this and seems almost frustrated with Belisarius' subservience to Justinian. So, was Belisarius too subservient to Justinian? Should he have tried to seize the throne? My sense is that there was an opportunity to do this in 542–3 when Justinian was ill with the plague. Belisarius was enormously popular at that time. So, it's possible he could have staged a successful coup. Would it have been good for the empire? Again, it's impossible to know but I suggest he would have done more to expand the army than Justinian did. It's difficult to imagine Belisarius paying tribute to the Persians and Avars in the way Justinian did.

To conclude, Belisarius was central to the age of Justinian. Indeed, it's impossible to imagine Justinian without Belisarius' victories. Belisarius delivered the clever battlefield tactics to realise Justinian's vaulting ambitions. Together they achieved the impossible and made all things seem possible. The age of Justinian could just as well be called the age of Belisarius.

57

Were Justinian's Wars of Reconquest Worth It?

We are nearing the end of Justinian's reign. Yet there is a question that demands an answer. What was the economic value of the territories he conquered and did they benefit the empire?

The economic historian Michael Hendy has examined this.[220] His conclusion is unequivocal. He describes the economic benefit of Justinian's conquests as a 'dead loss'. His work is so important that it is worth quoting his summary before we look in more detail at the numbers behind it.

The financial position of the prefectures of Africa, Italy and Illyricum, vis-à-vis that of the East, was almost absurdly weak. The budget of Africa alone amounted to barely a tenth of that of the east (on the basis of a budget of four million solidi for the latter), and the budgets of Africa, Italy and Illyricum combined amounted to barely a quarter of that of the east. In the long term (that is not forgetting the acquisition of the immediate

*contents of the Vandal and Ostrogothic treasuries), and
as a source of surplus revenue, Justinian's reconquest was
a dead loss.*[221]

Let's look at the most significant elements within Hendy's estimates. He reckons the annual expenditure of the eastern empire before the reconquest would have been at least 3 million *solidi* (equivalent to 42,000 pounds of gold at the exchange of rate of 72 *solidi* for a pound of gold). In Anastasius' reign, Procopius tells us that he accumulated a treasury surplus of 23 million *solidi* in the course of a 27-year reign (491–518). This implies a surplus of around a million *solidi* each year, suggesting the empire's annual tax revenue might have been around 4 million *solidi* to cover 3 million of expenses and save 1 million per annum.

Many of the assumptions underpinning Hendy's estimates are fascinating. For example, he believes Egypt was by far the largest contributor to Roman tax revenues at around 38 per cent of the total. A large part of the reason for this was its grain supply to the capital which he estimates as worth nearly 30 per cent of the total expenditure of the Roman state. This seems high to me. But I don't doubt Egypt's crucially important position within the Roman world. Its future loss to the Arabs can be seen as truly disastrous for Roman finances, as we will discuss in the next book in this series.

I confess I find some of the other constituents of Hendy's calculations open to question. For example, he estimates the cost of the army, the largest component of state expenditure, at only 36 per cent of the total. This seems low to me. It may have been true when the empire was at peace, but I suggest the army's cost would have rocketed to well over 50 per cent of the state budget when the empire was at war, as it was almost continuously in Justinian's reign. This would probably in itself explain why Justinian struggled and failed to balance his budget in contrast to Anastasius. War was an expensive business.

This leads us to the economic value of the newly conquered territories in Africa, Italy, Illyria (Illyria was taken from the Ostrogoths) and southern Spain. The starting point has to be what tax revenues these newly conquered provinces could actually generate. If they had been truly wealthy, Justinian would have been laughing. But they weren't. To cut a long piece of analysis short, Hendy reckons the newly conquered territories generated about a million *solidi* a year in total.

And this wasn't a surplus. He estimates the costs in terms of administration and defence were about the same – i.e. 1 million *solidi*. So, the economic benefit to the empire of the acquisitions was zero. Another way of looking at it is to compare this with Egypt which not only contributed 1.5 to 2 times the tax value of all Justinian's conquests combined, but also probably generated a large surplus since the costs of administration and defence were much less than its tax revenues. In other words, Egypt funded the conquest of the western territories.

The economic analysis is clear. Justinian's western conquests were simply not worth it. But I contend they were in fact worse than that. They were actually a serious drain on its resources.

Hendy's estimates are, I think, too generous. Most of them are based on sources *before* Justinian's conquests. This means they are almost certainly inflated compared with the tax generated *after* his conquests. This is because war and plague had devastated these territories, as discussed in Chapters 50 and 52. In particular, Italy was reduced from relative prosperity under the Ostrogoths, with large urban centres (such as Rome, Milan, Naples and Ravenna) to an economic wreck. Rome itself, as we have discussed, rapidly became a medieval village.

According to Procopius, Africa fared little better than Italy. While Belisarius' rapid demolition of the Vandal state in 533–534 was quick and successful, North Africa wasn't pacified until 548, when John Troglita finally crushed the Berber insurgency. Therefore, it took nearly 15 years after Belisarius' victory to stabilise the province. During those years, and probably for decades thereafter, tax revenues must have been well below those that the Vandals enjoyed. And this is before we take account of the effects of the plague which would have reduced tax revenues further.

Therefore, Hendy's estimate of 1 million *solidi* of tax revenue looks generous. We'll never know the true figure but perhaps it was more like half a million *solidi* per year.

Finally, Hendy doesn't try to estimate the cost of Justinian's wars of reconquest. Procopius mentions in *The Secret History*, John the Cappadocian, probably the most financially astute minister Justinian ever had, predicted they would bankrupt the empire.[222] As we will discuss in the next chapter, he was probably right.

58

The Price of Victory

Justinian's reign is normally associated with military glory. Not since Julius Caesar had so much territory been added to the empire. It is therefore nothing short of astounding to see how he neglected the army in the second half of his reign, paying tribute to his enemies rather than confronting them in battle.

The chronicler Agathias said: 'He allowed the quality of the legions to deteriorate, as though he thought he would have no further need of them.'[223] As mentioned in Chapter 54, Agathias blamed Justinian for having an army of only 150,000 soldiers, a force completely inadequate, he tells us, to defend the empire's extended frontiers.

Agathias was not alone in voicing his discontent with Justinian's military policies, or lack of them. In *The Secret History*, Procopius echoed Agathias' view, insisting Justinian's neglect of the Roman army was disastrous, particularly his policy of not paying them:

'The Roman Emperors before Justinian's time stationed huge numbers of soldiers on all the remote frontiers of

the Roman Empire, particularly in the eastern region as a means of stopping the incursions of the Persians and Saracens. These troops were called Limitanei. The Emperor Justinian treated them with such indifference and niggardliness from the start that their paymasters were four or five years in arrears with their pay...From then on, the frontiers of the Roman Empire were left ungarrisoned.[224]

Yet another source said the same. The poet and chronicler, Corippus, tells us Justinian's successor, Justin II, was scathing about the dead emperor once the required period of mourning was over. He told the senators in no uncertain terms that he was inheriting a poisoned chalice with a bankrupt treasury and a broken army:

'Many things were too much neglected while my father [Justinian who was his adopted father] was still alive and as a result the exhausted treasury contracted many debts... For lack of necessities, it [the army] has reached the point of collapse, with the result that the state is suffering from innumerable attacks and incursions by barbarians.'[225]

So, why was the army so neglected?

This question goes to the heart of why Justinian's reign was ultimately a failure. The answer lies with the financial crisis his western conquests created. As discussed in the last chapter, the western territories were not economically worth acquiring. Add to that the heavy costs of the wars of reconquest, and the result was a financial disaster.

Let us try to make a rough estimate of the costs of his western campaigns. The only starting point I can offer is

Procopius' comment that the emperor Leo's failed expedition to Carthage in 468 cost 130,000 pounds of gold, or 9.4 million *solidi* (72 *solidi* to a Roman pound). Imperfect as this is, if we use it as a yardstick for Justinian's later campaigns, perhaps we can make a very rough estimate of the cost of his wars of reconquest as follows.

First, if we assume Belisarius' expedition in 533 was half the size of Leo's in 468, we can hazard a guess it cost in the region of 5 million *solidi* (about half of Leo's 9.4 million in 468). His first expedition to Italy was smaller and might have cost 2.5 million *solidi*. His third expedition was hardly resourced at all, so let's say it cost only 1 million *solidi*. However, Narses' army fielded in 554 was huge and must have cost almost as much as Belisarius' entire expedition to Carthage, so let's say 4 million. Meanwhile, we also need to put in a figure for the fighting in Africa after Belisarius' conquest which lasted nearly 15 years. Let's say this cost the same as the initial expedition of 5 million *solidi*.

Adding all these up, the total estimated cost for Justinian's western campaigns is 19.5 million *solidi*. But that was only the *direct* cost.

For we should include the *indirect* costs such as the massive destruction in Mesopotamia and the Balkans, consequent upon the removal of the best troops from those regions to fight in the west. Although we can't put a number on the cost of the destruction wrought by the Kutrigurs and Slavs in the Balkans with any accuracy, or Chosroes' devastation of Mesopotamia in 540 and sack of Antioch (although, for example, we know Justinian invested 5,000 pounds of gold in rebuilding the city), we can be fairly certain there was a considerable loss of tax revenues and need for investment to rebuild destroyed cities (such as at Antioch). We can safely say this was an indirect cost of at least 10 million *solidi*, probably much more.

So, if we add that to the direct military costs of 19.5 million *solidi*, we have a grand total of 29.5 million *solidi*. I suggest this is a conservative estimate and the true cost might have been far larger. Even this is more than Anastasius' entire surplus of 23 million, leaving us with a deficit of 6.5 million *solidi*.

I think we can safely say this deficit wasn't funded from the tax revenues generated by the western conquests since, as discussed, these were probably barely sufficient to pay the administrators and garrison troops. The only one-off revenue boost might have been the Vandal treasure. Putting a value on this is anyone's guess but it was sufficiently famous to be worth probably around a million *solidi*, reducing our deficit to 5.5 million *solidi*. It's also worth noting we haven't considered the effect on the central budget of the cost of Justinian's massive building projects begun after the Nika riots. These would presumably have made the state deficit even larger.

However, for sake of simplicity, let's ignore the cost of Justinian's buildings and focus instead on the deficit of 5.5 million solidi caused by his wars. This deficit alone would surely have meant the state was effectively bankrupt. The anecdotal evidence supports this view. As mentioned earlier, Procopius says repeatedly, both in the *Wars* and *The Secret History*, Justinian could not pay his troops. For example, in 540, when Chosroes sacked Antioch, he hadn't even paid the garrison troops – the *limitanei* – on the eastern front. He even hints he spent Anastasius' surplus in Justin's reign – so, before his own reign had even begun – but this sounds like hyperbole.

Therefore, it seems likely the Roman state went into a funding deficit at some point in the 530s, and Justinian spent the rest of his reign trying to shore up this weak financial position. Of course, the situation only got worse when the plague struck in 541–542. The signs of this are evident in Justinian's monetary policy. In the early 540s, he debased the coinage. He was also borrowing money. One revealing incident is recounted by the chronicler John Malalas who tells us of a failed assassination attempt by a group of bankers in 562.[226] Apparently the attempt was made as he was eating his evening meal in the Great Palace. Unfortunately, Malalas doesn't say what the bankers were unhappy about but presumably their loans to the government hadn't been repaid.

In conclusion, Justinian's wars of reconquest bankrupted the empire. The main casualty of this was the army which thereafter suffered from chronic under-funding. Of course, it was the army which had brought him success in the first place. It was an ironic price for victory.

59

Justinian's Last Days

Late at night, the oil lamp flickers.

The Great Palace is silent. Everyone is asleep except for the old emperor. Wrapped in blankets, he stares grimly from his desk out across the cold, dark sea of the Bosphorus. There are only ghosts here now. His beloved Theodora was so cruelly stolen from him 17 years ago. Just months ago Belisarius died. Soon it will be his turn, he knows. Now he's worried. What punishment does God have in store for him, he wonders? Why did he turn away from him at the height of his success, bringing famine and plague? What did he do wrong? Was he too merciful towards the Monophysites? Did he not build the most magnificent church the world has ever seen? Did he not crush the Arians and restore the Chalcedonian faith in Africa and Italy?

But he suspects he's offended his lord in some way he can't understand. Was it his marriage to Theodora? Yes, she had led an immoral life but did she not repent for it? He thinks of her and smiles. He remembers when they first met. She was a dancer and looked so beautiful. Her eyes were so intelligent, so mischievous. He closes his eyes and falls asleep, dreaming of his beloved Theodora.

Justinian's last years were relatively uneventful, certainly in comparison with the tumult of most of his reign. With peace acquired through paying tribute to the Avars in the north, and to the Persians in the east, he made one last military adventure. In 551, a Roman fleet sailed for southern Spain at the invitation of a Visigothic pretender to the throne, Athanagild. In the ensuing Visigothic civil war, a Roman outpost was established at Cartagena. The southern Spanish coast was now officially Roman. With control secured of the entire Mediterranean coastline except for southern Gaul and northern Spain, Justinian could claim his conquests had in effect returned the Mediterranean to the 'Mare Nostrum' of the old Roman Empire.

Another success, probably of much greater value to the empire, was achieved at some point in the 550s, although we don't know precisely when. This was the theft of silkworm eggs from China. Until then, silk had always been bought at enormous cost from China. In the classical empire, Pliny the Elder was so worried by the amount of gold flowing east to buy silk, which he claimed was only wanted by Roman women to flatter their appearance, that he feared it would bankrupt Rome. In fact, the barbarians got there first. But silk had remained popular in the eastern empire until some monks offered to travel to China and smuggle back silkworm eggs feeding on mulberry leaves. Justinian paid them a fortune to do this, and soon a thriving silk industry was established in the environs of Constantinople.

But in his last years, Justinian's principal focus was on finding religious salvation for the empire, perhaps reflecting his own personal search for the same. For him, the religious divide was further complicated because he and Theodora stood on opposite sides. While he had identified as a Chalcedonian, she was a Monophysite. The strong-willed personality she was, there was no giving into him on this issue.

These factors motivated him to find a solution. But he never succeeded. Instead, he vacillated between accommodating the Monophysites after the Nika riots in 532, and then expelling the Monophysite patriarch of Alexandria, Theodosius, in 537.

Sixteen years later, in 553, he staged his most serious attempt to find a compromise similar to what Zeno had done with the *Henotikon*. He convened the Second Council of Constantinople. This was a big event, with 152 bishops attending. Ecumenical councils like this could only be initiated by the emperor, the last one having been held in 381 by Theodosius I. Justinian's strategy was to propose something that everyone could agree on. You recall that the basic disagreement between Chalcedonians and Monophysites was over the nature of Jesus Christ. Chalcedonians said he was both human and divine at the same time; Monophysites said he was entirely divine. Justinian's idea was to unify the two sides by getting them to agree on something they could both condemn.

This was another obscure part of Christian doctrine called the Three Chapters. This referred to the writings of three Nestorian bishops who had long ago been expelled as heretics and had fled to Persia. It was agreed both sides would unite in condemning the Three Chapters. One notable exception was Pope Vigilius, who Justinian had summoned from Rome. Justinian actually had him imprisoned until he recanted.

Justinian hoped he had brought Chalcedonians and Monophysites closer together. But in reality, they were still far apart. Indeed, arguably even more so than at the beginning of his reign since the Monophysites developed their own separate Church hierarchy, in defiance of the fact that their senior bishops, like Severus of Antioch and Theodosius of Alexandria, had been deposed and replaced with pro-Chalcedonian ones. These religious differences represented a growing division in the empire that would, in due course, prove especially damaging when, in the seventh century, a new faith – Islam – arose in the deserts of Arabia.

On a cold night, 14 November 565, at the age of 83, Justinian died in his sleep.

His nephew, Justin, rushed to the palace. He had been waiting for this moment for months, if not years, and now he seized it with consummate political skill. His allies were lined up. The Patriarch of Constantinople, the palace guards, his senatorial supporters. They all joined in proclaiming him emperor. Next stop was the hippodrome, where the mob could make or break emperors. They gave him the thumbs up. No one wanted trouble.

There was enough of that lying in wait for the empire already.

Conclusion

The Beginning of the End

Like a shooting star, Justinian's reign glowed briefly in an otherwise dark firmament of Roman history between the end of the western empire and the Arab invasions. The eastern empire rose again to prominence not just militarily but also culturally. It left a legacy more tangible perhaps than that of almost any other period in Rome's history apart from the high classical period.

One reason for this was Justinian's legal code, the *Corpus Juris Civilis*. Ask any lawyer, and they will tell you it was vital to developing modern law across the world. In the *Divine Comedy*, Dante held Justinian in high esteem for ensuring Roman law was accessible to posterity.

Next was Hagia Sophia. It is impossible to enter the building as it stands today in Istanbul and not to be astonished by its size, grandeur, and architectural perfection. It is as breath-taking as any other great Roman building, the Pantheon and Colosseum included. And Justinian's buildings are not just limited to Hagia Sophia. The Basilica Cistern and Hagia Eirene, both in Istanbul, have also survived as two magnificent examples of many others that have been lost.

Then of course there were his western conquests. Dante admired his attempt to restore the Roman Empire. Procopius has left us with a pulsating history of those wars, undertaken by the noble Belisarius. The reader is transported to a magical time when Roman arms triumphed once again over the barbarians, surpassing even Caesar's Gallic Wars.

It seems we can only gaze in wonder at the lost glories of the age of Justinian.

But there was another side. Procopius knew it well. *The Secret History* provides our most valuable insight into the reality of Justinian's age. For underneath the glorious veneer there lurked a more sinister truth. Justinian had overstretched the empire. The people and the senate knew his victories were a sham. Chosroes was the real victor of the war in the east. The Avars were also playing with an aged emperor, extorting gold to ensure a temporary peace along the Danube. Outwardly, in its last days, Justinian's empire appeared victorious, but inwardly it was a house of cards.

Of course, the plague exacerbated the scale of Justinian's mistakes. The extraordinary natural catastrophes that struck the Roman Empire like hammer blows from 536 and into the 540s – climate cooling, famine and bubonic plague – were not Justinian's fault and nor could they have been predicted. They caused economic recession and depopulation which wreaked havoc with his military and economic policies. But do they exonerate him from the mistakes he made?

The evidence suggests not. In Chapter 57, we discussed how his western conquests did not add up either economically or strategically. Aside from the unexpected effect of famine and plague, the 'cost-benefits analysis' still appears woeful.

In short, the plague exacerbated a pre-existing financial crisis caused by Justinian's western wars. Without the plague, there would still have been a crisis, albeit less severe.

Justinian has also attracted criticism for his Christian zeal which seemed to hasten the end of classical civilisation and accelerate the march towards the religious intolerance of the Middle Ages. Edward Gibbon said: '[he] was regulated not by the prudence of a philosopher, but the superstition of a monk.'[227] Procopius detested him as a betrayer of Rome's ancient values.

But this book suggests his greatest failure lay with something more mundane than divine contemplation. It was his neglect of the army. Both Agathias and Procopius highlight his failure to pay the army adequately and to expand it sufficiently to defend the extended borders. Justinian may have risen through the ranks of the imperial guard but he was no soldier. He inherited a powerful army and he squandered it.

This mistake would be the single most important reason why, within a hundred years of Justinian's death, the Roman Empire would be reduced to the struggling medieval state we call Byzantium. The fall of the western empire had been due to military failure. And Justinian's policy of paying tribute to his enemies instead of defeating them in battle was the first step towards military failure in the east. His successors would do everything they could to unwind this error and restore Roman military supremacy.[228] They would nearly succeed. But ultimately they would fail.

Justinian's reign was brilliant, bustling and beset with unforgettable characters, high ambition and impossible victories. But it was also the beginning of the end.

Acknowledgements

I would like to give my heartfelt thanks to all my readers. Thank you so much for your interest in this book, and others in this series as well. Without you, I wouldn't be able to do what I love doing. A special thanks to my American readers who have taken such an interest in the series despite having to put up with my use of UK English instead of US English!

I would also like to thank my family. My wonderful wife, Sarah, and my amazing children, William and Anna – all roads lead to Rome, and all my roads lead to you. This book is dedicated to my late father, George Holmes, Chichele Professor of History at Oxford and author of so many fascinating history books. Thank you for inspiring me with a love for history, and for first showing me many years ago the unforgettable mosaics depicting Justinian and his court at San Vitale in Ravenna.

Finally, I would like to thank all those people who have kindly helped me create this book, in particular my editor, Scott Pack, who has given me so much valuable input. Nick Castle for his striking front cover. Bek Cruddace for making the clear and elegant maps. Sara Hall for proof-reading and indexing. I would like to thank the London Library and its staff for providing an excellent haven of study and creativity in the middle of central London, and a supportive coffee machine!

Roman Emperors

(Augustus to Heraclius)

Augustus	27 BC – AD 14
Tiberius	AD 14 – 37
Caligula	37 – 41
Claudius	41 – 54
Nero	54 – 68
Galba	68 – 69
Otho	69
Vitellius	69
Vespasian	69 – 79
Titus	79 – 81
Domitian	81 – 96
Nerva	96 – 98
Trajan	98 – 117
Hadrian	117 – 38
Antoninus Pius	138 – 61
Marcus Aurelius	161 – 80
Commodus	180 – 92
Pertinax	193

Didius Iulianus	193
Septimius Severus	193 – 211
Caracalla	211 – 17
Macrinus	217 – 18
Elagabalus	218 – 22
Severus Alexander	222 – 35
Maximinus Thrax	235 – 38
Gordian III	238 – 44
Philip the Arab	244 – 49
Decius	249 – 51
Trebonianus	251 – 53
Aemilianus	253
Valerian	253 – 60
Gallienus	260 – 68
Claudius Gothicus	268 – 70
Aurelian	270 – 75
Tacitus	275 – 76
Probus	276 – 82
Carus	282 – 83
Numerian	283 – 84
Diocletian (*Sole then Tetrarch*)	284 – 305
Maximian (*Tetrarch*)	286 – 305

Constantius (*Tetrarch*)	292 – 306
Galerius (*Tetrarch*)	293 – 311
Licinus (*Tetrarch*)	308 – 24
Constantine I (*Tetrarch then Sole*)	306 – 37
Constantine II (*West*)	337 – 40
Constans I (*Middle then West*)	337 – 50
Constantius II (*East then Sole*)	337 – 61
Magnentius (*Rebel in West*)	350 – 53
Nepotianus (*Rebel in West*)	350 – 50
Vetranio (*Rebel in West*)	350 – 50
Julian 'The Apostate' (*Sole*)	361 – 63
Jovian (*Sole*)	363 – 64
Valentinian I (*Sole then West*)	364 – 75
Valens (*East*)	364 – 78
Procopius (*Rebel in East*)	365 – 66
Gratian (*West*)	375 – 83
Magnus Maximus (*Rebel in West*)	383 – 88
Valentinian II (*West*)	388 – 92
Eugenius (*Rebel in West*)	392 – 94
Theodosius I (*East then Sole*)	379 – 95
Arcadius (*East*)	395 – 408

Honorius (*West*)	395 – 423
Constantine III (*Rebel in West*)	407 – 11
Theodosius II (*East*)	408 – 50
Johannes (*usurper in West*)	423-25
Valentinian III (*West*)	425-55
Marcian (*East*)	451-7
Leo I (*East*)	457-74
Petronius Maximus (*West*)	455
Avitus (*West*)	455-56
Majorian (*West*)	457-61
Libius Severus (*West*)	461-5
Anthemius (*West*)	467-72
Olybrius (*West*)	472
Zeno (*East*)	473-91
Basiliscus (*East – interregnum during Zeno's reign*)	474-76
Glycerius (*West*)	473-74
Julius Nepos (*West*)	474-75
Romulus Augustulus (*West*)	475-76
End of Western Empire	476
Zeno (again)	476-91
Anastasius	491-518

Justin I	518-27
Justinian	527-65
Justin II	565-78
Tiberius II	578-82
Maurice	582-602
Phocas	602-10
Heraclius	610-41

Timeline

(AD 376–578)

376-377   Migration of Goths across the Danube, fleeing the Huns

378   Battle of Adrianople: catastrophic defeat of the eastern Roman army and death of eastern emperor, Valens

379   Theodosius made emperor of east by Gratian

382   Treaty with Goths after several years of warfare; they are given land south of the Danube in unprecedented Roman capitulation to barbarians

383-394   Long period of civil wars and rebellions until Theodosius reunites the empire

395   Death of Theodosius; succeeded by his sons Arcadius in the east and Honorius in the west; Stilicho guardian of the west; Huns raid Middle East from Caucasus

395-397   Rebellion of Goths led by Alaric; Alaric made *magister militum* for Illyria

401-402   Stilicho defeats Alaric's first invasion of Italy at the battles of Pollentia and Verona

405-406   Treaty between Stilicho and Alaric; Radagaisus invades Italy and is defeated by Stilicho

406-407   Germans cross Rhine and devastate Gaul; Constantine III leads rebellion in the West

408   Stilicho executed; Alaric invades Italy and lays siege to Rome; minor Hunnic leader Uldin invades eastern empire;

409	Germans cross into Spain
410	Sack of Rome by Alaric
418	Goths settle in Aquitaine
423	Death of Honorius and usurpation of Johannes
425	East Roman army puts Valentinian III on western throne
427	Gaiseric secures leadership of Vandals
429	Vandals cross straits of Gibraltar to Africa
433	Aetius becomes generalissimo of western empire
433-439	Aetius expands Roman control of Gaul
439	Vandals seize Carthage
441-442	Huns led by Attila and Bleda cross Danube and sack Naissus; Constantinople agrees to pay annual tribute of 1,400 pounds of gold to Huns but reneges on this in 443 or 444
444	Treay with Vandals recognises their control of Carthage
445?	Attila murders Bleda and assumes sole leadership of Huns
447	Attila invades Balkans to force reinstatement of tribute; defeats eastern Roman armies at battles beside the Utus River and the Chersonesus but suffers heavy casualties; Constantinople agree to pay tribute of 2,100 pounds of gold.
449	Priscus participates in embassy to assassinate Attila
450	Marcian succeeds Theodosius II and stops payment of tribute to Huns
451	Attila invades Gaul and is defeated at the Battle of the Catalaunian Plains
452	Attila invades Italy; sacks Aquileia and Milan but not Rome
453	Death of Attila
454	Hunnic Empire starts to fragment at Battle of Nedao River; Aetius murdered by Valentinian III
455	Valentinian III murdered by Petronius Maximus who is killed by mob; Vandals sack Rome

457   Majorian becomes western emperor

461   Majorian's fleet destroyed in Spain; he is murdered by Ricimer; Libius Severus made western emperor

465   Libius Severus dies; no western emperor for two years

467-469   Attila's son, Dengizich defeated and killed; head displayed in Constantinople; Leo prepares major expedition to recapture Carthage; in preparation for this, he makes Anthemius western emperor

468   Leo's expedition to recapture Carthage defeated

472   Olybrius made western emperor by Ricimer; Ricimer dies; Olybrius dies

473   Glycerius declared western emperor

474   Glycerius deposed by Julius Nepos

475   Julius Nepos flees Italy and return to Dalmatia; Orestes declares his son, Romulus Augustulus western emperor

476   Odoacer deposes Romulus Augustulus; widely-recognised formal end of western empire although Julius Nepos claims he is still the true emperor

480   Julius Nepos dies – death of last claimant on western throne

482/3   Birth of Justinian

486   Last remnant of western empire extinguished when Franks eliminate kingdom of Soissons in Gaul

489-493   Theodoric the Amal conquers Italy

491   Anastasius becomes emperor

c. 500-   Birth of Procopius, Theodora and Belisarius
505

502-506   War with Persia; after early reverses Romans win the war

511   Anastasius' triumph in Hippodrome when he appeases the mob

511-515   Revolt of Vitalian

518   Justin succeeds Anastasius as emperor

520   Murder of Vitalian; Justinian's rise to power accelerates as he is appointed *Magister Militum Praesentalis* and consul designate

521/2   Marriage law changed to allow Justinian to marry Theodora

523   Hilderic becomes king of Vandals

525   Justinian becomes Caesar; Kavad's peace embassy asks Justin to adopt Chosroes which is rejected

526   Death of Theodoric the Great, king of the Ostrogoths

527   Death of Justin; Justinian becomes emperor with Theodora as empress

529   First edition of the Code of Justinian

530   Belisarius defeats Persians at Battle of Dara; Gelimer overthrows Hilderic to become king of the Vandals

531   Belisarius defeated by Persians at Battle of Callinicum with heavy casualties on both sides

532   Nika riots crushed by Belisarius; Justinian signs 'Eternal Peace' with Persia

533   Belisarius sails for North Africa; defeats Vandals at Battles of Ad Decimum and Tricamarum and captures Carthage

534   Gelimer surrenders and Belisarius returns to Constantinople for first Roman triumphal procession in centuries; Solomon campaigns against Berbers in North Africa

535   Belisarius takes Sicily

536   *Dust Veil Event* as volcanic eruptions around globe cause temperatures to fall by as much as three degrees centigrade; Roman army in North Africa mutinies; Belisarius invades Italy and captures Naples and Rome

537-538   Hagia Sophia completed; Goths besiege Belisarius in Rome from March 537 to March 538

538   Belisarius traps Wittigis in Ravenna; Germanus fights Berbers in North Africa

539   Cutrigur Huns raid Balkans

540   Belisarius takes Ravenna by trickery; Chosroes sacks Antioch; Belisarius returns to Constantinople

541   First outbreak of Justinianic Plague at Pelusium; Belisarius campaigns on eastern front and takes Sisauranon; Chosroes takes Petra in Lazica; Totila becomes king of the Ostrogoths

542   Plague spreads to Constantinople and beyond causing massive death toll; Totila defeats Romans at Verona and Faenza and recovers most of Belisarius' Italian conquests; Belisarius recalled to Constantinople and arrested for treason

543   Second Berber revolt in North Africa; Belisarius pardoned and restored to office

544   Belisarius undertakes second campaign in Italy which lasts until 549 with no positive results

545   Truce with Chosroes in Mesopotamia but fighting continues in Lazica

547-556   War with Persia in Lazica

548   Death of Theodora probably due to cancer

549   Belisarius recalled from Italy; end of his military career except for one last triumph in 559

550   High point for Totila as he captures Rome and raids Sicily

551   Roman recovery begins as Bessas takes Petra from Persians and Narses is appointed to recover Italy

552   Victory in Italy as Narses defeats and kills Totila at Busta Gallorum, and does the same to his successor Teias at Mons Lactarius

553	Franks invade Italy
554	Narses defeats the Franks at the Battle of Capua; Justinian issues 'Pragmatic Sanction' which reduced Italy and Rome to a province run by Constantinople; the Roman senate ceases to exist
557	Truce with Chosroes ends fighting in Lazica
558	First Avar embassy to Constantinople; Justinian agrees to pay tribute to Avars
559	Cutrigur Huns raid Balkans and approach Constantinople; Belisarius recalled from retirement and defeats them
562	Peace for fifty years agreed with Persia; plot of the bankers to assassinate Justinian fails
565	Deaths of Belisarius (March) and Justinian (14 November); Justin II becomes emperor and cancels tribute to Avars
568	Lombards invade Italy
573	Justin II cancels tribute to Persians, breaking the fifty year peace, and reopening war; his general Marcian wins victories in Armenia and lays siege to Nisibis, expecting Turks to attack Persia from the east
574	Turkish attack never materialises; Marcian dismissed; Chosroes forces Romans to retreat from Nisibis and captures Dara; Justin II goes mad; his wife, Sophia, arranges for Tiberius to rule in his place as Caesar
578	Justin II dies and Tiberius II crowned emperor

Further Reading

Primary Sources on Justinian

Procopius is by far our most important source on Justinian. A number of others provide us with further insights into the events both before and during his reign, including most prominently Agathias, Jordanes, Corippus, John of Ephesus and the anonymous Chronicon Paschale. But nothing comes close to Procopius' thrilling history of the campaigns of Belisarius where he was personally present, as well as the notorious *Secret History.* Thankfully, given the paucity of other source material, he also provided us with information about the half century before Justinian much of it taken from the now lost history of Priscus of Panium (our most reliable Roman source on the fifth century). See Chapter 15 for a full discussion of Procopius' life.

Procopius did not record the end of Justinian's reign, so Agathias picks up where he left off and supplies us with the final military chapter. We're also reliant on the writings of other more obscure chroniclers like John of Ephesus (whose description of the plague is vivid – see Chapter 44), the poet and chronicler Corippus for a description of Justin II's succession and his disenchantment with Justinian's legacy, the anonymous Chronicon Paschale (or Easter Chronicle) provides additional insights into the Nika riots, as well as contributions from John of Antioch, John Malalas, Malchus of Philadelphia and others.

Jordanes is probably our most important source on the western kingdoms in the fifth and sixth centuries. His Gothic History or 'Getica' in Latin, records the migration of the Gothic people which was central to Roman history . It's worth noting that while Jordanes was of Gothic origins and identified himself with the Goths, he was of a firmly Roman disposition and education. However, some historians are sceptical about what he wrote because he copied most of it from the now lost writings of a man called Cassiodorus, who lived in Rome when the Ostrogoths took control of it, and wrote a history of the Goths for Theodoric the Great in the 520s which seems to have been strongly biased in his favour.

Procopius' writings are widely available and I recommend these four volumes in particular, including two different versions of the *Secret History* which each provide a valuable perspective on this important work. All of Procopius' writings have also been published by the Loeb Classical Library.

Prokopios, *The Wars of Justinian*, translated by HB Dewing and modernized by Anthony Kaldellis, (Hackett Publishing Company, 2014).

Prokopios, *The Secret History*, translated with introduction by Anthony Kaldellis, Hackett Publishing Company, 2010).

Procopius, *The Secret History*, translated by GA Williamson with introduction by Peter Sarris (Penguin, 2007).

Procopius, *The Buildings*, translated by HB Dewing, (Loeb Classical Library, Harvard University Press, 1940).

It is more difficult to get hold of the writings of the other chroniclers relevant to Justinian, and below I list most of those published in formats that can be bought or accessed via academic libraries or online are:

Agathias, *The Histories*, translated by Joseph Frendo, (published by Walter de Gruyter, 1975).

Ammianus Marcellinus, *The Later Roman Empire*, translated by Walter Hamilton, (Penguin, 1986)

Cassiodorus, *The Letters of Cassiodorus*, translated by Thomas Hodgkin (Legare Street Press, 2022)

Chronicon Paschale, translated by Michael Whitby and Mary Whitby, (Liverpool UP, 1989)

Corippus, *In Laudem Iustini Augusti Minoris*, translated by Averil Cameron, (The Athlone Press, 2000)

Gregory of Tours, *The History of the Franks* (Penguin, 1974)

John of Antioch, *Ioannis Antiocheni Fragmenta Quae Supersunt Omnia*, translated by Sergei Mariev, (De Gruyter, 2008)

John of Ephesus, *Church History*, translated by Witold Witakowski and titled Chronicle of Pseudo-Dionysius of Tel-Mahre, (Liverpool University Press, 1996)

Jordanes, *The Gothic History* (Sophron Editor, 2018) Jordanes, *Romana and Getica*, translated by Peter Van Nuffelen (Translated Texts for Historians Vol 75, Liverpool University Press, 2020)

Lactantius, *On the Deaths of the Persecutors* (Oxford UP, 1984)

Maurice, *Maurice's Strategicon*, translated by George T Dennis (published by University of Pennsylvania Press, 1984).

Priscus, *The Fragmentary History of Priscus* (translated by John Given), Christian Roman Empire Series Vol 2, (Evolution Publishing, 2014)

Zosimus, *The New History* (Byzantina Australiensia, 1984)

Secondary Sources on Justinian

Quite a few books have been written on Justinian's reign and I will limit this selection to what I consider the main scholarly works. My top pick, and very good on the military history, is Peter Heather's *Rome Resurgent* (Oxford UP , 2018). Peter Sarris' *Justinian: Emperor, Soldier, Saint* (Basic Books, 2023) is good on the legal, climate and plague related aspects. Anthony Kaldellis' *Procopius of Caesarea* (University of Pennsylvania Press, 2004) presents a fascinating analysis of Procopius' writings. David Alan Parnell's *Belisarius and Antonina* (Oxford UP, 2023) is an interesting investigation into the life of the great general and his notorious wife. Hans-Ulrich Wiemer's *Theodoric the Great*, translated by JN Dillon, (Yale UP, 2023) is a must read on Theodoric and the Ostrogoths. Three books on the economic background to Justinian's empire are Jairus Banaji, *Agrarian Change in Late Antiquity*, (Oxford UP, 2001), Peter Sarris' *Economy and Society in the Age of Justinian* (Cambridge UP, 2006) and Michael Hendy's *Studies in the Byzantine Monetary Economy c.300-1450* (Cambridge UP, 1985) which contains analysis of Justinian's reign within a large book of much broader scope. Finally, Kyle Harper's *The Fate of Rome: Climate, Disease, and the End of an Empire* (Princeton UP, 2017) contains sections relevant to Justinian within a broader and ground-breaking book.

Other Secondary Sources on the Fall of the Roman Empire

Given this book is the fourth in a series on the fall the Roman Empire, which covers a wide number of different topics and periods, all relevant to this book, I have listed further reading on a number of related areas.

My Top Five on the Fall of the Roman Empire

These are all landmark academic works which are also very readable. Two outstanding examples are Peter Heather's *The Fall of the Roman Empire* (Oxford UP, 2006), and Bryan Ward-Perkins' *The Fall of Rome and the End of Civilisation* (Oxford UP, 2005). They are both updates on Peter Brown's classic, *The World of Late Antiquity* (Thames & Hudson, 1971), which has had an enduring influence on academic scholarship. Arther Ferrill's *The Fall of the Roman Empire: The Military Explanation* (Thames and Hudson, 1988) is a somewhat forgotten classic on Rome's military decline, in my view. More recently, a compelling work which provides new and thought-provoking research, especially about the effects of climate change and pandemics on the Roman Empire, is Kyle Harper's *The Fate of Rome: Climate, Disease, and the End of an Empire* (Princeton UP, 2017).

Attila and the Huns

The two most influential scholarly works on Attila and the Huns are Otto Maenchen-Helfen's *The World of the Huns* (University of California Press, 1973) and EA Thompson's *The Huns* (Oxford UP, 1948, updated in 1999 with an afterword by Peter Heather, Blackwell Publishing, 1999).

Maenchen-Helfen was a meticulous German scholar, who spent a lifetime compiling a huge amount of information and analysis on the Huns which was published after his death in 1969. It remains the most extensive analysis of the Huns used by scholars worldwide. Peter Heather has also developed clear views of the impact of the Huns on the Roman Empire described in *The Fall of the Roman Empire* (Oxford UP, 2006) mentioned above. More recently, an interesting new scholarly perspective of the impact of the Huns on Rome and Europe is presented, somewhat controversially, by Hyun Jin Kim, in *The Huns* (Routledge, 2016). Also relevant are Christopher Kelly's *The End of Empire: Attila the Hun and the Fall of Rome* (Norton, 2009); Ian Hughes' *Attila the Hun: Arch-enemy of Rome* (Pen & Sword, 2019) and John Man's *Attila the Hun: A Barbarian King and the Fall of Rome* (Bantam, 2005).

General Overview of the Later Roman Empire

For many decades, the most famous scholarly work on the late Roman Empire was by AHM Jones, *The Later Roman Empire 284–602*, Volumes I and II (Blackwell, 1964), although archaeological discoveries since it was written have made much of Jones' economic analysis redundant. JB Bury's two volumes on the *History of the Later Roman Empire: From the Death of Theodosius I to the Death of Justinian* (Dover Publications, 1958) still make compelling if somewhat outdated reading. Essential reading for the Roman economy is Richard Duncan-Jones, *Money and Government in the Roman Empire* (Cambridge UP, 1994). The difficult subject of the impact of the Huns on Rome and Europe is presented, somewhat controversially, by Hyun Jin Kim, *The Huns* (Routledge, 2016). Walter

Scheidel provides an entertaining new view of Rome's legacy in his *Escape from Rome: The Failure of Empire and the Road to Prosperity* (Princeton UP, 2019). Going further back in time, the classic work remains Edward Gibbon's *The History of the Decline and Fall of the Roman Empire* (first published in 1776 and more recently by Penguin, 1994). Hugely influential are two older works published in French with English translations – Ferdinand Lot's *The End of the Ancient World* (first published in 1931 and more recently by Routledge, 1996) and Henri Pirenne's *Mohammed and Charlemagne* (first published in 1939 and more recently by Martino, 2017).

The Crisis of the Third Century

The crisis of the third century was of huge significance not just for Rome but also for world history, and yet remains sadly under-researched because of the lack of surviving source material. Probably the most insightful works are Alaric Watson's *Aurelian and the Third Century* (Routledge, 1999) and John F White's *The Roman Emperor Aurelian: Restorer of the World* (Pen and Sword, 2015). Edward Luttwak's *The Grand Strategy of the Roman Empire: From the First Century A.D. to the Third* (John Hopkins, 1976) is interesting. More recent and thought-provoking are Ilkka Syvanne's *The Reign of Emperor Gallienus: The Apogee of Roman Cavalry* (Pen and Sword, 2019) and, by the same author, *Aurelian and Probus: The Soldier Emperors Who Saved Rome* (Pen and Sword, 2020).

Diocletian and Constantine

Diocletian and Constantine have received more attention than the crisis of the third century. Strongly recommended on

Diocletian are Stephen Williams' *Diocletian and the Roman Recovery* (Routledge, 1985) and Roger Rees' *Diocletian and the Tetrarchy* (Edinburgh UP, 2004). On Constantine: AHM Jones' *Constantine and the Conversion of Europe* (first published in 1948 and more recently by Medieval Academy of America, 1994); Timothy Barnes' *Constantine: Dynasty, Religion and Power in the Later Roman Empire* (Wiley-Blackwell, 2014) and David Potter's *Constantine: The Emperor* (Oxford UP, 2013). Extremely valuable on Christianity is Rodney Stark's *The Rise of Christianity* (Princeton UP, 1996).

Julian the Apostate

Of the many books written about Julian, three stand out: GW Bowersock's *Julian the Apostate* (Harvard UP, 1978); Robert Browning's *The Emperor Julian* (Weidenfeld and Nicolson, 1975); and Adrian Murdoch's *The Last Pagan: Julian the Apostate and the Death of the Ancient World* (Inner Traditions, 2008).

From Valentinian to the Sack of Rome in AD 410

The Valentinian and Theodosian dynasties are relatively under-researched. A good overview is provided in David Potter's *The Roman Empire at Bay: AD 180–395* (Routledge, 2004). The reign of Theodosius is well covered by Stephen Williams and Gerard Friell in *Theodosius: The Empire at Bay* (Routledge, 1998). Books on other main fourth-century figures are Neil McLynn's *Ambrose of Milan: Church and Court in a Christian Capital* (University of California Press, 1994); Ian Hughes' *Stilicho: The Vandal Who Saved Rome* (Pen and Sword, 2010); and Douglas Boin's *Alaric the Goth: An Outsider's History of the Fall of Rome* (Norton, 2020).

The Fifth Century

Since most of the main scholarly works on the fifth century are already included in the section above on *Attila and the Huns*, and in the other sections both above and below, I highlight the useful works by Ian Hughes which I have not listed elsewhere, and which provide a reliable and detailed narrative on many of the key figures of the fifth century. His works include: Ian Hughes, *Constantius III: Rome's Lost Hope* (Pen and Sword 2021); Ian Hughes, *Gaiseric: the Vandal who Destroyed Rome* (Pen and Sword, 2017); Ian Hughes, *Patricians and Emperors: The Last Rulers of the Western Empire* (Pen and Sword, 2015) and Ian Hughes, *Aetius: Attila's Nemesis* (Pen and Sword, 2012). I would also add another classic by Peter Brown, *Augustine of Hippo: A Biography* (University of California Press, 2000).

Roman Army

There are a number of good books on the Roman army including the outstanding recent work by Anthony Kaldellis and Marion Kruse, *The Field Armies of the East Roman Empire, 361-630* (Cambridge UP, 2023). Otherwise, the most interesting works on the late Roman army are Pat Southern and Karen Dixon's *The Late Roman Army* (Yale UP, 1996) and Hugh Elton's *Warfare in Roman Europe AD 350–425* (Oxford UP, 1996). For an understanding of the development of the Roman army, Lawrence Keppie's *The Making of the Roman Army: From Republic to Empire* (Routledge, 1998) and Adrian Goldsworthy's *The Roman Army at War 100 BC–AD 200* (Oxford UP, 1996) are strongly recommended. For the Praetorian Guard, see Sandra Bingham's *The Praetorian*

Guard: A History of Rome's Elite Special Forces (Baylor UP, 2013).

Persia

Sasanian Persia remains somewhat under-researched. Three useful books are Beate Dignas and Engelbert Winter's *Rome and Persia in Late Antiquity* (Cambridge UP, 2007); Eberhard Sauer's *Sasanian Persia* (Edinburgh UP, 2017); and Touraj Daryaee's *Sasanian Persia: The Rise and Fall of an Empire* (I.B. Tauris, 2013).

Climate Change

Paleoclimatology is rapidly becoming a major focus for historians. Kyle Harper's *The Fate of Rome* (Princeton UP, 2017) is the most comprehensive scholarly analysis yet published of how the climate (and pandemics) affected Roman history. I also strongly recommend Brian Fagan's *The Great Warming: Climate Change and the Rise and Fall of Civilisations* (Bloomsbury, 2008) for a fascinating account of the medieval warm period. The view put forward in this book that it was probably a megadrought that prompted the Huns to migrate west is informed by the research paper called 'Megadroughts, ENSO, and the Invasion of Late Roman Europe by the Huns and Avars' presented by Edward R. Cook to the Dumbarton Oaks Workshop for Climate Change Under the Late Roman Empire in April 2009. Another relevant research paper is 'Climate and the Decline and Fall of the Western Roman Empire: A Bibliometric View on an Interdisciplinary Approach to Answer a Most Classic Historical Question' by Werner Marx, Robin Haunschild and Lutz Bornmann, published on 15 November 2018 in the Multidisciplinary Digital Publishing Institute (MDPI).

Other Primary Sources on Roman History

The sources listed below are only those referenced in my series on the Fall of the Roman Empire that can currently be purchased in paperback/hardback. Other versions and more material are accessible online and in academic libraries. It should be noted that the history of the republic and early empire is so rich in sources that my list is very concise. In contrast, the third, fourth and fifth centuries have relatively few sources, the most significant of which are listed.

Republic/Early Empire

Cicero, *Selected Works* (Penguin, 1971)

Livy, *The Rise of Rome* (Oxford UP, 1998)

Marcus Aurelius, *Meditations* (Oxford UP, 2011)

Polybius, *The Histories* (Digireads, 2019)

Suetonius, *The Twelve Caesars* (Penguin, 1957)

Tacitus, *Annals and Histories* (Everyman, 2009)

Virgil, *The Aeneid* (Oxford UP, 1986)

Later Empire (AD 180–476)

Ambrose (Saint), *On the Mysteries and on Repentance* (Veritatis Splendor Publications, 2014)

Ammianus Marcellinus, *The Later Roman Empire* (Penguin, 1986)

Augustan History (Historia Augusta) – first half published as *Lives of the Later Caesars*, translated by Antony Birley (Penguin, 1976); full work published by Loeb Classical

Library in three volumes as *Scriptores Historiae Augustae*, translated by D. Magie (Loeb, 1932)

Cassius Dio – the first and last sections of his incomplete *Roman History* have been published i) by Penguin (1987) covering Books 50–6 from 32 BC to AD 14, and ii) by Echo Library (2007) covering Books 77–80 from AD 211 to 229

Claudian, *Volumes I and II* (Loeb Classical Library, 1922)

Eusebius, *Life of Constantine* (Oxford UP, 1999)

Eusebius, *Ecclesiastical History* (Baker Book House, 1989)

Gregory of Tours, *The History of the Franks* (Penguin, 1974

Jerome, *Chronicle* (Akademie Verlag, 1956)

Jerome, *Letters* (Aeterna Press, 2016)

Jordanes, *The Gothic History* (Sophron Editor, 2018) Jordanes, *Romana and Getica*, translated by Peter Van Nuffelen (Translated Texts for Historians Vol 75, Liverpool University Press, 2020)

Julian, *Volumes I to III* (Loeb Classical Library, 1923)

Lactantius, *On the Deaths of the Persecutors* (Oxford UP, 1984)

Notitia Dignitatum – the original version in Latin compiled by Otto Seeck in 1876 has been reproduced by Forgotten Books (2018); a summarised English translation compiled by William Fairley in 1899 has been reproduced by BiblioLife

Procopius, *History of the Wars, Book 3* (Loeb Classical Library, 1916)

Priscus, *The Fragmentary History of Priscus* (translated by John Given), Christian Roman Empire Series Vol 2, (Evolution Publishing, 2014)

'*Res Gestae Divi Saporis*' ('The Great Inscription of Shapur

I') are rock carvings located in modern Iran containing essential information on the Roman/Sasanian wars in the third century (see online for best accessibility)

Saint Severinus, *The Life of Saint Severinus*, translated by George Robinson, published by Leopold Classic Library (reprint of 1914 original by Harvard Translations)

Sidonius Apollonaris, *Poems and Letters* (Loeb Classical Library, 1936)

Themistius, *The Private Orations of Themistius*, translated by Robert Penella (University of California Press, 1999)

Vegetius, *The Military Institutions of the Romans (De Re Militari)*, (Ancient World Books, 2018)

Victor (Aurelius), *De Caesaribus* (Liverpool UP, 1994)

Zosimus, *The New History* (Byzantina Australiensia, 1984)

Endnotes

Introduction

1   *Prokopios, The Wars of Justinian*, translated by HB Dewing with revisions by Anthony Kaldellis, (Hackett Publishing Company, 2014), p. 287.

2   Something Gibbon was deeply aware of. He did his best to de-emphasise Justinian although he couldn't help admiring Belisarius' victories.

3   This is the subject of the previous book in this series.

4   Prokopios, *The Wars of Justinian*, translated by HB Dewing with revisions by Anthony Kaldellis, (Hackett Publishing Company, 2014), p. 61.

5   Robert Graves, Preface to *Count Belisarius* (Penguin, 1954).

Part I New Rome, New Romans

6   Attila's tribute from the eastern empire rose to a high of 2,100 pounds of gold in 447.

7   *The Fragmentary History of Priscus* (translated by John Given). Christian Roman Empire Series Vol 2, (Evolution Publishing, 2014), p. 158.

8   *Procopius, The Wars of Justinian*, translated by HB Dewing with revisions by Anthony Kaldellis, (Hackett Publishing Company, 2014), p. 157.

9   Ibid., p. 158.

10 Ibid., p. 158.

11 Ibid., p. 158.

12   Ibid., p. 158.

13   Anthony Kaldellis, *The New Roman Empire* (Oxford UP, 2024), p. 19 citing Herodian.

14   See recent research putting forward this view contained in Anthony Kaldellis and Marion Kruse, *The Field Armies of the East Roman Empire, 361-630,* (Cambridge UP, 2023).

15   Procopius, *History of the Wars* Book 1, p. 7.

16   *Maurice's Strategicon* (translated by George T Dennis), University of Pennsylvania Press, 1984.

17   For a full discussion of this subject, see Books Two and Three in this series.

18   JB Bury, *History of the Later Roman Empire Vol I*, (Dover Publications, 1958), p. 392.

19   Peter Heather, The Goths, (Blackwell, 1998).

20   JB Bury, *History of the Later Roman Empire Vol 1*, (Dover Publications, 1958), p. 430.

21   Prokopios, *The Wars of Justinian*, translated by HB Dewing with revisions by Anthony Kaldellis, (Hackett Publishing Company, 2014), p. 17.

22   JB Bury, *History of the Later Roman Empire Vol 2*, (Dover Publications, 1958), p. 11.

23   Anthony Kaldellis and Marion Kruse, *The Field Armies of the East Roman Empire, 361–630,* (Cambridge UP, 2023), p. 67.

24   JB Bury, *History of the Later Roman Empire Vol II*, (Dover Publications, 1958), p. 13.

25   Ibid., p. 14.

26   Bryan Ward-Perkins, *The Fall of Rome and the End of Civilization,* (Oxford UP. 2005).

27   Kyle Walker, *The Fate of Rome*, (Princeton UP, 2019).

28   JB Bury, *The History of the Later Roman Empire, Vol 1*, (Dover Publications, 1958), p. 441.

29   Procopius, *The Secret History*, translated by GA Williamson with introduction by Peter Sarris (published by Penguin, 2007), p. 78.

30   Prokopios, *The Wars of Justinian*, translated by HB Dewing with revisions by Anthony Kaldellis, (Hackett Publishing Company, 2014), p. 257.

31 Procopius, *The Secret History*, translated by GA Williamson with introduction by Peter Sarris (Penguin, 2007), p. 78.

Part II The Peasant and the Prostitute

32 Procopius, *The Secret History*, translated by GA Williamson with introduction by Peter Sarris (Penguin, 2007), p. 25.

33 Peter Sarris *Justinian: Emperor, Soldier, Saint,* (Basic Books, 2023), p. 61.

34 Ibid., p. 62.

35 Ibid., p. 63.

36 Ibid., p. 64.

37 Procopius, *The Secret History*, translated by GA Williamson with introduction by Peter Sarris (Penguin, 2007), p. 41.

38 Peter Heather, *Rome Resurgent,* (Oxford UP, 2018), p. 2.

39 Procopius, *The Buildings*, translated by HB Dewing, (Loeb Classical Library, Harvard University Press, 1940), p.5.

40 Procopius, *The Secret History* translated by GA Williamson and Peter Sarris (Penguin, 2007), p. 52.

41 Edward Gibbon, *The History of the Decline and Fall of the Roman Empire*, Vol IV, (Penguin, 1994, first published 1781), p. 731.

42 Procopius, *The Secret History*, translated by GA Williamson with introduction by Peter Sarris (Penguin, 2007), p. 43.

43 Ibid., p. 40.

44 Ibid., p. 42.

45 Prokopios, *The Wars of Justinian*, translated by HB Dewing with revisions by Anthony Kaldellis, (Hackett Publishing Company, 2014), p. 28.

46 Ibid., p. 26.

47 Prokopios, *The Wars of Justinian*, translated by HB Dewing with revisions by Anthony Kaldellis, (Hackett Publishing Company, 2014), p. 36.

48 Ibid., p. 37.

49 Ibid., p. 37.

50 Peter Sarris *Justinian: Emperor, Soldier, Saint,* (Basic Books, 2023), p. 139.

51 Ibid., p. 139.

52 Ibid., p. 140.

53 Procopius, *The Secret History,* translated by GA Williamson with introduction by Peter Sarris (Penguin, 2007), p. 78.

54 Peter Sarris *Justinian: Emperor, Soldier, Saint,* (Basic Books, 2023), p. 116.

55 Prokopios, *The Wars of Justinian,* translated by HB Dewing with revisions by Anthony Kaldellis, (Hackett Publishing Company, 2014), p. 46.

56 Ibid, p. 49.

57 Ibid, p. 49.

58 Prokopios, *The Wars of Justinian,* translated by HB Dewing with revisions by Anthony Kaldellis, (Hackett Publishing Company, 2014), p. 60-61.

59 Peter Sarris *Justinian: Emperor, Soldier, Saint,* (Basic Books, 2023), p. 61.

60 Ibid., p. 145.

61 Ibid., p. 145.

62 Malalas and the Chronicon Paschale are our best sources on this part of the riots.

63 Peter Sarris *Justinian: Emperor, Soldier, Saint,* (Basic Books, 2023), p. 149.

64 Prokopios, *The Wars of Justinian,* translated by HB Dewing with revisions by Anthony Kaldellis, (Hackett Publishing Company, 2014), p. 64.

65 Ibid, p. 64.

66 Ibid, p. 64.

67 *Chronicon Paschale,* translated by Michael Whitby and Mary Whitby, (Liverpool UP, 1989), p. 122.

68 *Chronicon Paschale,* translated Michael Whitby and Mary Whitby, (Liverpool UP), p. 127.

69 Peter Sarris *Justinian: Emperor, Soldier, Saint,* (Basic Books, 2023), p. 158.

70 Procopius, *The Secret History*, translated by GA Williamson with introduction by Peter Sarris (Penguin, 2007), p. 80.

71 Peter Sarris seems inclined to give Justinian the benefit of the doubt in *Justinian: Emperor, Soldier, Saint,* (Basic Books, 2023), p. 104.

72 While Peter Heather is more critical of Justinian in *Rome Resurgent,* (Oxford UP, 2018), p. 114.

Part III The Age of Conquest

73 Prokopios, *The Wars of Justinian*, translated by HB Dewing with revisions by Anthony Kaldellis, (Hackett Publishing Company, 2014), p. 166.

74 Ibid., p. 166.

75 Ibid., p. 170.

76 Ibid., p. 182.

77 Ibid., p. 104.

78 Ibid., p. 184.

79 Ibid., p. 186.

80 Ibid., p. 186.

81 Ibid., p. 193.

82 Ibid., p. 195.

83 Ibid., p. 197.

84 Ibid., p. 198.

85 Ibid. p. 198.

86 Ibid., p. 198.

87 Robert Graves, *Count Belisarius* (Penguin, 1938).

88 Prokopios, *The Wars of Justinian*, translated by HB Dewing with revisions by Anthony Kaldellis, (Hackett Publishing Company, 2014), p. 209.

89 Peter Sarris *Justinian: Emperor, Soldier, Saint,* (Basic Books, 2023), p. 163.

90 Peter Brown, *The World of Late Antiquity*, (Thames and Hudson, 1971), p. 123.

91 Hans-Ulrich Wiemer, *Theodoric the Great*, translated by JN Dillon, (Yale UP, 2023), p. 10.

92 Ibid., p. 323.

93 Ibid., p. 3.

94 Cassiodorus, *Orationum Reliquiae*, taken from *Ravenna in Late Antiquity*, translated by Deborah Mauskopf Deliyannis, (Cambridge UP, 2010), p. 120.

95 Hans-Ulrich Wiemer, *Theodoric the Great*, translated by JN Dillon, (Yale UP, 2023).

96 Ibid., p. 389.

97 Prokopios, *The Wars of Justinian*, translated by HB Dewing with revisions by Anthony Kaldellis, (Hackett Publishing Company, 2014), p. 255.

98 Ibid., p. 257

99 Ibid., p. 221.

100 Ibid., p. 222.

101 Ibid., p. 276.

102 Ibid., p. 277.

103 Ibid., p. 278.

104 Ibid., p. 287.

105 Constantine's conversion is fraught with controversy – for the details see Book I in this series called The Roman Revolution, Chapter 38.

106 Prokopios, *The Wars of Justinian*, translated by HB Dewing with revisions by Anthony Kaldellis, (Hackett Publishing Company, 2014), p. 304.

107 Ibid., p. 302.

108 Ibid., p. 314.

109 Edward Gibbon, *The History of the Decline and Fall of the Roman Empire* (Penguin, 1994), Vol II, Chapter XLI, p. 669.

110 Prokopios, *The Wars of Justinian*, translated by HB Dewing with revisions by Anthony Kaldellis, (Hackett Publishing Company, 2014), p. 339

111 Ibid., p. 339.

112 Ibid., p. 356.

113 Ibid., p. 362.

114 Ibid., p. 380.

115 Ibid., p. 80

116 Ibid., p. 383.

117 Ibid., p. 383.

118 Ibid., p. 383.

Part IV Apocalypse Now

119 See Chapter 20 in the first book in this series, *The Roman Revolution*.

120 JB Bury, *History of the Later Roman Empire*, Vol II, p. 89.

121 *The History of al-Tabari*, translated by Franz Rosenthal, (State University of New York Press, 1989) – al-Tabari was a Sunni Muslim scholar (839-923) who lived in Baghdad.

122 Prokopios, *The Wars of Justinian*, translated by HB Dewing with revisions by Anthony Kaldellis, (Hackett Publishing Company, 2014), p. 78.

123 Ibid., p. 73.

124 Ibid., p. 82.

125 Ibid., p. 83.

126 Ibid., p. 84.

127 Ibid., p. 84.

128 See Book 3 in this series, *Rome and Attila*, Chapter 27.

129 Prokopios, *The Wars of Justinian*, translated by HB Dewing with revisions by Anthony Kaldellis, (Hackett Publishing Company, 2014), p. 92.

130 Ibid., p. 89.

131 Peter Sarris *Justinian: Emperor, Soldier, Saint*, (Basic Books, 2023), p. 317.

132 Prokopios, *The Wars of Justinian*, translated by HB Dewing with revisions by Anthony Kaldellis, (Hackett Publishing Company, 2014), p. 221.

133 Peter Sarris *Justinian: Emperor, Soldier, Saint*, (Basic Books, 2023), p. 319.

134 Ibid., p. 318.

135 Kyle Harper, *The Fate of Rome: Climate, Disease, and the End of an Empire* (Princeton UP, 2017), p. 253.

136 Peter Sarris *Justinian: Emperor, Soldier, Saint,* (Basic Books, 2023), p. 318.

137 Kyle Harper, *The Fate of Rome: Climate, Disease, and the End of an Empire* (Princeton UP, 2017), p. 254.

138 This is discussed in the Swiss Federal Research Institute's publication *'New Little Ice Age coincides with fall of Eastern Roman Empire and growth of Arab Empire',* February 8, 2016.

139 Prokopios, *The Wars of Justinian,* translated by HB Dewing with revisions by Anthony Kaldellis, (Hackett Publishing Company, 2014), p. 359.

140 Kyle Harper, *The Fate of Rome: Climate, Disease, and the End of an Empire* (Princeton UP, 2017), p. 253-259.

141 Ibid., p. 258.

142 Centers for Disease Control and Prevention, Maps and Statistics.

143 Peter Sarris *Justinian: Emperor, Soldier, Saint,* (Basic Books, 2023), p. 320.

144 Klunk, J., Vilgalys, T.P., Demeure, C.E. et al. *Evolution of immune genes is associated with the Black Death,* (Nature 611, 312–319, 2022).

145 Peter Sarris *Justinian: Emperor, Soldier, Saint,* (Basic Books, 2023), p. 322.

146 Peter Frankopan, *The Earth Transformed: An Untold History,* (London, 2023), p. 303-304.

147 David Keys, *Catastrophe: An Investigation into the Origins of the Modern World,* (Arrow Books, 2000).

148 John of Ephesus, *Church History,* translated by Witold Witakowski and titled *Chronicle of Pseudo-Dionysius of Tel-Mahre,* (Liverpool University Press, 1996).

149 Ibid., p. 74.

150 Ibid., p. 75.

151 Ibid., p. 81.

152 Ibid., p. 81.

153 Ibid., p. 75.

154 Ibid., p. 81.

155 Prokopios, *The Wars of Justinian,* translated by HB Dewing with revisions by Anthony Kaldellis, (Hackett Publishing Company,

2014), p. 121.

156 John of Ephesus, *Church History*, translated by Witold Witakowski and titled *Chronicle of Pseudo-Dionysius of Tel-Mahre*, (Liverpool University Press, 1996), p. 88.

157 Prokopios, *The Wars of Justinian*, translated by HB Dewing with revisions by Anthony Kaldellis, (Hackett Publishing Company, 2014), p. 121.

158 Ibid., p. 122.

159 Ibid., p. 122.

160 John of Ephesus, *Church History*, translated by Witold Witakowski and titled *Chronicle of Pseudo-Dionysius of Tel-Mahre*, (Liverpool University Press, 1996), p. 86.

161 Ibid., p. 89.

162 Prokopios, *The Wars of Justinian*, translated by HB Dewing with revisions by Anthony Kaldellis, (Hackett Publishing Company, 2014), p. 123.

163 Ibid., p. 124.

164 Peter Sarris, *Economy and Society in the Age of Justinian* (Cambridge UP, 2006), p. 218.

165 Ibid., p. 224.

166 Peter Heather, *Rome Resurgent,* (Oxford UP, 2018).

167 Kyle Harper, *The Fate of Rome: Climate, Disease, and the End of an Empire* (Princeton UP, 2017), p. 234.

168 Prokopios, *The Wars of Justinian*, translated by HB Dewing with revisions by Anthony Kaldellis, (Hackett Publishing Company, 2014), p. 97.

169 Ibid., p. 93.

170 Ibid., p. 107.

171 Ibid., p. 109.

172 Ibid., p. 113.

173 Ibid., p. 115.

174 Ibid., p. 117.

175 Ibid., p. 117.

176 Ibid., p. 118.

177 Ibid., p. 119.

178 Ibid., p. 132.

179 David Alan Parnell, *Belisarius and Antonina* (Oxford UP, 2023), p. 150.

180 Prokopios, *The Wars of Justinian*, translated by HB Dewing with revisions by Anthony Kaldellis, (Hackett Publishing Company, 2014), p. 384.

181 Ibid., p. 386.

182 Ibid., p. 534.

183 Ibid., p. 398.

184 Ibid., p. 398.

185 Procopius, *The Secret History*, translated by GA Williamson with introduction by Peter Sarris (Penguin, 2007), p. 18.

186 Prokopios, *The Wars of Justinian*, translated by HB Dewing with revisions by Anthony Kaldellis, (Hackett Publishing Company, 2014), p. 404.

187 Ibid., p. 425.

188 Ibid., p. 424.

189 Ibid., p. 432.

190 Peter Heather, *Rome Resurgent*, (Oxford UP, 2018), p. 243.

191 Prokopios, *The Wars of Justinian*, translated by HB Dewing with revisions by Anthony Kaldellis, (Hackett Publishing Company, 2014), p. 210.

192 Ibid., p. 217.

193 Ibid., p. 250.

194 Ibid., p. 444.

195 Ibid., p. 453.

196 Ibid., p. 523.

197 Ibid., p. 460.

198 Ibid., p. 534.

199 Ibid., p. 542.

200 Ibid., p. 543.

201 Ibid., p. 543.

202 Peter Heather, *Rome Resurgent*, (Oxford UP, 2018), p. 289.

203 Prokopios, *The Wars of Justinian*, translated by HB Dewing with

revisions by Anthony Kaldellis, (Hackett Publishing Company, 2014), p. 539.

204 Peter Sarris *Justinian: Emperor, Soldier, Saint,* (Basic Books, 2023), p. 377.

205 Prokopios, *The Wars of Justinian*, translated by HB Dewing with revisions by Anthony Kaldellis, (Hackett Publishing Company, 2014), p. 409.

206 Ibid., p. 408.

207 Ibid., p. 456.

208 Ibid., p. 520.

209 Edward R Cook, *Megadroughts, ENSO, and the invasion of Late Roman Europe by the Huns and Avars*, (Dumbarton Oaks Workshop for Climate Change under the Late Roman Empire, 2009).

210 Peter Sarris *Justinian: Emperor, Soldier, Saint,* (Basic Books, 2023), p. 284.

211 He also forced Cunimund's daughter, Rosamund, to marry him and drink from her father's skull. She got her own back by murdering him a few years later.

212 Prokopios, *The Wars of Justinian*, translated by HB Dewing with revisions by Anthony Kaldellis, (Hackett Publishing Company, 2014), p. 487.

213 Agathias, *The Histories*, translated by Joseph Frendo, (Walter de Gruyter, 1975), p. 148.

214 Michael Hendy, *Studies in the Byzantine Monetary Economy c. 300-1450,* (Cambridge UP, 1985), p. 172.

215 Peter Sarris *Justinian: Emperor, Soldier, Saint,* (Basic Books, 2023), p. 267.

216 Ibid., p. 271.

217 See the third book in this series, Nick Holmes, *Rome and Attila* (Puttenham Press, 2024), p. 214.

218 DA Parnell, *Belisarius and Antonina*, (Cambridge UP, 2023), p. 188.

219 Ibid., p. 193.

220 Michael Hendy, *Studies in the Byzantine Monetary Economy c.300-1450,* (Cambridge UP, 1985).

221 Ibid., p. 171.

222 Prokopios, *The Wars of Justinian*, translated by HB Dewing with revisions by Anthony Kaldellis, (Hackett Publishing Company, 2014), p. 167.

223 Agathias, *The Histories*, translated by Joseph Frendo, (Walter de Gruyter, 1975), p. 149.

224 Procopius, *The Secret History*, translated by GA Williamson with introduction by Peter Sarris (Penguin, 2007), p. 98.

Conclusion

225 Ibid., p. 405.

226 Peter Sarris *Justinian: Emperor, Soldier, Saint,* (Basic Books, 2023), p. 395.

227 Edward Gibbon, *The History of the Decline and Fall of the Roman Empire Vol 2* (Penguin, 1994) Vol 2, p.769.

228 This is the subject of the fifth book in this series.

Index

Nick Holmes is a British author, podcaster and historian. He is currently writing a multi-volume series on the fall of the Roman Empire. He has also written about the Crusades and the Byzantine Empire. His podcast *The Fall of the Roman Empire* accompanies his books. In 2021, he gave up a career in investment banking to write full-time.

Justinian's Empire is the fourth book in his series on the Fall of the Roman Empire.

For more information see his website
www.nickholmesauthor.com